Solutions Manual for Actuarial Mathematics for Life Contingent Risks

This must-have manual provides detailed solutions to all of the 200+ exercises in Dickson, Hardy and Waters' *Actuarial Mathematics for Life Contingent Risks*, Second Edition. This ground-breaking text on the modern mathematics of life insurance is required reading for the Society of Actuaries' Exam MLC and also provides a solid preparation for the life contingencies material of the UK actuarial profession's Exam CT5.

Beyond the professional examinations, the textbook and solutions manual offer readers the opportunity to develop insight and understanding, and also offer practical advice for solving problems using straightforward, intuitive numerical methods. Companion spreadsheets illustrating these techniques are available for free download.

DAVID C. M. DICKSON is Professor of Actuarial Studies in the Department of Economics at the University of Melbourne. He is a Fellow of the Faculty of Actuaries and of the Institute of Actuaries of Australia. He has twice been awarded the H. M. Jackson Prize of the Institute of Actuaries of Australia, most recently for his book *Insurance Risk and Ruin* (Cambridge University Press, 2005).

MARY R. HARDY holds the CIBC Chair in Financial Risk Management at the University of Waterloo, Ontario. She is a Fellow of the UK Institute and Faculty of Actuaries and of the Society of Actuaries. She is a past Vice President of the Society of Actuaries. In 2013 she was awarded the Finlaison Medal of the Institute and Faculty of Actuaries for services to the actuarial profession, in research, teaching and governance.

HOWARD R. WATERS is Professor in the Department of Actuarial Mathematics and Statistics at Heriot-Watt University, Edinburgh. He is a Fellow of the Institute and Faculty of Actuaries, by whom he was awarded the Finlaison Medal for services to the actuarial profession in 2006.

INTERNATIONAL SERIES ON ACTUARIAL SCIENCE

SOLUTIONS MANUAL FOR ACTUARIAL MATHEMATICS FOR LIFE CONTINGENT RISKS

SECOND EDITION

DAVID C. M. DICKSON

University of Melbourne

MARY R. HARDY

University of Waterloo, Ontario

HOWARD R. WATERS

Heriot-Watt University, Edinburgh

CAMBRIDGE
UNIVERSITY PRESS

CAMBRIDGE
UNIVERSITY PRESS

University Printing House, Cambridge CB2 8BS, United Kingdom

Cambridge University Press is part of the University of Cambridge.

It furthers the University's mission by disseminating knowledge in the pursuit of education, learning and research at the highest international levels of excellence.

www.cambridge.org
Information on this title: www.cambridge.org/9781107620261

© David C. M. Dickson, Mary R. Hardy and Howard R. Waters 2012, 2013

First published 2012
3rd printing 2013
Second Edition 2013
5th printing 2016

Printed in the United States of America by Sheridan Books, Inc.

A catalogue record for this publication is available from the British Library

ISBN 978-1-107-62026-1 Paperback

Contents

Preface

This manual presents solutions to all exercises from

Actuarial Mathematics for Life Contingent Risks, 2nd edition (AMLCR),
by David C. M. Dickson, Mary R. Hardy, Howard R. Waters,
Cambridge University Press, 2013
ISBN 9781107044074

It should be read in conjunction with the spreadsheets posted at the website
www.cambridge.org\9781107620261 which contain details of the calculations required. However, readers are encouraged to construct their own spreadsheets before looking at the authors' approach. In the manual, exercises for which spreadsheets are posted are indicated with an [E].

In some cases the answers in the manual will differ from answers calculated using tables such as those provided in Appendix D of AMLCR. The differences arise from rounding errors. The numbers given in this manual are calculated directly, without using rounded table values, unless otherwise indicated.

From time to time, updates to this manual may appear at www.cambridge.org\9781107620261.

Solutions for Chapter 1

1.1 The insurer will calculate the premium for a term or whole life insurance policy assuming that the policyholder is in relatively good health; otherwise, if the insurer assumed that all purchasers were unhealthy, the cost of insurance would be prohibitive to those customers who are healthy. The assumption then is that claims will be relatively rare in the first few years of insurance, especially since most policies are sold to lives in their 30s and 40s.

This means that the price is too low for a life who is very unwell, for whom the risk of a claim shortly after purchase might be 10 or 100 times greater than for a healthy life. The insurer therefore needs evidence that the purchaser is in good health, to avoid the risk that insurance is bought too cheaply by lives who have a much higher probability of claim.

The objective of underwriting is to produce a relatively homogeneous insured population when policies are issued. The risk that the policyholder purchases the insurance because they are aware that their individual risk is greater than that of the insured population used to calculate the premium, is an example of adverse selection risk. Underwriting is a way of reducing the impact of adverse selection for life insurance.

Adverse selection for an annuity purchaser works in the other direction – a life might buy an annuity if they considered their mortality was lighter than the general population. But, since adverse selection is likely to affect all lives purchasing annuities, more or less, it does not generate heterogeneity, and the impact can be managed by assuming lower overall mortality rates for annuitants.

In addition, the difference in the net cost to the insurer arising from adverse selection will be smaller compared with the term insurance example.

1.2 The insurer will be more rigorous with underwriting for term insurance than for whole life insurance because the potential financial consequence of adverse selection is greater. Note that the insurer expects few claims to arise from the term insurance portfolio. Premiums are small, relative to the death benefit, because the probability of payment of the death benefit is assumed to be small. For whole life insurance, premiums are substantially larger as payment of the death benefit is a certain event (ignoring surrenders). The only uncertainty is the timing of the benefit payment.

The main risk to the insurer is that a life with a very high mortality risk, much higher than the assumed insured population, purchases life insurance. It is likely in this case that the life will pay very few premiums, and the policy will involve a large death benefit payout with very little premium income. Since term insurance has much lower premiums for a given sum insured than whole life insurance, it is likely that such a policyholder would choose term insurance. Hence, the risk of adverse selection is greater for term insurance than for whole life insurance, and underwriting is used to reduce the adverse selection risk.

1.3 The principle of charging in advance for life insurance is to eliminate the potential for policyholders to benefit from short-term life insurance cover without paying for it. Suppose premiums were payable at the end of the policy year. A life could sign up for the insurance, and lapse the contract at the end of the year. The life would have benefited from free insurance cover for that year.

In addition, life insurance involves significant acquisition expenses. The first premium is used to meet some or all of these expenses.

Background note: The fact that the insurance for a policyholder did not result in a claim does not make it free to the insurer. The insurer's view is of a portfolio of contracts. Suppose 100 people buy term life insurance for one year, with a sum insured of $1000, at a premium of $11 each. The insurer expects a mortality rate of 1%, which means that, on average, one life out of the 100 dies. If all the policyholders pay their first year's premiums in advance, and one life dies, then the insurer receives $1100 (plus some interest) and pays out $1000. On the other hand, if premiums were due at the year end, it is possible that many of the 99 expected to survive might decide not to pay. It would be difficult and expensive for the insurer to pursue payment. The policyholders have benefited collectively from the insurance and the insurer has not been appropriately compensated.

1.4 (a) Without term insurance, the homeowner's dependents may struggle to meet mortgage payments in the even of the homeowner's death. The lending company wishes to reduce as far as possible the risk of having to foreclose on the loan. Foreclosure is expensive and creates hardship for the homeowner's family at the worst possible time. Term insurance is used to pay off the mortgage balance in the event of the homeowner's death, thus avoiding the foreclosure risk for both the lender and homeowner's family.

(b) If the homeowner is paying regular instalments of capital and interest to pay off the mortgage, then the term insurance sum insured will decrease as the loan outstanding decreases. The reduction in loan outstanding is slow in the early years of, say, a 25-year mortgage, but speeds up later. The reduction in the term insurance sum insured is therefore not linear. Different loan provisions, including interest-only loan periods, cliff-edge repayment schedules (where the interest is very low for some period and then increases substantially), fixed or variable interest rates, fixed or variable repayment instalments will all affect the sum insured.

(c) In Section 1.3.5 it is noted that around 2% of applicants for insurance are considered to be too high risk. If these lives are, in consequence, unable to purchase property, then that is a social cost for these lives that may not be acceptable.

1.5 In with-profit whole life insurance, the insurer invests the premiums, and excess investment returns over the minimum required to fund the original benefits are shared between the policyholders and the insurer.

With a cash bonus, the policyholder's share of profits can be paid out in cash, similar to a dividend on shares. In this case, the investments need to be realized (i.e. assets sold for cash). The payout is immediate.

With a reversionary bonus, the policyholder's share of profits is used to increase the sum insured. The assets can remain in the capital markets until the sum insured is due.

Cash Bonus System – Insurer Perspective
Advantages

- Bonuses are transparent and easy to explain to policyholders.

- It does not involve maintenance of records of payouts and does not impact schedules for surrender values.

- The prospect of cash bonuses may persuade policyholders to continue with their policies rather than surrender.

Disadvantages

- It creates a liquidity risk – that assets need to be sold to meet bonus expectations, possibly at unfavourable times.

- Investment proceeds are volatile; volatility in cash bonuses may be difficult to explain to policyholders. There may be a temptation to over-distribute in an attempt to smooth, that could cause long-term losses.

- There may be problems determining equitable payouts, resulting in possible policyholder grievances.

Cash Bonus System – Policyholder Perspective
Advantages

- Cash is immediate and it is easy to understand the distribution.

Disadvantages

- May not be tax efficient.

- The risks to the insurer may lead to under-distribution to avoid risk.

- Possible volatility of bonuses.

Reversionary Bonus System – Insurer Perspective
Advantages

- Assets remain invested as long as a policy is in force, reducing liquidity risk.

- Bonuses appear larger as they are generally delayed many years.

- Bonuses may not be paid in full if a policy is surrendered subsequently, allowing higher rates of bonus to be declared for remaining policyholders.

- Over-distribution can be mitigated with lower bonuses between the declaration year and the claim event.

Disadvantages

- More complex to value, to keep records.

- Policyholders may not understand the approach, and there may be resentment (e.g. on surrender).

- Difficult to determine an equitable distribution.

- Easy to over-declare, as profits are based on asset values which may subsequently decrease.

- It is difficult to reduce bonus rates, even when justified. This may lead to loss of new and existing business.

Reversionary Bonus System – Policyholder Perspective
Advantages

- It may be tax efficient to receive profit share with sum insured.

- The system allows more investment freedom for the insurer, with higher upside potential for the policyholder.

Disadvantages

- Difficult to understand, especially 'super-compound' systems.

- Possible loss of profit share on surrender.

- Opaque system of distribution. It is difficult to compare how different companies perform.

1.6 Insurers prefer policies to remain in force, as their profits from long-term business arise largely from the interest spread, which is the difference between the interest earned on the accumulated premiums, and the interest needed to support the benefits. After age 80 few policyholders will be receiving salary, so there is greater risk that the premiums will not be affordable. Policyholders may then surrender their policies, cutting off the profit stream to the insurer. By designing the contract such that no premiums are due after age 80, the insurer increases significantly the proportion of policies that remain in force at that time, which we call the **persistency**.

1.7 For a comprehensive answer, we need to understand Andrew's age, health and family responsibilities and support. The answers for an average 65-year old retiree in good health would be different from those for a 50-year old retiree in poor health. Also, we should consider the impact of governmental benefits (old age pension, social security, health costs), and any potential support from family in the event that he faces financial ruin.

In the absence of more detailed information, we assume that Andrew is a person in average health at an average retirement age of, say, 65. We also assume that the $500 000 represents the capital on which he wishes to live reasonably comfortably for the remainder of his life. We also ignore tax issues, though these are likely to be very significant in this kind of decision in practice.

Consider the risks Andrew faces at retirement.

(1) Outliving his assets – this is the risk that at some point the funds are all spent and Andrew must live on whatever government benefit or family support that might be available.

(2) Inflation risk – that is, that his standard of living is gradually eroded by increases in the cost of living that are not matched by increases in his income.

(3) Catastrophe costs – this is the risk that a large liability arises and Andrew does not have the assets (or cannot access the assets) to meet the costs. Examples might include the cost of health care for Andrew or a dependent (where health care is not freely available); catastrophic uninsured liability; cost of long-term care in older age.

Andrew may also have some 'wants' – for example

(1) Bequest – Andrew may want to leave some assets to dependents if possible.

(2) Flexible spending – Andrew may want the freedom of full access to all his capital at all times.

We now consider the options listed in the question in light of the risks and potential 'wants' listed.

(a) With a level life annuity, Andrew is assured of income for his whole life, and eliminates the risk of outliving his assets. However, he retains the inflation risk, and he may not have sufficient assets to meet catastrophe costs. If he uses all his capital for an annuity, there will be no bequest funds available on his death, and no flexibility in spending during his lifetime.

(b) As in (a), Andrew will not outlive his assets, and this option also covers inflation risk to some extent. There may be some residual inflation risk, as the cost of living increases that Andrew is exposed to may differ from the inflation adjustments applied to his annuity. In order to purchase the cost of living cover, Andrew will receive a significantly lower starting annual payment than under option (a). All other issues are similar to those under option (a).

(c) A 20-year annuity-certain will offer a similar or slightly higher benefit to a life annuity for a 65-year old man in average health. Andrew's life expectancy might be around 18 years, so on average the annuity will be sufficient to give Andrew a life income and allow a small bequest. An annuity-certain can be reasonably easily converted to cash in the event of a catastrophe or a change in circumstances. However, there is a significant risk that Andrew will live more than 20 years, and it will be difficult to manage the dramatic change in income at such an advanced age.

(d) Investing the capital and living off the interest would involve much risk. The interest income will be highly variable, and will be insufficient to live on in some years. If Andrew invests the capital in safe, stable long-term bonds, he might make only 2–3% after expenses (or less, this figure has been highly variable over the last 20 years) which would be insufficient if it is his only income. There is also reinvestment risk, as he could live longer than the longest income he could lock-in in the market, and there will be counterparty risk (that is, the risk that the borrower will default on the interest and capital) if his investment is not in solid risk-free assets.

If Andrew needs a higher income, he will have to take more risk. For example, he might invest in corporate bonds with counterparty risk, or he might put some of his capital in stocks, which have upside potential but downside risk. Using riskier investments would increase the volatility of his income and threaten his capital. If he invests heavily in shares, he may see negative returns in some years. This strategy just might not be sustainable.

Income would also not be inflation hedged, in general.

On the other hand, the capital would be accessible in the event of a catastrophe or for flexible spending (although that would raise the risk of outliving assets). This system would allow for a significant bequest, assuming that Andrew managed to live on the investment, but at the expense of income level and stability for Andrew. Also, Andrew would have the added complication of managing a portfolio of assets, or paying someone to manage them for him. On the other hand, purchasing an annuity involves substantial hidden expenses that would not be incurred under this option.

(e) $40 000 is 8% of the capital. If this rate is higher than the interest rate achievable on capital, then Andrew will be drawing down the capital and risks outliving his assets. The income is not inflation hedged, but the system does allow spending flexibility. Other issues are as for option (d).

Solutions for Chapter 2

2.1 (a) $F_0(60) = 1 - \left(1 - \frac{60}{105}\right)^{1/5} = 0.1559$.

(b) $S_0(70)/S_0(30) = 0.8586$.

(c) $(S_0(90) - S_0(100))/S_0(20) = 0.1394$.

(d) We may use either

$$\mu_x = -\frac{1}{S_0(x)} \frac{d}{dx} S_0(x)$$

or

$$\mu_x = -\frac{d}{dx} \log S_0(x) = -\frac{d}{dx} \frac{1}{5} \log\left(1 - \frac{x}{105}\right) = \frac{1}{525 - 5x},$$

so $\mu_{50} = 0.0036$.

(e) We must solve

$$\frac{S_0(50 + t)}{S_0(50)} = \frac{1}{2}$$

which is the same as

$$\left(1 - \frac{t}{55}\right)^{1/5} = \frac{1}{2}.$$

This gives $t = 53.28$.

(f) We have

$$\overset{\circ}{e}_{50} = \int_0^{55} {}_t p_{50}\, dt = \int_0^{55} \left(1 - \frac{t}{55}\right)^{1/5} dt = 45.83.$$

9

(g) We have

$$e_{50} = \sum_{t=1}^{54} {}_t p_{50} = \sum_{t=1}^{54} \left(1 - \frac{t}{55}\right)^{1/5} = 45.18.$$

2.2 (a) $G(x)$ can be written as

$$G(x) = \frac{(90 - x)(x + 200)}{18\,000}$$

and since $G(\omega) = 0$ at the limiting age (and $x > 0$), $\omega = 90$.

(b) First, we have $G(0) = 1$. Next, setting $x = 90$ we see that the function equals 0 at the limiting age. Third, the derivative of $G(x)$ is

$$\frac{-110 - 2x}{18\,000}$$

which is negative for $x > 0$. Hence all three conditions for a survival function are satisfied.

(c) $S_0(20)/S_0(0) = 0.8556$.

(d) The survival function is

$$\begin{aligned}
S_{20}(t) &= \frac{S_0(20 + t)}{S_0(20)} \\
&= \frac{18\,000 - 110(20 + t) - (20 + t)^2}{18\,000 - 110(20) - 20^2} \\
&= \frac{15\,400 - 150t - t^2}{15\,400}.
\end{aligned}$$

(e) $(S_0(30) - S_0(40))/S_0(20) = 0.1169$.

(f) $\mu_x = -S_0'(x)/S_0(x)$. Using part (b) we obtain

$$\begin{aligned}
\mu_x &= \left(\frac{110 + 2x}{18\,000}\right)\left(\frac{18\,000}{18\,000 - 110x - x^2}\right) \\
&= \frac{110 + 2x}{18\,000 - 110x - x^2}
\end{aligned}$$

so that $\mu_{50} = 0.021$.

2.3 The required probability, ${}_{19|17}q_0$ in actuarial notation, is equal to

$$S_0(19) - S_0(36) = \frac{1}{10}\left(\sqrt{81} - \sqrt{64}\right) = 0.1.$$

^{E}2.4 (a) We can check that S_0 is a survival function as follows:

$$S_0(0) = \exp\{0\} = 1,$$
$$\lim_{x \to \infty} S_0(x) = \exp\{-\infty\} = 0,$$

and the derivative, $\dfrac{d}{dx} S_0(x)$, is

$$- (A + Bx + CD^x) \exp\left\{ - \left(Ax + \frac{1}{2} Bx^2 + \frac{C}{\log D} D^x - \frac{C}{\log D} \right) \right\}$$
$$< 0 \quad \text{for } x > 0.$$

(b) The survival function S_x is given by

$$S_x(t) = \frac{S_0(x+t)}{S_0(x)}$$
$$= \exp\left\{ -A(x+t) - \frac{1}{2} B(x+t)^2 - \frac{C}{\log D} D^{x+t} + \frac{C}{\log D} D \right.$$
$$\left. + Ax + \frac{1}{2} Bx^2 + \frac{C}{\log D} D^x - \frac{C}{\log D} \right\}$$
$$= \exp\left\{ -At - \frac{1}{2} B(2xt + t^2) - \frac{C}{\log D} D^x (D^t - 1) \right\}.$$

(c) The force of mortality at age x is

$$\mu_x = -\frac{1}{S_0(x)} \frac{d}{dx} S_0(x) = -\frac{d}{dx} \log S_0(x)$$
$$= \frac{d}{dx} \left(Ax + \frac{1}{2} Bx^2 + \frac{C}{\log D} D^x - \frac{C}{\log D} \right).$$

Recall that

$$\frac{d}{dx} D^x = \frac{d}{dx} e^{\log D x} = (\log D) e^{\log D x} = (\log D) D^x$$

so that

$$\mu_x = A + Bx + CD^x.$$

(d) Numerical results are given below.

Part	Function	1	5	10	20	50	90
					t		
(i)	$_tp_{30}$	0.9976	0.9862	0.9672	0.9064	0.3812	3.5×10^{-7}
(ii)	$_tq_{40}$	0.0047		0.0629	0.1747		
(iii)	$_{t|10}q_{30}$	0.0349		0.0608	0.1082		

		70	71	72	73	74	75
					x		
(iv)	e_x	13.046	12.517	12.001	11.499	11.009	10.533
(v)	$\overset{\circ}{e}_x$	13.544	13.014	12.498	11.995	11.505	11.029

2.5 (a) The survival function S_x is given by

$$S_x(t) = S_0(x+t)/S_0(x)$$
$$= \frac{e^{-\lambda(x+t)}}{e^{-\lambda x}}$$
$$= e^{-\lambda t}.$$

(b) $\mu_x = -\dfrac{d}{dx} \log S_0(x) = -\dfrac{d}{dx} \log e^{-\lambda x} = \dfrac{d}{dx} \lambda x = \lambda.$

(c) As $_tp_x = e^{-\lambda t}$, which is independent of x,

$$e_x = \sum_{t=1}^{\infty} {_tp_x} = \sum_{t=1}^{\infty} e^{-\lambda t}.$$

This is a geometric series, so that

$$e_x = \frac{e^{-\lambda}}{1 - e^{-\lambda}} = \frac{1}{e^{\lambda} - 1}.$$

(d) This lifetime distribution is unsuitable for human mortality as survival probabilities, and therefore expected future lifetimes, are independent of attained age. The force of mortality for this lifetime distribution is constant. The force of mortality for humans increases significantly with age.

2.6 (a) $p_{x+3} = 1 - q_{x+3} = 0.98.$

(b) $_2p_x = p_x\, p_{x+1} = 0.99 \times 0.985 = 0.97515.$

(c) As $_3p_{x+1} = {_2p_{x+1}}\, p_{x+3}$, we have $_2p_{x+1} = 0.95/0.98 = 0.96939.$

(d) $_3p_x = p_x\, {_3p_{x+1}} / p_{x+3} = 0.95969.$

(e) $_{1|2}q_x = p_x(1 - {}_2p_{x+1}) = 0.03031$.

2.7 (a) $S_0(x) = 1/(1 + x)$.

(b) $f_0(x) = F'_0(x) = 1/(1 + x)^2$.

(c) $S_x(t) = S_0(x + t)/S_0(x) = (1 + x)/(1 + x + t)$.

(d) $p_{20} = S_{20}(1) = 0.95455$.

(e) $_{10|5}q_{30} = (S_0(40) - S_0(45))/S_0(30) = 31/41 - 31/46 = 0.08218$.

2.8 (a) $f_0(x) = -S'_0(x) = 0.002xe^{-0.001x^2}$.

(b) $\mu_x = f_0(x)/S_0(x) = 0.002x$.

2.9 Write

$$_tp_x = \exp\left\{-\int_0^t \mu_{x+s}ds\right\} = \exp\left\{-\int_x^{x+t} \mu_s ds\right\}.$$

In this case, we are treating t as fixed and x as variable. Let $h(x) = -\int_x^{x+t} \mu_s \, ds$. Then

$$_tp_x = e^{-h(x)} \implies \frac{d}{dx}\,_tp_x = -h'(x)e^{-h(x)} = -h'(x)\,_tp_x.$$

Now

$$h'(x) = \frac{d}{dx}\int_x^{x+t} \mu_s \, ds = \frac{d}{dx}\left(\int_0^{x+t} \mu_s \, ds - \int_0^x \mu_s \, ds\right) = \mu_{x+t} - \mu_x,$$

so that

$$\frac{d}{dx}\,_tp_x = {}_tp_x(\mu_x - \mu_{x+t})$$

as required.

2.10 As $\mu_x = Bc^x$, we have

$$\mu_{50}/\mu_{30} = c^{20} = \frac{0.000344}{0.000130} = 2.6462,$$

giving $c = 1.04986$. As $\mu_{30} = Bc^{30}$ we have

$$\frac{0.000130}{c^{30}} = B = 3.0201 \times 10^{-5}.$$

Then using $g = \exp\{-B/\log c\}$,

$$_{10}p_{40} = g^{c^{40}(c^{10}-1)} = 0.9973.$$

2.11 (a) As $\mu_x = A + Bc^x$,

$$_tp_x = \exp\left\{-\int_0^t (A + Bc^{x+s})\,ds\right\}$$

$$= \exp\left\{-\int_0^t A\,ds\right\}\exp\left\{-\int_0^t Bc^{x+s}\,ds\right\}.$$

From Example 2.3 we know that the second exponential term is $g^{c^x(c^t-1)}$ where $g = \exp\{-B/\log c\}$, so

$$_tp_x = e^{-At}g^{c^x(c^t-1)}$$

$$= s^t g^{c^x(c^t-1)}$$

where $s = \exp\{-A\}$.

(b) Using part (a), we have

$$_{10}p_{50} = s^{10}g^{c^{50}(c^{10}-1)}$$

so that

$$\log(_{10}p_{50}) = 10\log(s) + c^{50}(c^{10} - 1)\log(g).$$

Similarly,

$$\log(_{10}p_{60}) = 10\log(s) + c^{60}(c^{10} - 1)\log(g)$$

and

$$\log(_{10}p_{70}) = 10\log(s) + c^{70}(c^{10} - 1)\log(g)$$

so that

$$\log(_{10}p_{70}) - \log(_{10}p_{60}) = c^{60}(c^{10} - 1)^2\log(g)$$

and

$$\log(_{10}p_{60}) - \log(_{10}p_{50}) = c^{50}(c^{10} - 1)^2\log(g),$$

giving

$$\frac{\log(_{10}p_{70}) - \log(_{10}p_{60})}{\log(_{10}p_{60}) - \log(_{10}p_{50})} = c^{10}.$$

E2.12 (a) We show an excerpt from the table below.

x	p_x
0	0.99954
1	0.99951
2	0.99948
3	0.99945
4	0.99942
$\vdots$	$\vdots$

(b) The probability that (70) dies at age $70 + k$ last birthday is $\Pr[K_{70} = k]$ where K_x is the curtate future lifetime. The most likely age at death is the value of k that maximizes $\Pr[K_{70} = k] = {}_{k|}q_{70}$.

The maximum value for ${}_{k|}q_{70}$ can be found by constructing a table of values and selecting the largest value; it is ${}_{3|}q_{70} = 0.05719$, so the most likely age at death is 73.

(c) The curtate expectation of life at age 70 is

$$e_{70} = \sum_{t=1}^{\infty} {}_tp_{70} = 9.339.$$

(d) The complete expectation of life at age 70 is

$$\overset{\circ}{e}_{70} = \int_0^{\infty} {}_tp_{70}\, dt = 9.834,$$

using numerical integration.

E2.13 (a) As $\mu_x^* = 2\mu_x$ for all x, we have

$$ {}_tp_x^* = \exp\left\{-\int_0^t \mu_{x+s}^*\, ds\right\} = \exp\left\{-2\int_0^t \mu_{x+s}\, ds\right\} = ({}_tp_x)^2.$$

(b) Using numerical integration, $\overset{\circ}{e}_{50} - \overset{\circ}{e}_{50}^* = 6.432$.

(c) Using numerical integration, $E[T_{50}^2] = 575.40$ and $E[(T_{50}^*)^2] = 298.25$, giving $V[T_{50}] = 125.89$ and $V[T_{50}^*] = 80.11$.

2.14 (a) We have

$$\overset{\circ}{e}_x = \int_0^\infty {}_t p_x \, dt$$

$$= \int_0^1 {}_t p_x \, dt + \int_1^\infty {}_t p_x \, dt$$

$$\leq 1 + \int_1^\infty {}_t p_x \, dt$$

$$= 1 + \int_1^\infty p_x \, {}_{t-1} p_{x+1} \, dt$$

$$\leq 1 + \int_1^\infty {}_{t-1} p_{x+1} \, dt$$

$$= 1 + \int_0^\infty {}_t p_{x+1} \, dt$$

$$= 1 + \overset{\circ}{e}_{x+1} \, .$$

(b) We have

$$\overset{\circ}{e}_x = \int_0^\infty {}_t p_x \, dt$$

$$= \int_0^1 {}_t p_x \, dt + \int_1^2 {}_t p_x \, dt + \int_2^3 {}_t p_x \, dt + \cdots$$

and since ${}_t p_x$ is a decreasing function of t,

$$\int_{s-1}^s {}_t p_x \, dt \geq {}_s p_x \, ,$$

so

$$\overset{\circ}{e}_x \geq p_x + {}_2 p_x + {}_3 p_x + \cdots$$

$$= e_x \, .$$

(c) Using the repeated trapezium rule for numerical integration we have

$$\overset{\circ}{e}_x = \int_0^\infty {}_t p_x \, dt$$

$$\approx \frac{1}{2}(1 + {}_1 p_x + {}_1 p_x + {}_2 p_x + {}_2 p_x + \cdots)$$

$$= \frac{1}{2} + e_x \, .$$

(d) It is almost always the case in practice that $\overset{\circ}{e}_x$ is a decreasing function of x, but, in principle, it need not be. Consider a hypothetical population where people die only at ages 1 or 50. Of all those born, precisely one half die at age 1 and the remainder all die at age 50. Then

$$\overset{\circ}{e}_0 = \frac{1}{2}(1 + 50) = 25.5 \qquad \text{and} \qquad \overset{\circ}{e}_2 = 48.$$

2.15 (a) We use the result from Exercise 2.9, that $\frac{d}{dx}\,_tp_x = \,_tp_x(\mu_x - \mu_{x+t})$. Then

$$\frac{d}{dx}\overset{\circ}{e}_x = \frac{d}{dx}\int_0^\infty \,_tp_x\,dt$$

$$= \int_0^\infty \frac{d}{dx}\,_tp_x\,dt$$

$$= \int_0^\infty \,_tp_x(\mu_x - \mu_{x+t})\,dt$$

$$= \int_0^\infty \,_tp_x\,\mu_x\,dt - \int_0^\infty \,_tp_x\,\mu_{x+t}\,dt$$

$$= \mu_x\,\overset{\circ}{e}_x - 1.$$

The final line follows as μ_x is not a function of t, so may be moved out of the integral in the first term, and the second term is the integral of the probability density function of T_x, over all values of t, and so the integral equals 1.

(b) $\dfrac{d}{dx}\left(x + \overset{\circ}{e}_x\right) = 1 + \dfrac{d}{dx}\overset{\circ}{e}_x = \mu_x\,\overset{\circ}{e}_x > 0$, so that $x + \overset{\circ}{e}_x$ increases with x.

Note that $\left(x + \overset{\circ}{e}_x\right)$ is the expected age at death of a life, given that the life has survived to age x. This is clearly an increasing function of x.

2.16 We have

$$e_{x:\overline{n}|} = \mathrm{E}[\min(K_x, n)]$$

$$= \sum_{k=0}^{n-1} k\,\Pr[K_x = k] + \sum_{k=n}^{\infty} n\,\Pr[K_x = k]$$

$$= \sum_{k=0}^{n-1} k\,(\,_kp_x - \,_{k+1}p_x) + n\,\Pr[K_x \geq n]$$

$$= (\,_1p_x - \,_2p_x) + 2(\,_2p_x - \,_3p_x) + \ldots + (n-1)(\,_{n-1}p_x - \,_np_x) + n\,_np_x$$

$$= \,_1p_x + \,_2p_x + \ldots + \,_np_x$$

$$= \sum_{k=1}^{n} \,_kp_x.$$

Solutions for Chapter 3

3.1 Figures S3.1, S3.2 and S3.3 are graphs of μ_x, l_x and d_x, respectively, as functions of age x up to $x = 100$. Each graph has been drawn using the values from ELT 15, Males and Females.

(a) The key feature of Figure S3.1 is that the value of μ_x is very low until around age 55, from where it increases steeply. Numerically, μ_x is very close to q_x provided q_x is reasonably small, so that the features in Figure S3.1 are very similar to those shown in Figure 3.1 in AMLCR. The features at younger ages show up much better in Figure 3.1 in AMLCR because the y-axis there is on a logarithmic scale. Note that the near-linearity in Figure 3.1 in AMLCR for ages above 35 is equivalent to the near-exponential growth we observe in Figure S3.1.

(b) The key feature of Figure S3.2 is that, apart from a barely perceptible drop in the first year due to mortality immediately following birth, the graph is more or less constant until around age 55 when it starts to fall at an increasing rate before converging towards zero at very high ages. This reflects the pattern seen in Figure S3.1.

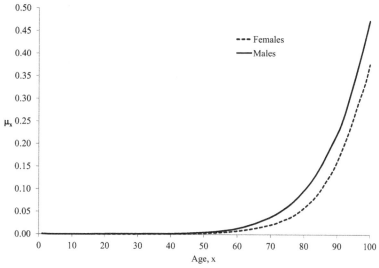

Figure S3.1 A graph of μ_x as a function of x.

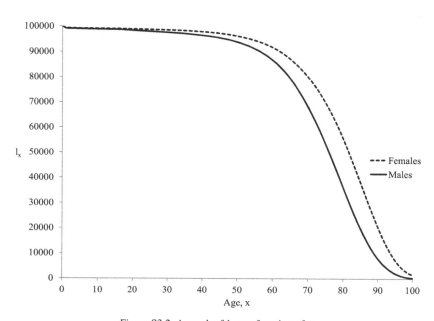

Figure S3.2 A graph of l_x as a function of x.

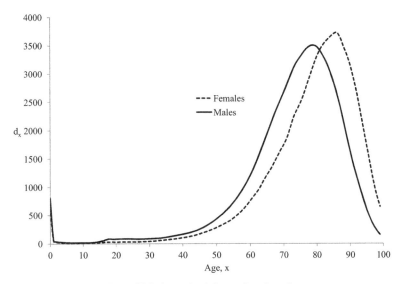

Figure S3.3 A graph of d_x as a function of x.

(c) The function d_x is the expected number of deaths between exact ages x and
     $x + 1$ out of l_0 lives aged 0. The relatively high mortality in the first year
     of life shows clearly in Figure S3.3, as does the increase in the expected
     number of deaths for males in the late teenage years – the so-called 'ac-
     cident hump'. See the comments on Figure 3.1 in AMLCR. The expected
     number of deaths increases gradually from around age 30 and sharply
     from around age 55. It reaches a peak at around ages 77 (males) and 87
     (females) even though the force of mortality continues to increase beyond
     these ages, as can be seen in Figure S3.1. The peak occurs because the
     expected number of survivors to high ages, l_x, is decreasing sharply (see
     Figure S3.2) and so the expected number of deaths from these survivors,
     d_x, eventually has to fall as well.

3.2 The assumption of a uniform distribution of deaths between integer ages im-
     plies that

$$l_{x+s} = (1 - s)l_x + sl_{x+1}$$

for integer x and $0 \le s \le 1$. This follows directly from formula (3.8) in
AMLCR.

The assumption of a constant force of mortality between integer ages means that for integer x and $0 \le s \le s + t \le 1$

$$_s p_{x+t} = (p_x)^s .$$

See Section 3.3.2 in AMLCR. Note that if $s + t > 1$, then we must calculate survival probabilities for fractions of a year at different (integer) ages. See part (d) for an example.

(a) $_{0.2}q_{52.4} = 1 - \dfrac{l_{52.6}}{l_{52.4}} = 1 - \dfrac{0.4 l_{52} + 0.6 l_{53}}{0.6 l_{52} + 0.4 l_{53}}$ using UDD

$\qquad = 0.001917.$

(b) $_{0.2}q_{52.4} = 1 - {}_{0.2}p_{52.4}$

$\qquad = 1 - (p_{52})^{0.2}$ using the constant force assumption

$\qquad = 1 - \left(\dfrac{89\,089}{89\,948} \right)^{0.2} = 0.001917.$

(c) $_{5.7}p_{52.4} = \dfrac{l_{58.1}}{l_{52.4}} = \dfrac{0.9 l_{58} + 0.1 l_{59}}{0.6 l_{52} + 0.4 l_{53}}$ using UDD

$\qquad = 0.935422.$

(d) $_{5.7}p_{52.4} = {}_{0.6}p_{52.4} \times {}_{5}p_{53} \times {}_{0.1}p_{58}$

$\qquad = (p_{52})^{0.6} \, {}_{5}p_{53} \, (p_{58})^{0.1}$ using the constant force assumption

$\qquad = 0.935423.$

(e) $_{3.2|2.5}q_{52.4} = \dfrac{l_{55.6} - l_{58.1}}{l_{52.4}}$

$\qquad = \dfrac{0.4 l_{55} + 0.6 l_{56} - 0.9 l_{58} - 0.1 l_{59}}{0.6 l_{52} + 0.4 l_{53}}$ using UDD

$\qquad = 0.030957.$

(f) $_{3.2|2.5}q_{52.4} = {}_{3.2}p_{52.4}(1 - {}_{2.5}p_{55.6})$

$\qquad = {}_{0.6}p_{52.4} \times_{2} p_{53} \times {}_{0.6}p_{55}(1 - {}_{0.4}p_{55.6} \times {}_{2}p_{56} \times {}_{0.1}p_{58})$

$\qquad = (p_{52})^{0.6} \, {}_{2}p_{53} \, (p_{55})^{0.6}(1 - (p_{55})^{0.4} \, {}_{2}p_{56} \, (p_{58})^{0.1})$

$\qquad\qquad\qquad\qquad$ using the constant force assumption

$\qquad = 0.030950.$

3.3 The required probabilities are calculated as follows:

(a) $\dfrac{l_{85}}{l_{[75]}} = \dfrac{10\,542}{15\,930} = 0.66177.$

(b) $_{9|2}q_{[75]+1} = \dfrac{l_{85} - l_{87}}{l_{[75]+1}} = \dfrac{10\,542 - 9\,064}{15\,668} = 0.09433.$

(c) $_{4|2}q_{[77]+1} = \dfrac{l_{82} - l_{84}}{l_{[77]+1}} = \dfrac{12\,576 - 11\,250}{14\,744} = 0.08993.$

3.4 The required probabilities are calculated as follows:

(a) $_2p_{[72]} = (1 - q_{[72]})(1 - q_{[72]+1})$

$\qquad = 0.994764 \times 0.992544$

$\qquad = 0.987347.$

(b) $_3q_{[73]+2} = 1 - {_3p_{[73]+2}}$

$\qquad = 1 - (1 - q_{[73]+2})(1 - q_{[73]+3})(1 - q_{[73]+4})$

$\qquad = 1 - 0.98863 \times 0.985012 \times 0.980684$

$\qquad = 0.044998.$

(c) $_{1|}q_{[65]+4} = p_{[65]+4} \times q_{70} = 0.992006 \times 0.010599 = 0.010514.$

(d) $_7p_{[70]} = (1 - q_{[70]})(1 - q_{[70]+1})(1 - q_{[70]+2})(1 - q_{[70]+3})(1 - q_{[70]+4})$

$\qquad \times (1 - q_{75})(1 - q_{76})$

$\qquad = 0.995715 \times 0.994033 \times 0.991934 \times 0.989371 \times 0.986302$

$\qquad \times 0.981226 \times 0.978947$

$\qquad = 0.920271.$

3.5 (a) The calculation is the same as for Exercise 3.4(d), with different numbers:

$\qquad _7p_{[70]} = (1 - q_{[70]})(1 - q_{[70]+1})(1 - q_{[70]+2})(1 - q_{[70]+3})(1 - q_{[70]+4})$

$\qquad\qquad \times (1 - q_{75})(1 - q_{76})$

$\qquad\qquad = 0.989627 \times 0.985670 \times 0.980808 \times 0.974977 \times 0.968141$

$\qquad\qquad \times 0.956314 \times 0.951730$

$\qquad\qquad = 0.821929.$

Note that this survival probability is considerably smaller than the corresponding probability for non-smokers calculated in Exercise 3.4(d).

(b) We have

$$
\begin{aligned}
_{1|2}q_{[70]+2} &= p_{[70]+2} \times {}_2q_{[70]+3} \\
&= (1 - q_{[70]+2})(q_{[70]+3} + (1 - q_{[70]+3}) \times q_{[70]+4}) \\
&= 0.980808\,(0.025023 + 0.974977 \times 0.031859) \\
&= 0.055008.
\end{aligned}
$$

(c) Probably the easiest way to calculate this probability is to express it first in terms of ls, as follows:

$$
\begin{aligned}
_{3.8}q_{[70]+0.2} &= 1 - \frac{l_{[70]+4}}{l_{[70]+0.2}} \\
&= 1 - \frac{l_{[70]+4}}{0.8l_{[70]} + 0.2l_{[70]+1}} \quad \text{using UDD} \\
&= 1 - \frac{{}_4p_{[70]}}{0.8 + 0.2p_{[70]}} \\
&= 1 - \frac{(1 - q_{[70]})(1 - q_{[70]+1})(1 - q_{[70]+2})(1 - q_{[70]+3})}{0.8 + 0.2(1 - q_{[70]})} \\
&= 0.065276.
\end{aligned}
$$

3.6 Working in terms of ls we need l_{56}/l_{53}. We have

$$
\begin{aligned}
l_{[50]+1} &= l_{[50]}(1 - q_{[50]}), \\
l_{[50]+2} &= l_{[50]}\,{}_2p_{[50]}, \\
l_{53} &= l_{[50]+2} - l_{[50]} \times {}_2|q_{[50]}, \\
l_{56} &= l_{53} - l_{[50]+1} \times {}_2|_3q_{[50]+1}.
\end{aligned}
$$

Hence $_3p_{53} = 0.90294$.

3.7 Use the superscript A to denote the mortality of country A. Other functions refer to US Life Tables, 2002, Females. The required probability is

$$
_{10}p_{[30]}^{A} = {}_5p_{[30]}^{A}\, {}_5p_{35}^{A}
$$

where

$$
\begin{aligned}
_5p_{[30]}^{A} &= (1 - 6q_{30})(1 - 5q_{31})(1 - 4q_{32})(1 - 3q_{33})(1 - 2q_{34}) \\
&= 0.98599
\end{aligned}
$$

and

$$5p_{35}^A = \exp\left\{-\int_0^5 \mu_{35+t}^A \, dt\right\}$$

$$= \exp\left\{-1.5 \times \int_0^5 \mu_{35+t} \, dt\right\}$$

$$= (5p_{35})^{1.5}$$

$$= 0.99139.$$

Hence $10p_{[30]}^A = 0.977497$.

3.8 (a) We start by showing that $l_x^* = l_{x+1}$ for all x. We are given that this is true
for $x = 25$. Consider first $x = 26$. We have

$$l_{26}^* = p_{25}^* \, l_{25}^* = l_{27}$$

since $p_{25}^* = p_{26}$ and $l_{25}^* = l_{26}$. Similarly

$$l_{27}^* = p_{26}^* \, l_{26}^* = l_{28}$$

and the same argument gives

$$l_x^* = l_{x+1} \quad \text{for } x = 26, 27, 28, \ldots$$

Consider now l_x^* for $x \leq 24$. We have

$$l_{24}^* = l_{25}^* / p_{24}^*$$

$$= l_{26} / p_{25}$$

$$= l_{25}.$$

This argument gives $l_x^* = l_{x+1}$ for $x = 24, 23, 22, \ldots, 0$.

The next step is to show that $l_{[x]+2}^* = l_{x+2}$ for all x. As $p_{[x]+2}^* = {}_2 p_{x+2}$,

$$p_{[x]+2}^* \, l_{[x]+2}^* = l_{[x]+3}^* = l_{x+3}^* = l_{x+4}$$

$$\implies {}_2 p_{x+2} \, l_{[x]+2}^* = l_{x+4}$$

$$\implies l_{[x]+2}^* = l_{x+4} \, \frac{l_{x+2}}{l_{x+4}} = l_{x+2} \, .$$

Next we show that $l_{[x]+1}^* = l_{x-1}$ for all x. As $p_{[x]+1}^* = {}_3 p_{x-1}$,

$$p_{[x]+1}^* \, l_{[x]+1}^* = l_{[x]+2}^* = l_{x+2}$$

$$\implies l_{[x]+1}^* = \frac{l_{x+2}}{{}_3 p_{x-1}} = l_{x-1} \, .$$

Finally we show that $l^*_{[x]} = l_{x-5}$ for all x. As $p^*_{[x]} = {}_4p_{x-5}$,

$$p^*_{[x]} l^*_{[x]} = l^*_{[x]+1} = l_{x-1}$$

$$\implies l^*_{[x]} = \frac{l_{x-1}}{{}_4p_{x-5}} = l_{x-5} .$$

In summary,

$$l^*_{[x]} = l_{x-5} , \quad l^*_{[x]+1} = l_{x-1} , \quad l^*_{[x]+2} = l_{x+2} , \quad l^*_x = l_{x+1} .$$

The required life table is as follows:

x	$l^*_{[x]}$	$l^*_{[x]+1}$	$l^*_{[x]+2}$	l^*_{x+3}
20	99 180	98 942	98 700	98 529
21	99 135	98 866	98 615	98 444
22	99 079	98 785	98 529	98 363

(b) Using the results from part (a),

(i) ${}_{2|38}q^*_{[21]+1} = (l^*_{24} - l^*_{62})/l^*_{[21]+1} = 0.121265,$

(ii) ${}_{40}p^*_{[22]} = l^*_{62}/l^*_{[22]} = 0.872587,$

(iii) ${}_{40}p^*_{[21]+1} = l^*_{62}/l^*_{[21]+1} = 0.874466,$

(iv) ${}_{40}p^*_{[20]+2} = l^*_{62}/l^*_{[20]+2} = 0.875937,$

(v) ${}_{40}p^*_{22} = l^*_{62}/l^*_{22} = 0.876692.$

Note that in this model there is 'reverse selection', i.e. the probabilities (ii) to (v) above are in ascending order of magnitude.

3.9 (a) For integer x and $k = 0, 1, \ldots$, let μ^*_{x+k} denote the assumed constant force of mortality between ages $x + k$ and $x + k + 1$. Then

$$p_{x+k} = \exp\left\{-\int_0^1 \mu^*_{x+k} \, dt\right\} = \exp\{-\mu^*_{x+k}\}.$$

The probability in formula (3.17) can be written as

$$\Pr[R_x \le s | K_x = k] = \frac{\Pr[k < T_x \le k + s]}{\Pr[k < T_x \le k + 1]}$$

$$= \frac{{}_kp_x \, {}_sq_{x+k}}{{}_kp_x \, (1 - p_{x+k})}$$

$$= \frac{{}_sq_{x+k}}{1 - \exp\{-\mu^*_{x+k}\}}$$

$$= \frac{1 - \exp\left\{-\int_0^s \mu^*_{x+k} \, dt\right\}}{1 - \exp\{-\mu^*_{x+k}\}}$$

$$= \frac{1 - \exp\{-\mu^*_{x+k}s\}}{1 - \exp\{-\mu^*_{x+k}\}} \, ,$$

as required.

(b) Suppose formula (3.17) holds for integer x and for $k = 0, 1, 2, \ldots$. Then for $0 \le s \le 1$,

$$\frac{1 - \exp\{-\mu^*_{x+k}s\}}{1 - \exp\{-\mu^*_{x+k}\}} = \Pr[R_x \le s | K_x = k]$$

$$= \frac{\Pr[k < T_x \le k + s]}{\Pr[k < T_x \le k + 1]}$$

$$= \frac{{}_kp_x \, {}_sq_{x+k}}{{}_kp_x \, (1 - p_{x+k})}$$

$$= \frac{1 - {}_sp_{x+k}}{1 - \exp\{-\mu^*_{x+k}\}}$$

which implies that

$$_sp_{x+k} = \exp\{-\mu^*_{x+k} \, s\}.$$

The force of mortality at age $x + k + s$ can be written as

$$\mu_{x+k+s} = -\frac{d}{ds} \log \, {}_sp_{x+k} = \mu^*_{x+k}$$

using the formula for ${}_sp_{x+k}$ derived above. Thus μ_{x+k+s} does not depend on s, as required.

3.10 First note that for any constant a,

$$\int_0^t a^s \, ds = \int_0^t \exp\{s \log(a)\} \, ds$$

$$= \frac{1}{\log(a)} (\exp\{t \log(a)\} - 1)$$

$$= \frac{a^t - 1}{\log(a)}.$$

Using this formula, we have for $0 \le t \le 2$:

$$_tp_{[x]} = \exp\left\{ -\int_0^t \mu_{[x]+s} \, ds \right\}$$

$$= \exp\left\{ -\int_0^t 0.9^{2-s}(A + Bc^{x+s}) \, ds \right\}$$

$$= \exp\left\{ -0.9^2 \int_0^t (A(0.9^{-s}) + Bc^x(c/0.9)^s) \, ds \right\}$$

$$= \exp\left\{ -0.9^2 \left(\frac{A(1 - 0.9^{-t})}{\log(0.9)} + \frac{Bc^x((c/0.9)^t - 1)}{\log(c/0.9)} \right) \right\}$$

$$= \exp\left\{ -0.9^{2-t} \left(\frac{A(0.9^t - 1)}{\log(0.9)} + \frac{Bc^x(c^t - 0.9^t)}{-\log(0.9/c)} \right) \right\}$$

$$= \exp\left\{ 0.9^{2-t} \left(\frac{A(1 - 0.9^t)}{\log(0.9)} + \frac{Bc^x(c^t - 0.9^t)}{\log(0.9/c)} \right) \right\}$$

which is formula (3.16) in AMLCR.

Solutions for Chapter 4

4.1 (a) $_5E_{35} = v^5 l_{40}/l_{35} = 0.735942.$

(b) $A^1_{35:\overline{5}|} = A_{35} - {_5E_{35}} A_{40} = 0.012656.$

(c) $_5|A_{35} = {_5E_{35}} A_{40} = 0.138719.$

(d) $\bar{A}_{35:\overline{5}|} = (i/\delta)A^1_{35:\overline{5}|} + {_5E_{35}} = 0.748974.$

4.2 (a) $A^1_{30:\overline{20}|} = A_{30} - {_{20}E_{30}} A_{50}$

$$= 0.07698 - 0.37254 \times 0.18931 = 0.00645.$$

(b) $\bar{A}_{40:\overline{20}|} = \bar{A}^1_{40:\overline{20}|} + {_{20}E_{40}}$

$$= \tfrac{i}{\delta} (A_{40} - {_{20}E_{40}} A_{60}) + {_{20}E_{40}}$$

$$= \tfrac{0.05}{\log 1.05} (0.12106 - 0.36663 \times 0.29028) + 0.36663$$

$$= 0.38163.$$

(c) $_{10}|A_{25} = {_{10}E_{25}} A_{35}$

$$= 0.61198 \times 0.09653 = 0.05907.$$

4.3 Consider the whole life insurance as the sum of deferred one-year term insurances so that

$$A_x^{(m)} = \sum_{t=0}^{\infty} v^t \, {_t p_x} A^{(m)1}_{x+t:\overline{1}|}.$$

Now for any integer age y,

$$A^{(m)\ 1}_{y:\overline{1}|} = v^{1/m}\ _{1/m}q_y + v^{2/m}\ _{1/m|1/m}q_y + \cdots + v^{m/m}\ _{(m-1)/m|1/m}q_y,$$

and for $r = 0, 1, 2, \ldots, m - 1$,

$$\begin{aligned}
_{r/m|1/m}q_y &= \ _{(r+1)/m}q_y - \ _{r/m}q_y \\
&= \frac{r+1}{m}q_y - \frac{r}{m}q_y \quad \text{using UDD (formula (3.6))} \\
&= \frac{q_y}{m}.
\end{aligned}$$

Hence,

$$A^{(m)\ 1}_{y:\overline{1}|} = q_y \left\{ \frac{1}{m} \left(v^{1/m} + v^{2/m} + \cdots + v^{m/m} \right) \right\}.$$

You might recognize the term in the { } parentheses as $a^{(m)}_{\overline{1}|} = (1 - v)/i^{(m)}$. Alternatively, sum the geometric series to give

$$\begin{aligned}
\frac{1}{m} \left(v^{1/m} + v^{2/m} + \cdots + v^{m/m} \right) &= v^{1/m} \frac{1 - v}{m(1 - v^{1/m})} \\
&= \frac{1 - v}{m((1 + i)^{1/m} - 1)} = \frac{iv}{i^{(m)}}.
\end{aligned}$$

So

$$A^{(m)}_x = \sum_{t=0}^{\infty} v^t\ _tp_x\ q_{x+t} \frac{iv}{i^{(m)}} = \frac{i}{i^{(m)}} \sum_{t=0}^{\infty} v^{t+1}\ _t|q_x = \frac{i}{i^{(m)}} A_x.$$

E4.4 The EPV is

$$100\,000 \sum_{t=0}^{\infty} v^{t+1}\ 1.03^t\ _t|q_{30} = \frac{100\,000}{1.03} A_{30\,j}$$

where $A_{30\,j}$ is calculated at rate of interest $j = (0.05 - 0.03)/1.03$. The EPV is \$33\,569.47.

4.5 (a) Starting from formula (4.17), we have

$$\begin{aligned}
A_{x:\overline{n}|} &= \sum_{t=0}^{n-1} v^{t+1}\ _t|q_x + v^n\ _np_x \\
&= \sum_{t=0}^{n-2} v^{t+1}\ _t|q_x + v^n\ _{n-1}|q_x + v^n\ _np_x \\
&= \sum_{t=0}^{n-2} v^{t+1}\ _t|q_x + v^n\ _{n-1}p_x
\end{aligned}$$

since $_{n-1}|q_x + {}_np_x = {}_{n-1}p_x$.

(b) Formula (4.17) splits the EPV into a death benefit, covering the n-year term, and a benefit on survival to age $x+n$. The formula in part (a) splits the benefit according to the possible payment times. Payments may be made at any of the times $t = 1, 2, \ldots, n - 1$, if (x) dies in the year up to t, and a payment is made at time n if (x) dies in the year $n - 1$ to n, or if (x) survives to n.

That is, if (x) survives to the start of the final year (with probability $_{n-1}p_x$), then the benefit will be paid at the year end, whether (x) dies or survives the year.

4.6 We can consider a whole life insurance as a sum of deferred one-year term insurances, and hence write

$$A_x^{(m)} = \sum_{t=0}^{\infty} v^t {}_tp_x A_{x+t:\,\overline{1}|}^{(m)\,1},$$

and similarly

$$(IA^{(m)})_x = \sum_{t=0}^{\infty} (t + 1) v^t {}_tp_x A_{x+t:\,\overline{1}|}^{(m)\,1}.$$

Writing this equation in the following array form gives a clue as to how we can reorganize the expression:

$$(IA^{(m)})_x = \begin{cases} A_{x:\,\overline{1}|}^{(m)\,1} & + & v\,p_x A_{x+1:\,\overline{1}|}^{(m)\,1} & + & v^2\,{}_2p_x A_{x+2:\,\overline{1}|}^{(m)\,1} & + & \cdots \\ & & + & v\,p_x A_{x+1:\,\overline{1}|}^{(m)\,1} & + & v^2\,{}_2p_x A_{x+2:\,\overline{1}|}^{(m)\,1} & + & \cdots \\ & & & & + & v^2\,{}_2p_x A_{x+2:\,\overline{1}|}^{(m)\,1} & + & \cdots \\ & & & & & & + & \cdots \end{cases}$$

Now, considering each row separately,

$$(IA^{(m)})_x = A_x^{(m)}$$
$$+ v\,p_x \left(A_{x+1:\,\overline{1}|}^{(m)\,1} + v\,p_{x+1} A_{x+2:\,\overline{1}|}^{(m)\,1} + v^2\,{}_2p_{x+1} A_{x+3:\,\overline{1}|}^{(m)\,1} + \cdots \right)$$
$$+ v^2\,{}_2p_x \left(A_{x+2:\,\overline{1}|}^{(m)\,1} + v\,p_{x+2} A_{x+3:\,\overline{1}|}^{(m)\,1} + v^2\,{}_2p_{x+2} A_{x+4:\,\overline{1}|}^{(m)\,1} + \cdots \right)$$
$$+ \quad \cdots$$
$$= A_x^{(m)} + v\,p_x A_{x+1}^{(m)} + v^2\,{}_2p_x A_{x+2}^{(m)} + \cdots$$

The explanation for this formula is that we can view an increasing whole life insurance as the sum of deferred whole life insurance policies with deferred periods 0, 1, 2,... years and sum insured \$1, so that the death benefit in the tth policy year is $t + 1$. This argument applies whether the sum insured is payable at the moment of death, the end of the $\frac{1}{m}$th year of death, or at the end of the year of death.

4.7 (a) We have

$$(IA)^1_{x:\overline{n}|} = \sum_{k=0}^{n-1} (k + 1)v^{k+1} \,_{k|}q_x$$

$$= vq_x + 2v^2 \,_{1|}q_x + 3v^3 \,_{2|}q_x + \cdots + nv^n \,_{n-1|}q_x$$

$$= vq_x + 2v^2 \, p_xq_{x+1} + 3v^3 \,_{2}p_xq_{x+2} + \cdots + nv^n \,_{n-1}p_xq_{x+n-1}$$

$$= vq_x + vp_x(2v \, q_{x+1} + 3v^2 \, p_{x+1}q_{x+2} + \cdots + nv^{n-1} \,_{n-2}p_{x+1}q_{x+n-1})$$

$$= vq_x + vp_x(v \, q_{x+1} + 2v^2 \, p_{x+1}q_{x+2} +$$

$$\cdots + (n - 1)v^{n-1} \,_{n-2}p_{x+1}q_{x+n-1})$$

$$+ vp_x(v \, q_{x+1} + v^2 \, p_{x+1}q_{x+2} + \cdots + v^{n-1} \,_{n-2}p_{x+1}q_{x+n-1})$$

$$= vq_x + vp_x\left((IA)^1_{x+1:\overline{n-1}|} + A^1_{x+1:\overline{n-1}|}\right).$$

(b) This formula splits the EPV according to whether (x) survives for one year or not. The contribution to the EPV resulting from death in the first policy year is $v \, q_x$. If (x) survives the first policy year, the insurance benefit is an increasing benefit to a life now aged $x + 1$ with term $n - 1$ years and benefit levels $2, 3, \ldots, n$. This part of the benefit can be expressed as an increasing benefit of $1, 2, \ldots, n - 1$, with EPV at age $x + 1$ of $(IA)^1_{x+1:\overline{n-1}|}$, plus a level term benefit of 1 for the remaining $n - 1$ years of the contract, which has EPV at age $x+1$ of $A^1_{x+1:\overline{n-1}|}$. To get the EPV at age x of the benefits payable from age $x + 1$, discount for interest and survival for one year using $v \, p_x$.

(c) If we let $n \to \infty$ in part (a) we get

$$(IA)_{50} = v \, q_{50} + v \, p_{50} \, ((IA)_{51} + A_{51}).$$

We are given that $A^1_{50:\overline{1}|} = 0.00558$ and, as $A^1_{50:\overline{1}|} = v \, q_{50}$ and $i = 0.06$, we find that $p_{50} = 0.99409$. We are given A_{51}, so we calculate $(IA)_{51} = 5.07307$.

4.8 We start from

$$A_x - \,_{20}E_x \, A_{x+20} = A^1_{x:\overline{20}|}.$$

Adding $20E_x$ to each side gives

$$A_x - {}_{20}E_x (A_{x+20} - 1) = A_{x:\overline{20}|}$$

so that

$${}_{20}E_x = \frac{A_{x:\overline{20}|} - A_x}{1 - A_{x+20}} = \frac{0.55 - 0.25}{1 - 0.4} = 0.5$$

and so $A^1_{x:\overline{20}|} = A_{x:\overline{20}|} - {}_{20}E_x = 0.05$.

(a) Under claims acceleration,

$$10\,000\bar{A}_{x:\overline{20}|} = 10\,000 \left((1+i)^{1/2} A^1_{x:\overline{20}|} + {}_{20}E_x \right) = 5507.44.$$

(b) Under UDD,

$$10\,000\bar{A}_{x:\overline{20}|} = 10\,000 \left(\frac{i}{\delta} A^1_{x:\overline{20}|} + {}_{20}E_x \right) = 5507.46.$$

4.9 We have

$$(IA)^1_{x:\overline{n}|} = \sum_{k=0}^{n-1} v^{k+1}(k+1)_k|q_x$$

$$= \sum_{k=0}^{n-1} v^{k+1}(n+1)_k|q_x - \sum_{k=0}^{n-1} v^{k+1}{}_k|q_x - \sum_{k=0}^{n-2} v^{k+1}{}_k|q_x$$

$$- \sum_{k=0}^{n-3} v^{k+1}{}_k|q_x - \cdots - \sum_{k=0}^{0} v^{k+1}{}_k|q_x$$

$$= (n+1)A^1_{x:\overline{n}|} - \sum_{k=1}^{n} A^1_{x:\overline{k}|}.$$

The benefit being valued is a payment at the end of the year of death if this occurs within n years. The amount is 1 in the first year, 2 in the second year, and so on. We can regard this as an amount $n+1$ on death in any year minus n if death occurs in the first year, $n-1$ if death occurs in the second year, and so on.

4.10 We have

$$(\bar{I}\bar{A})_x = \int_0^\infty t \, v^t \, {}_tp_x \, \mu_{x+t} \, dt$$

$$= \sum_{j=0}^\infty \int_j^{j+1} t \, v^t \, {}_tp_x \, \mu_{x+t} \, dt$$

$$= \sum_{j=0}^\infty v^j \, {}_jp_x \int_0^1 (r+j) \, v^r \, {}_rp_{x+j} \, \mu_{x+j+r} \, dr$$

$$= \sum_{j=0}^\infty v^j \, {}_jp_x \, q_{x+j} \int_0^1 (r+j) \, v^r \, dr \quad \text{under UDD}$$

$$= \sum_{j=0}^\infty v^{j+1} \, {}_jp_x \, q_{x+j} \int_0^1 (r+j) \, e^{\delta(1-r)} \, dr.$$

Now

$$\int_0^1 e^{\delta(1-r)} \, dr = \frac{i}{\delta}$$

as in AMLCR and

$$\int_0^1 r \, e^{\delta(1-r)} \, dr = \frac{e^\delta - 1 - \delta}{\delta^2} = \frac{i - \delta}{\delta^2}$$

giving

$$\sum_{j=0}^\infty v^{j+1} \, {}_jp_x \, q_{x+j} \int_0^1 (r+j) \, e^{\delta(1-r)} \, dr = \frac{i-\delta}{\delta^2} A_x + \frac{i}{\delta} \sum_{j=0}^\infty j \, v^{j+1} \, {}_jp_x \, q_{x+j}$$

$$= \frac{i-\delta}{\delta^2} A_x + \frac{i}{\delta} \left((IA)_x - A_x \right).$$

4.11 As $v^t = (1+i)^{-t}$,

$$\frac{d}{di} v^t = -t \, (1+i)^{-t-1} = -t v^{t+1}.$$

Thus

$$\frac{d}{di} \bar{A}_x = \frac{d}{di} \int_0^\infty v^t \, {}_tp_x \, \mu_{x+t} \, dt$$

$$= \int_0^\infty \frac{d}{di} (1+i)^{-t} \, {}_tp_x \, \mu_{x+t} \, dt$$

$$= -\int_0^\infty t \, v^{t+1} \, {}_tp_x \, \mu_{x+t} \, dt$$

$$= -v(\bar{I}\bar{A})_x$$

which is negative since v and $(\bar{I}\bar{A})_x$ are positive. Thus $\bar{A}_x$ is a decreasing function of i. The result is intuitive if we think of $\bar{A}_x$ as the single premium required to provide a benefit of 1 immediately on the death of (x). The higher the rate of interest we can earn, the smaller the premium required.

4.12 We know that

$$A_{50} = A^1_{50:\overline{20}|} + {}_{20}E_{50}\, A_{70}$$

and

$$_{20}E_{50} = A_{50:\overline{20}|} - A^1_{50:\overline{20}|} = 0.27251.$$

Thus

$$A_{70} = \frac{A_{50} - A^1_{50:\overline{20}|}}{{}_{20}E_{50}} = 0.59704.$$

4.13 We have

$$X = \begin{cases} v^{T_x} & \text{if } T_x \le n, \\ v^n & \text{if } T_x > n, \end{cases} \qquad \text{and} \qquad Y = \begin{cases} v^{T_x} & \text{if } T_x \le n, \\ 0 & \text{if } T_x > n. \end{cases}$$

Let $Z = X - Y$ be the present value random variable for a pure endowment:

$$Z = \begin{cases} 0 & \text{if } T_x \le n, \\ v^n & \text{if } T_x > n. \end{cases}$$

Since $Y = X - Z$, we know that

$$E[X] = E[Y] + E[Z] \text{ and } V[Y] = V[X] + V[Z] - 2\mathrm{Cov}[X, Z].$$

Now

$$E[Z] = {}_nE_x = v^n \, {}_n p_x = 0.3 \times 0.8 = 0.24 \text{ and } E[Z^2] = v^{2n} \, {}_n p_x = 0.072,$$

so that $V[Z] = 0.0144$.

The covariance term is $E[XZ] - E[X]\,E[Z]$. We have

$$E[X] = E[Y] + E[Z] = 0.28$$

and as

$$XZ = \begin{cases} 0 & \text{if } T_x \le n, \\ v^{2n} & \text{if } T_x > n, \end{cases}$$

we have

$$E[XZ] = E[Z^2] = 0.072,$$

so that the covariance term is $0.072 - 0.28 \times 0.24 = 0.0048$, giving $V[Y] = 0.01$.

4.14 Again we use the technique of considering the whole life insurance as the sum of deferred one-year term insurances so that

$$\bar{A}_x = \sum_{t=0}^{\infty} v^t \, {}_tp_x \bar{A}^{\,1}_{x+t:\,\overline{1}|},$$

and

$$\bar{A}^{\,1}_{y:\,\overline{1}|} = \int_0^1 v^t \, {}_tp_y \, \mu_{y+t} \, dt.$$

Under the assumption of a constant force of mortality, such that $\mu_{y+t} = v_y$ between integer ages y and $y+1$, we have ${}_tp_y = \exp\{-v_y t\}$ for $0 \le t \le 1$, so that

$$\bar{A}^{\,1}_{y:\,\overline{1}|} = \int_0^1 {}_tp_x \, \mu_{x+t} \, v^t \, dt = \int_0^1 e^{-v_y t} \, v_y \, v^t \, dt = v_y \int_0^1 e^{-(\delta + v_y)t} \, dt$$

$$= \frac{v_y}{\delta + v_y} \left(1 - \exp\{-(\delta + v_y)\}\right)$$

$$= \frac{v_y}{\delta + v_y} \left(1 - v \, p_y\right).$$

Substituting this back into the original sum, replacing y with $x + t$, gives

$$\bar{A}_x = \sum_{t=0}^{\infty} v^t \, {}_tp_x \, \frac{v_{x+t}}{\delta + v_{x+t}} \left(1 - v \, p_{x+t}\right).$$

4.15 The covariance is $\mathrm{Cov}[Z_1, Z_2] = E[Z_1 Z_2] - E[Z_1]\,E[Z_2]$. Assuming that the benefit is payable immediately on death, we have

$$Z_1 = \begin{cases} v^{T_x} & \text{if } T_x \le n, \\ 0 & \text{if } T_x > n, \end{cases} \qquad \text{and} \qquad Z_2 = v^{T_x}$$

with expected values $E[Z_1] = \bar{A}^{\,1}_{x:\,\overline{n}|}$ and $E[Z_2] = \bar{A}_x$.

We see from the definitions that

$$Z_1 Z_2 = \begin{cases} v^{2T_x} & \text{if } T_x \le n, \\ 0 & \text{if } T_x > n, \end{cases}$$

so that

$$E[Z_1 Z_2] = {}^2\bar{A}^{\,1}_{x:\,\overline{n}|}$$

and so

$$\mathrm{Cov}[Z_1, Z_2] = {}^2\bar{A}^{\,1}_{x:\,\overline{n}|} - \bar{A}^{\,1}_{x:\,\overline{n}|} \bar{A}_x.$$

^{E}4.16 (a) We have

$$A_{[40]+1:\overline{4}|} = \sum_{t=0}^{3} v^{t+1} \,_t|q_{[40]+1} + v^4 \,_4p_{[40]+1}$$

$$= \frac{d_{[40]+1}v + d_{[40]+2}v^2 + d_{[40]+3}v^3 + d_{44}v^4 + l_{45}v^4}{l_{[40]+1}}$$

$$= 0.79267.$$

(b) Let Z denote the present value of the benefit. Then

$$E[Z] = 100\,000 \sum_{t=1}^{4} v^{t+1} \,_t|q_{[40]} = 701.35$$

and

$$E[Z^2] = 100\,000^2 \sum_{t=1}^{4} \left(v^{t+1}\right)^2 \,_t|q_{[40]} = 57\,037\,868,$$

giving a standard deviation of \$7519.71.

(c) The present value of the benefit is less than or equal to \$85 000 if the life dies in the deferred period or survives 5 years (since in either case no benefit is payable), or if the benefit is payable at time t years and

$$100\,000\,v^t < 85\,000,$$

which gives t as 3, 4 or 5. Thus the present value is strictly greater than \$85 000 only if the payment is at time 2, the probability of which is $_1|q_{[40]}$. Thus, the required probability is

$$1 - \,_1|q_{[40]} = 0.99825.$$

4.17 (a) (i) Z_1 is the present value of a benefit payable immediately on the death of (x), the amount of the benefit being 20 if death occurs before age $x + 15$ and 10 if death occurs after age $x + 15$.

(ii) Z_2 is the present value of a benefit of 10 payable immediately on the death of (x) should death occur between ages $x+5$ and $x+15$ or payable at age $x + 15$ should (x) survive to that age.

(b) (i) There are different ways in which the answer can be written. Viewing the benefit as being 10 immediately on death at any age plus an extra

10 on death before age $x + 15$, we get

$$E[Z_1] = 10\left(\int_0^\infty v^t \, {}_t p_x \, \mu_{x+t} dt + \int_0^{15} v^t \, {}_t p_x \, \mu_{x+t} dt \right).$$

Alternatively we can view the benefit as a term insurance plus a deferred whole life insurance giving

$$E[Z_1] = 20 \int_0^{15} v^t \, {}_t p_x \, \mu_{x+t} dt + 10 \int_{15}^\infty v^t \, {}_t p_x \, \mu_{x+t} dt.$$

(ii) We have

$$E[Z_2] = 10 \int_5^{15} v^t \, {}_t p_x \, \mu_{x+t} dt + 10 v^{15} \, {}_{15} p_x.$$

(c) (i) Corresponding to the first integral expression,

$$E[Z_1] = 10\left(\bar{A}_x + \bar{A}^1_{x:\overline{15|}} \right),$$

and corresponding to the second we get

$$E[Z_1] = 20 \bar{A}^1_{x:\overline{15|}} + 10 \, {}_{15}E_x \, A_{x+15}.$$

(ii) Using formula (4.22) to value the death benefit, we get

$$E[Z_2] = 10\left(\bar{A}^1_{x:\overline{15|}} - \bar{A}^1_{x:\overline{5|}} + {}_{15}E_x \right).$$

(d) Since $\text{Cov}[Z_1, Z_2] = E[Z_1 Z_2] - E[Z_1]E[Z_2]$ and since, from part (c), we already have expressions in terms of standard actuarial functions for $E[Z_1]$ and $E[Z_2]$, it remains to find an expression for $E[Z_1 Z_2]$.

From part (a) we have

$$Z_1 Z_2 = \begin{cases} 0 & \text{if } T_x \le 5, \\ 200 \, v^{2T_x} & \text{if } 5 < T_x \le 15, \\ 100 \, v^{15} \, v^{T_x} & \text{if } 15 < T_x. \end{cases}$$

Hence

$$E[Z_1 Z_2] = 200\left({}^2\bar{A}^1_{x:\overline{15|}} - {}^2\bar{A}^1_{x:\overline{5|}} \right) + 100 \, v^{15} \left(\bar{A}_x - \bar{A}^1_{x:\overline{15|}} \right)$$

and so

$$\text{Cov}[Z_1, Z_2] = 200\left({}^2\bar{A}^1_{x:\overline{15|}} - {}^2\bar{A}^1_{x:\overline{5|}} \right) + 100 \, v^{15} \left(\bar{A}_x - \bar{A}^1_{x:\overline{15|}} \right)$$
$$- 100(\bar{A}_x + \bar{A}^1_{x:\overline{15|}})(\bar{A}^1_{x:\overline{15|}} - \bar{A}^1_{x:\overline{5|}} + {}_{15}E_x).$$

Note that there are several ways to express the covariance using standard actuarial functions.

4.18 (a) The benefit is a death benefit, payable immediately on death, equal to t should (30) die at time t years from the issue of the policy if $t < 25$, and equal to 25 if death occurs more than 25 years after the issue of the policy.

  (b) $(\bar{I}\bar{A})^{1}_{30:\overline{25}|} + 25 \, {}_{25}E_{30} \, \bar{A}_{55}$.

4.19 (a) Let $S = 100\,000$. The present value random variable is

$$Z = S v^{K_{30}+1} \, .$$

The EPV is

$$S A_{30} = 10^5 \times 0.07698 = 7698$$

and $E[Z^2]$ is

$$S^2 \, ({}^2A_{30}) = 10^{10} \times 0.01109 = 110\,900\,000$$

so the standard deviation of the present value is

$$\sqrt{51\,640\,796} = 7186.$$

  (b) The present value random variable is

$$Z = \begin{cases} S v^{K_{30}+1} & \text{if } K_{30} \le 19, \\ 0 & \text{if } K_{30} \ge 20. \end{cases}$$

The EPV is

$$
\begin{aligned}
S A^{1}_{30:\overline{20}|} &= S(A_{30} - {}_{20}E_{30} A_{50}) \\
&= 10^5 (0.07698 - 0.37254 \times 0.18931) \\
&= 645.45
\end{aligned}
$$

and $E[Z^2]$ is

$$
\begin{aligned}
S^2 \, ({}^2A^{1}_{30:\overline{20}|}) &= S^2({}^2A_{30} - v^{20} \, {}_{20}E_{30} \, {}^2A_{50}) \\
&= 10^{10}(0.01109 - 0.37689 \times 0.37254 \times 0.05108) \\
&= 39\,180\,407
\end{aligned}
$$

so the standard deviation of the present value is

$$\sqrt{39\,180\,407 - 645.45^2} = 6226.$$

E4.20 (a) (i) We use the formula

$$A_x = v\,q_x + v\,p_x A_{x+1}$$

and start the recursion by setting $A_x = v$ for a suitably large value of x such as 119 (i.e. assume $\omega = 120$).

(ii) We use the formula

$$A_x^{(4)} = v^{1/4}\,_{1/4}q_x + v^{1/4}\,_{1/4}p_x A_{x+1/4}^{(4)}$$

and start the recursion by setting $A_x^{(4)} = v^{1/4}$ for a suitably large value of x such as $119\frac{3}{4}$. (For consistency with part (i), we have set the age to be $\frac{1}{4}$ less than the value of ω assumed there.)

(iii) We get the following values:

$$A_{50} = 0.33587, \qquad A_{100} = 0.87508,$$
$$A_{50}^{(4)} = 0.34330, \qquad A_{100}^{(4)} = 0.89647.$$

(b) Under UDD we have $A_x^{(4)} = (i/i^{(4)})A_x$ and when $i = 0.06$, we have $i/i^{(4)} = 1.02223$, giving the approximate values as

$$A_{50}^{(4)} = 0.34333 \quad \text{and} \quad A_{100}^{(4)} = 0.89453.$$

(c) The approximation is very good at age 50 (with an error less than 0.01%) but not as good at age 100 (although still fairly accurate with an error of around 0.2%). The reason for this is that UDD is fairly accurate when the mortality probabilities are low for adult ages, but UDD becomes rather less accurate at older ages. In the approximation of $A_{50}^{(4)}$ the older ages have less impact on the overall value, partly due to the dampening effect of discounting, but in the approximation of $A_{100}^{(4)}$ the mortality rates are very high, the discount factors are low, and the impact of the UDD approximation is more significant.

E4.21 (a) The EPV is

$$2000A_{50:\overline{15}|}^{(4)\,1} + 1000\,_{15|}A_{50}^{(4)}$$
$$= 2000A_{50:\overline{15}|}^{(4)\,1} + 1000\left(A_{50}^{(4)} - A_{50:\overline{15}|}^{(4)\,1}\right)$$
$$= 1000A_{50:\overline{15}|}^{(4)\,1} + 1000A_{50}^{(4)} = 218.83.$$

Using the UDD approximation gives an estimated EPV of \$218.87.

(b) For the variance, letting Z denote the present value of the benefit and $K^{(4)}$ denote the quarterly curtate future lifetime of (50), we have

$$Z^2 = \begin{cases} 2000^2 \, v^{2(K^{(4)}+1/4)} & \text{if } K^{(4)} + 1/4 \le 15, \\ 1000^2 \, v^{2(K^{(4)}+1/4)} & \text{if } K^{(4)} + 1/4 > 15. \end{cases}$$

The expected value is

$$E[Z^2] = 2000^2 \left({}^2 A^{(4)\,1}_{50:\overline{15}|} \right) + 1000^2 \left({}^2 A^{(4)}_{50} - {}^2 A^{(4)}_{65} \right)$$

$$= 105\,359$$

so that the standard deviation required is $239.73.

(c) The cost of benefits will exceed the accumulated premium on death at time T, say, if the present value of the benefits up to T is greater than the premium.

During the first 15 years

$$\Pr[Z > 500] = \Pr[2000 v^{K^{(4)}+1/4} > 500]$$
$$= \Pr[v^{K^{(4)}+1/4} > 1/4]$$
$$= \Pr[K^{(4)} + 1/4 < 28.4]$$

so that the EPV of the benefit will exceed the single premium for any payment during the first 15 years.

If the benefit is paid after the first 15 years, the amount drops to $1000, and the maximum present value is $1000 \, v^{15.25} = 475.2$ which is less than the premium. That is, if (50) survives the first 15 years, the accumulated premium will exceed the value of the benefit whenever it is paid.

So, the probability that the EPV of benefit exceeds the premium is the probability that (50) dies in the first 15 years, which is ${}_{15}q_{50} = 0.04054$.

E4.22 (a) We use

$$_t p_{60} = \exp\left\{ -\int_0^t \mu_{60+s} \, ds \right\} = {}_{t-h}p_{60} \times \exp\left\{ -\int_0^h \mu_{60+t-h+s} \, ds \right\}.$$

We calculate the table of values for $_t p_{60}$ recursively, with $_0 p_{60} = 1$, and using the trapezium rule for $-\int_0^h \mu_{60+t-h+s} \, ds$, for each period of $h = 1/40$ years. An excerpt from the table is shown below.

t	μ_{60+t}	$_tp_{60}$
0	0.003850	1.000000
0.025	0.003855	0.999904
0.050	0.003860	0.999807
0.075	0.003866	0.999711
$\vdots$	$\vdots$	$\vdots$

(b) We use

$$\bar{A}^{\,1}_{60:\overline{2|}} = \int_0^2 v^t \, _tp_{60} \, \mu_{60+t} \, dt$$

and evaluate the integral numerically using the repeated Simpson's method, with a step of $h = 1/40$, giving

$$\bar{A}^{\,1}_{60:\overline{2|}} \approx (1 \times {}_0p_{60} \times \mu_{60} \times v^0 + 4 \times {}_hp_{60} \times \mu_{60+h} \times v^h$$

$$+ 2 \times {}_{2h}p_{60} \times \mu_{60+2h} \times v^{2h} + 4 \times {}_{3h}p_{60} \times \mu_{60+3h} \times v^{3h}$$

$$+ \cdots + 4 \times {}_{79h}p_{60} \times \mu_{60+79h} \times v^{79h} + 1 \times {}_2p_{60} \times \mu_{62} \times v^2)h/3$$

$$= 0.007725.$$

Solutions for Chapter 5

5.1 (a) The benefit is an annuity of 1 per year payable continuously to (x) for at most 15 years, with payments being made only when (x) is alive. The EPV is $\bar{a}_{x:\overline{15}|}$.

(b) The benefit is an annuity of 1 per year payable annually in arrear to (x), with payments being guaranteed for the first 15 years and being payable thereafter only if (x) is alive. The EPV is

$$a_{\overline{x:15}|} = a_{\overline{15}|} + {}_{15}E_x\, a_{x+15}.$$

5.2 (a) The random variable Y is the present value of an annuity payable continuously at rate 1 per year following the death of (x) before time n (years). The annuity payments are guaranteed to be paid from the death of (x) until time n, and cease at time n. If (x) survives to time n, there are no payments.

(b) To determine the EPV of the benefit, we can sum the product of the amount paid, probability of payment and discount factor, over all possible payment dates. Because the benefit is payable continuously, the sum here is an integral.

Consider the interval $(t, t + dt)$, for $t < n$. The probability that the annuity is paid is the probability that (x) has died at that time, which is ${}_t q_x$. The discount factor is v^t and the amount of benefit is dt. The EPV therefore is

$$E[Y] = \int_0^n {}_t q_x\, v^t\, dt = \int_0^n (1 - {}_t p_x)\, v^t\, dt = \int_0^n v^t\, dt - \int_0^n {}_t p_x v^t\, dt$$
$$= \bar{a}_{\overline{n}|} - \bar{a}_{x:\overline{n}|}.$$

(c) The term $\bar{a}_{\overline{n}|}$ values a benefit payable continuously for n years, and the term $\bar{a}_{x:\overline{n}|}$ values a benefit payable continuously for n years provided that (x) is alive. The difference between these two terms must therefore value a benefit payable continuously for n years provided that (x) is not alive.

5.3 We know that

$$\ddot{a}_{50:\overline{10}|} = 1 + vp_{50} + v^2 {}_2p_{50} + \cdots + v^9 {}_9p_{50}$$

and

$$a_{50:\overline{10}|} = vp_{50} + v^2 {}_2p_{50} + \cdots + v^9 {}_9p_{50} + v^{10} {}_{10}p_{50},$$

giving

$$\ddot{a}_{50:\overline{10}|} - a_{50:\overline{10}|} = 1 - v^{10} {}_{10}p_{50}.$$

The values in the question give $v^{10} = 0.675476$, so $i = 4.0014\%$.

5.4 Using the recursive relationship $a_x = vp_x(1 + a_{x+1})$ we have

$$p_x = (1 + i)\frac{a_x}{1 + a_{x+1}}$$

giving $p_{60} = 0.99147$ and $p_{61} = 0.99065$, so that $_2p_{60} = 0.98220$.

5.5 (a) We have

$$\ddot{a}_{40:\overline{20}|} = \ddot{a}_{40} - {}_{20}E_{40}\,\ddot{a}_{60}$$
$$= 18.458 - 0.36663 \times 14.904$$
$$= 12.994.$$

(b) Using Woolhouse's formula with two terms

$$\ddot{a}^{(4)}_{40:\overline{20}|} = \ddot{a}_{40:\overline{20}|} - \frac{3}{8}(1 - {}_{20}E_{40})$$
$$= 12.994 - \frac{3}{8}(1 - 0.36663)$$
$$= 12.756.$$

(c) Under the UDD assumption

$$\bar{a}_{25:\overline{10}|} = \alpha(\infty)\,\ddot{a}_{25:\overline{10}|} - \beta(\infty)(1 - {}_{10}E_{25})$$

where

$$\alpha(\infty) = \frac{id}{\delta^2} = 1.000198, \quad \beta(\infty) = \frac{i-\delta}{\delta^2} = 0.508232$$

which gives

$$\bar{a}_{25:\overline{10}|} = 1.000198(19.709 - 0.61198 \times 18.973) - 0.508232(1 - 0.61198)$$

$$= 7.902.$$

(d) Using Woolhouse's formula with two terms

$$a^{(12)}_{50:\overline{20}|} = \ddot{a}^{(12)}_{50:\overline{20}|} - \frac{1}{12}(1 - {}_{20}E_{50})$$

$$= \ddot{a}_{50:\overline{20}|} - \frac{11}{24}(1 - {}_{20}E_{50}) - \frac{1}{12}(1 - {}_{20}E_{50})$$

$$= \ddot{a}_{50} - {}_{20}E_{50}\,\ddot{a}_{70} - \frac{13}{24}(1 - {}_{20}E_{50})$$

$$= 17.025 - 0.34824 \times 12.008 - \frac{13}{24}(1 - 0.34824)$$

$$= 12.490.$$

(e) Under the UDD assumption,

$$\alpha(12) = \frac{id}{i^{(12)}d^{(12)}} \text{ and } \beta(12) = \frac{i - i^{(12)}}{i^{(12)}d^{(12)}}$$

and

$$_{20|}\ddot{a}^{(12)}_{45} = {}_{20}E_{45}\,\ddot{a}^{(12)}_{65}$$

$$= {}_{20}E_{45}\,(\alpha(12)\ddot{a}_{65} - \beta(12))$$

$$= 0.35994(1.000197 \times 13.550 - 0.466508)$$

$$= 4.710.$$

5.6 The present value random variable is

$$Z = 50\,000\,\frac{1 - v^{K_{[60]}+1}}{d}$$

which gives

$$V[Z] = \left(\frac{50\,000}{d}\right)^2 V[v^{K_{[60]}+1}]$$

$$= \left(\frac{50\,000}{d}\right)^2 \left({}^2A_{[60]} - A^2_{[60]}\right)$$

$$= \left(\frac{50\,000}{d}\right)^2 (0.10781 - 0.28984^2).$$

Hence, the standard deviation of Z is $161\,996$.

5.7 We use

$$A^1_{x:\overline{10|}} = A_{x:\overline{10|}} - {}_{10}E_x$$

and

$$A_{x:\overline{10|}} = 1 - d\,\ddot{a}_{x:\overline{10|}}.$$

From the given information we calculate

$$\ddot{a}_{x:\overline{10|}} = \ddot{a}_x - {}_{10|}\ddot{a}_x = 6,$$

giving

$$A_{x:\overline{10|}} = 1 - (1 - 0.94)6 = 0.64$$

and hence

$$A^1_{x:\overline{10|}} = 0.64 - 0.375 = 0.265.$$

5.8 (a) $\ddot{a}_{[40]:\overline{4|}} = \dfrac{l_{[40]} + l_{[40]+1}v + l_{42}v^2 + l_{43}v^3}{l_{[40]}} = 3.66643.$

(b) $a_{[40]+1:\overline{4|}} = \dfrac{l_{42}v + l_{43}v^2 + l_{44}v^3 + l_{45}v^4}{l_{[40]+1}} = 3.45057.$

(c) $(Ia)_{[40]:\overline{4|}} = \dfrac{l_{[40]+1}v + 2l_{42}v^2 + 3l_{43}v^3 + 4l_{44}v^4}{l_{[40]}} = 8.37502.$

(d) $(IA)_{[40]:\overline{4|}} = \dfrac{d_{[40]}v + 2d_{[40]+1}v^2 + 3d_{42}v^3 + 4d_{43}v^4 + 4l_{44}v^4}{l_{[40]}} = 3.16305.$

(e) Let Y denote the present value of the annuity. Then

$$Y = \begin{cases} 1000\,\ddot{a}_{\overline{1|}} & \text{with probability} & q_{[41]}, \\ 1000\,\ddot{a}_{\overline{2|}} & \text{with probability} & {}_{1|}q_{[41]}, \\ 1000\,\ddot{a}_{\overline{3|}} & \text{with probability} & {}_{2|}q_{[41]}, \\ 1000\,\ddot{a}_{\overline{4|}} & \text{with probability} & {}_{3}p_{[41]}. \end{cases}$$

So $E[Y] = 3665.58$ and $E[Y^2] = 13\,450\,684$ which gives a standard deviation of 119.14.

(f) At 6% per year, $\ddot{a}_{\overline{n|}} < 3$ if and only if

$$\frac{1 - v^n}{1 - v} < 3,$$

which gives $n < 3.19$. As the term n must be an integer, the present value is less than 3 if at most three annuity payments are made (i.e. if the life does not survive to age 43 since payments are in advance), and the required probability is

$$_3q_{[40]} = 1 - \frac{l_{43}}{l_{[40]}} = 0.00421.$$

5.9 If $\mu_x = 0.5(\mu_x^A + \mu_x^B)$, then

$$\begin{aligned}
_tp_x &= \exp\left\{-\int_0^t \mu_{x+r}dr\right\} \\
&= \exp\left\{-0.5\int_0^t \left(\mu_{x+r}^A + \mu_{x+r}^B\right)dr\right\} \\
&= \left(_tp_x^A\right)^{1/2}\left(_tp_x^B\right)^{1/2}.
\end{aligned}$$

For positive α and β, $(\alpha\beta)^{1/2} \leq (\alpha+\beta)/2$ since a geometric mean is less than an arithmetic mean. Alternatively, note that for positive α and β,

$$\alpha + \beta - 2(\alpha\beta)^{1/2} = (\alpha^{1/2} - \beta^{1/2})^2 \geq 0.$$

Thus

$$\left(_tp_x^A\right)^{1/2}\left(_tp_x^B\right)^{1/2} \leq 0.5\left(_tp_x^A + _tp_x^B\right)$$

and so

$$\begin{aligned}
a_x &= \sum_{t=1}^\infty v^t\, _tp_x = \sum_{t=1}^\infty v^t\left(_tp_x^A\right)^{1/2}\left(_tp_x^B\right)^{1/2} \\
&\leq 0.5\left(a_x^A + a_x^B\right).
\end{aligned}$$

Hence, the approximation overstates the true value.

5.10 The present value of the increasing annuity is $(I\ddot{a})_{\overline{K_x+1}|}$ and the present value of the death benefit is $(K_x + 1)v^{K_x+1}$. Also,

$$(I\ddot{a})_x = \mathrm{E}\left[(I\ddot{a})_{\overline{K_x+1}|}\right]$$

and

$$(IA)_x = \mathrm{E}\left[(K_x + 1)v^{K_x+1}\right].$$

We then have

$$(I\ddot{a})_x = E\left[\frac{\ddot{a}_{\overline{K_x+1}|} - (K_x + 1)v^{K_x+1}}{d}\right]$$

$$= \frac{1}{d}\left(\ddot{a}_x - (IA)_x\right),$$

giving $(IA)_x = \ddot{a}_x - d(I\ddot{a})_x$.

5.11 (a) With $H = \min(K_x, n)$, we have

$$a_{\overline{H}|} = \ddot{a}_{\overline{H+1}|} - 1$$

and so

$$V[a_{\overline{H}|}] = V[\ddot{a}_{\overline{H+1}|} - 1] = V[\ddot{a}_{\overline{H+1}|}]$$

$$= V\left[\frac{1 - v^{\min(K_x+1, n+1)}}{d}\right]$$

$$= \frac{1}{d^2}\left(^2A_{x:\overline{n+1}|} - (A_{x:\overline{n+1}|})^2\right).$$

(b) We have (similarly to Exercise 4.5)

$$A_{x:\overline{n+1}|} = A^1_{x:\overline{n+1}|} + {}_{n+1}p_x v^{n+1}$$

$$= \left(A^1_{x:\overline{n}|} + {}_np_x q_{x+n} v^{n+1}\right) + {}_np_x p_{x+n} v^{n+1}$$

$$= A^1_{x:\overline{n}|} + {}_np_x v^{n+1}.$$

Then

$$V\left[a_{\overline{H}|}\right] = \frac{1}{d^2}\left(^2A^1_{x:\overline{n}|} + v^{2(n+1)} {}_np_x - \left(A^1_{x:\overline{n}|} + v^{n+1} {}_np_x\right)^2\right)$$

$$= \frac{1}{d^2}\left(^2A^1_{x:\overline{n}|} - \left(A^1_{x:\overline{n}|}\right)^2 + v^{2(n+1)} {}_np_x - v^{2(n+1)} ({}_np_x)^2\right)$$

$$- \frac{2}{d^2}A^1_{x:\overline{n}|}v^{n+1} {}_np_x$$

$$= \left(\frac{1+i}{i}\right)^2\left(^2A^1_{x:\overline{n}|} - \left(A^1_{x:\overline{n}|}\right)^2\right) + \frac{v^{2n} {}_np_x(1 -{}_n p_x)}{i^2}$$

$$- \frac{2(1+i)v^n {}_np_x}{i^2}A^1_{x:\overline{n}|}.$$

5.12 (a) As future lifetime increases, the annuity present value (Y) increases whereas the insurance present value (Z) decreases, so Y and Z are negatively correlated and hence have a negative covariance.

(b) For two random variables X and Y, $\text{Cov}[X, Y] = E[XY] - E[X]E[Y]$. Thus,

$$
\begin{aligned}
\text{Cov}\left[\bar{a}_{\overline{T_x}|}, v^{T_x}\right] &= E\left[\bar{a}_{\overline{T_x}|} v^{T_x}\right] - E\left[\bar{a}_{\overline{T_x}|}\right] E\left[v^{T_x}\right] \\
&= E\left[\frac{1 - v^{T_x}}{\delta} v^{T_x}\right] - \bar{a}_x \bar{A}_x \\
&= \frac{1}{\delta}\left(\bar{A}_x - {}^2\bar{A}_x\right) - \frac{1 - \bar{A}_x}{\delta} \bar{A}_x \\
&= \frac{\left(\bar{A}_x\right)^2 - {}^2\bar{A}_x}{\delta}.
\end{aligned}
$$

(c) As $V[v^{T_x}] = {}^2\bar{A}_x - \left(\bar{A}_x\right)^2 > 0$, we see that $\text{Cov}\left[\bar{a}_{\overline{T_x}|}, v^{T_x}\right] < 0$.

5.13 (a) We know that $\frac{d}{dx}\, {}_tp_x = {}_tp_x(\mu_x - \mu_{x+t})$ (see Exercise 2.9). Then

$$
\begin{aligned}
\frac{d}{dx}\ddot{a}_x &= \frac{d}{dx}\sum_{t=0}^{\infty} v^t\, {}_tp_x = \sum_{t=0}^{\infty} v^t\, {}_tp_x(\mu_x - \mu_{x+t}) \\
&= \mu_x\, \ddot{a}_x - \sum_{t=0}^{\infty} v^t\, {}_tp_x\, \mu_{x+t}.
\end{aligned}
$$

(b) Similarly,

$$
\frac{d}{dx}\ddot{a}_{x:\overline{n}|} = \mu_x\, \ddot{a}_{x:\overline{n}|} - \sum_{t=0}^{n-1} v^t\, {}_tp_x\, \mu_{x+t}.
$$

E5.14 (a) The EPV is

$$
10\,000\,(40\,\ddot{a}_{60} + 30\,\ddot{a}_{70} + 10\,\ddot{a}_{80}) = 10\,418\,961.
$$

(b) For a life aged x, the variance of the present value is $10^8 \sigma_x^2$ where

$$
\sigma_x^2 = \frac{{}^2A_x - A_x^2}{d^2}.
$$

By the independence of the lives, the variance of the present value is

$$
10^8\left(40\,\sigma_{60}^2 + 30\,\sigma_{70}^2 + 10\,\sigma_{80}^2\right)
$$

and so the standard deviation is

$$
10^4\sqrt{40\,\sigma_{60}^2 + 30\,\sigma_{70}^2 + 10\,\sigma_{80}^2} = 311\,534.
$$

(c) The 95th percentile of the standard normal distribution is 1.644854 so the 95th percentile of the distribution of the present value is

$$10\,418\,961 + 1.644854 \times 311\,534 = 10\,931\,390.$$

5.15 Write everything in terms of δ:

$$i = \delta + \frac{1}{2}\delta^2 + \frac{1}{6}\delta^3 + \cdots,$$

$$d = \delta - \frac{1}{2}\delta^2 + \frac{1}{6}\delta^3 - \cdots,$$

$$i^{(m)} = \delta + \frac{1}{2m}\delta^2 + \frac{1}{6m^2}\delta^3 + \cdots,$$

$$d^{(m)} = \delta - \frac{1}{2m}\delta^2 + \frac{1}{6m^2}\delta^3 - \cdots.$$

Then ignoring terms in δ^4 and higher powers,

$$id \approx \delta^2 \quad \text{and} \quad i^{(m)}d^{(m)} \approx \delta^2$$

so that

$$\alpha(m) = \frac{id}{i^{(m)}d^{(m)}} \approx 1.$$

Similarly, ignoring terms in δ^3 and higher powers,

$$i - i^{(m)} \approx \frac{1}{2}\delta^2\left(1 - \frac{1}{m}\right)$$

and so

$$\beta(m) = \frac{i - i^{(m)}}{i^{(m)}d^{(m)}} \approx \frac{1}{2}\left(1 - \frac{1}{m}\right) = \frac{m-1}{2m}.$$

E5.16 (a) The formulae for the EPV is

$$\text{EPV} = \sum_{t=1}^{10} (I\ddot{a})_{\overline{t}|}\;{}_{t-1|}q_{50} + {}_{10}p_{50}\,(I\ddot{a})_{\overline{10}|},$$

and for the variance is

$$\sum_{t=1}^{10} \left((I\ddot{a})_{\overline{t}|}\right)^2 {}_{t-1|}q_{[50]} + {}_{10}p_{[50]}\,((I\ddot{a})_{\overline{10}|})^2 - (\text{EPV})^2.$$

For a recursive calculation we can use

$$(I\ddot{a})_{\overline{t}|} = (I\ddot{a})_{\overline{t-1}|} + t\,v^{t-1}$$

with $(I\ddot{a})_{\overline{1}|} = 1$.

(b) The present value of the annuity if it were payable for t years certain would be

$$PV_t = 1 + 1.03v + 1.03^2v^2 + \cdots + 1.03^{t-1}v^{t-1} = \frac{1 - 1.03^t v^t}{1 - 1.03v} = \ddot{a}_{\overline{t}|j}$$

where $\ddot{a}_{\overline{t}|j}$ is the present value of an annuity-certain evaluated at effective interest rate j, where $1 + j = (1 + i)/1.03$. Hence the formulae for the first two moments of the present value are respectively

$$\sum_{t=1}^{10} \ddot{a}_{\overline{t}|j}\,{}_{t-1|}q_{50} + {}_{10}p_{50}\,\ddot{a}_{\overline{10}|j}$$

and

$$\sum_{t=1}^{10} \left(\ddot{a}_{\overline{t}|j}\right)^2 {}_{t-1|}q_{50} + {}_{10}p_{50}(\ddot{a}_{\overline{10}|j})^2.$$

For a recursive calculation, $\ddot{a}_{\overline{1}|j} = 1$ and for $t = 2, 3, \ldots,$

$$\ddot{a}_{\overline{t}|j} = \ddot{a}_{\overline{t-1}|j} + 1.03^{t-1}v^{t-1}.$$

^{E}5.17 (a) The EPV is calculated as

$$\sum_{t=1}^{\infty} \ddot{a}_{\overline{t}|}\,{}_{t-1|}q_{65} = 13.550$$

and the second moment is calculated as

$$\sum_{t=1}^{\infty} \left(\ddot{a}_{\overline{t}|}\right)^2 {}_{t-1|}q_{65} = 196.094,$$

which gives a variance of 12.497.

(b) The EPV is calculated as

$$\sum_{t=1}^{10} {}_{t-1|}q_{65}\,\ddot{a}_{\overline{10}|} + \sum_{t=11}^{\infty} {}_{t-1|}q_{65}\,\ddot{a}_{\overline{t}|}$$

$$= {}_{10}q_{65}\,\ddot{a}_{\overline{10}|} + \sum_{t=11}^{\infty} {}_{t-1|}q_{65}\,\ddot{a}_{\overline{t}|} = 13.814$$

and the second moment is calculated as

$$\sum_{t=1}^{10} {}_{t-1|}q_{65}\left(\ddot{a}_{\overline{10}|}\right)^2 + \sum_{t=11}^{\infty} {}_{t-1|}q_{65}\left(\ddot{a}_{\overline{t}|}\right)^2$$

$$= {}_{10}q_{65}\left(\ddot{a}_{\overline{10}|}\right)^2 + \sum_{t=11}^{\infty} {}_{t-1|}q_{65}\left(\ddot{a}_{\overline{t}|}\right)^2$$

$$= 199.209$$

which gives a variance of 8.380.

The EPV is greater in part (b) because of the guarantee. The value of the benefit is greater for those who die in the first 10 years, and the same for those who survive 10 years, compared with the annuity in (a), so, overall, the expected value must be larger with the guarantee than without.

However, the guarantee reduces the variance of the present value as there is less variability in the payment terms – in part (a) the possible payment terms are $1, 2, 3, \ldots$ years, whereas in part (b) they are $10, 11, 12, \ldots$ years.

5.18 We have

$$\bar{a}_x = E\left[\bar{a}_{\overline{T_x}|}\right] = E\left[\frac{1 - e^{-\delta T_x}}{\delta}\right] = E\left[f(T_x)\right]$$

where

$$f(x) = (1 - e^{-\delta x})/\delta.$$

Hence $f'(x) > 0$ and $f''(x) < 0$, and (as given in the question) Jensen's inequality for concave functions gives

$$E\left[f(T_x)\right] \leq f(E[T_x])$$

so

$$\bar{a}_x \leq f(E[T_x]) = \bar{a}_{\overline{E[T_x]}|}.$$

Solutions for Chapter 6

6.1 (a) Let P be the annual premium. Then

$$L_0 = 200\,000\, v^{K_{[30]}+1} - P\, \ddot{a}_{\overline{\min(K_{[30]+1},20)}} .$$

(b) The equation of value is

$$P\, \ddot{a}_{[30]:\overline{20}|} = 200\,000\, A_{[30]}$$

giving $P = \$1\,179.73$ since $\ddot{a}_{[30]:\overline{20}|} = 13.04178$ and $A_{[30]} = 0.07693$.

(c) We want the least integer, n, such that the accumulation of premiums to time n exceeds the sum insured. Thus, assuming $n > 20$, we want n such that

$$P\, \ddot{s}_{\overline{20}|}\, (1.05^{n-20}) > 200\,000$$

which gives $n = 53$. The probability of a profit is thus $_{53}p_{[30]} = 0.67804$.

6.2 (a) Let P be the single premium. Then

$$L_0 = \begin{cases} 10^6\, v^{T_{[40]}} - P & \text{if } T_{[40]} \leq 5, \\ -P & \text{if } T_{[40]} > 5. \end{cases}$$

(b) The equation of value is

$$P = 10^6\, \bar{A}^{\,1}_{[40]:\overline{5}|}$$

and, under UDD, $\bar{A}^{\,1}_{[40]:\overline{5}|} = \frac{i}{\delta} A^{\,1}_{[40]:\overline{5}|} = 0.002535$, leading to $P = \$2597.95$.

(c) Note that $P(1.05^5) < 10^6$, meaning that there is a loss if the death benefit is payable at time 5 years (or earlier). Hence the probability of a profit is $_5p_{[40]} = 0.99704$.

6.3 (a) Let S be the sum insured. Then

$$350\,\ddot{a}_{[41]:\,\overline{3}|} = S A^{\,1}_{[41]:\,\overline{3}|}$$

gives $S = \$216\,326.38$ since

$$\ddot{a}_{[41]:\,\overline{3}|} = \sum_{t=0}^{2} v^t\, {}_t p_{[41]} = 2.82965$$

and

$$A^{\,1}_{[41]:\,\overline{3}|} = \sum_{t=0}^{2} v^{t+1}\, {}_t|q_{[41]} = 0.00458.$$

(b) The possible values of L_0 and the associated probabilities are as follows:

$$
\begin{array}{ll}
S v - 350 & \text{with probability } q_{[41]}, \\
S v^2 - 350\,\ddot{a}_{\overline{2}|} & \text{with probability } {}_1|q_{[41]}, \\
S v^3 - 350\,\ddot{a}_{\overline{3}|} & \text{with probability } {}_2|q_{[41]}, \\
-350\,\ddot{a}_{\overline{3}|} & \text{with probability } {}_3p_{[41]}.
\end{array}
$$

Now $E[L_0] = 0$ since the calculation in part (a) uses the equivalence principle and so

$$
\begin{aligned}
V[L_0] &= E[L_0^2] \\
&= \sum_{t=1}^{3} \left(S v^t - 350\,\ddot{a}_{\overline{t}|} \right)^2 {}_{t-1}|q_{[41]} + \left(350\,\ddot{a}_{\overline{3}|} \right)^2 {}_3p_{[41]} \\
&= 188\,541\,300,
\end{aligned}
$$

giving the standard deviation as $\$13\,731.03$.

(c) We can see from part (b) that L_0 will be positive if and only if the life dies before age 44, so

$$\Pr[L_0 > 0] = 1 - {}_3p_{[41]} = 0.0052.$$

6.4 (a) Let P be the annual premium. Then

$$
L_0 = \begin{cases}
100\,000\, v^{K_{[50]}+1} - P\,\ddot{a}_{\overline{\min(K_{[50]}+1,10)}|} & \text{if } K_{[50]} < 10, \\[2mm]
-P\,\ddot{a}_{\overline{\min(K_{[50]}+1,10)}|} & \text{if } K_{[50]} \leq 10,
\end{cases}
$$

or, using an indicator random variable,

$$L_0 = 100\,000\, v^{K_{[50]}+1}\, I(K_{[50]} < 10) - P\,\ddot{a}_{\overline{\min(K_{[50]}+1,10)}}\,.$$

(b) The equation of value is

$$P\,\ddot{a}_{[50]:\overline{10}} = 100\,000\, A^{\,1}_{[50]:\overline{10}}$$

and as $\ddot{a}_{[50]:\overline{10}} = 8.05665$ and $A^{\,1}_{[50]:\overline{10}} = 0.01439$, we find $P = \$178.57$.

E6.5 (a) Let P be the annual premium. Treating the premium related expenses as 3% of each premium plus an additional 17% of the first premium, we have

$$L_0 = 100\,000\, v^{\min(K_{[35]}+1,\,20)} + 3000 + 0.17P - 0.97P\,\ddot{a}_{\overline{\min(K_{[35]}+1,\,20)}}\,.$$

(b) The equation of value is

$$100\,000\, A_{[35]:\overline{20}} + 3000 = P\left(0.97\,\ddot{a}_{[35]:\overline{20}} - 0.17\right)$$

giving $P = \$3287.57$ since $\ddot{a}_{[35]:\overline{20}} = 13.02489$ and $A_{[35]:\overline{20}} = 0.37977$.

(c) We can write

$$L_0 = v^{\min(K_{[35]}+1,\,20)}\left(100\,000 + \frac{0.97P}{d}\right) - 3000 - 0.17P - \frac{0.97P}{d}$$

so that

$$V[L_0] = \left(100\,000 + \frac{0.97P}{d}\right)^2 V\left[v^{\min(K_{[35]}+1,\,20)}\right]$$

$$= \left(100\,000 + \frac{0.97P}{d}\right)^2 \left({}^2A_{[35]:\overline{20}} - \left(A_{[35]:\overline{20}}\right)^2\right).$$

We determine that ${}^2A_{[35]:\overline{20}} = 0.14511$, giving a standard deviation of $\$4981.10$.

(d) If the sum insured is payable at time k, there is a profit if the present value of premiums is greater than the present value of the sum insured and expenses, i.e. if

$$0.97\,P\,\ddot{a}_{\overline{k}} > 100\,000\, v^k + 3000 + 0.17\,P$$

which gives

$$1.05^k > \frac{100\,000 + 0.97\,P/d}{0.97\,P/d - 0.17\,P - 3000} = 2.6332 \Longrightarrow k > 19.8.$$

The payment date must be an integer, so there is a profit only if the benefit is payable (on death or survival) at time $k = 20$, i.e. if the life survives to time 19. The required probability is $_{19}p_{[35]} = 0.98466$.

6.6 Let P be the annual premium. We equate the EPV of premiums with the EPV of the sum insured plus expenses. When the cashflows are complicated, it is often convenient to value each element separately.

EPV of premiums:

$$P\ddot{a}_{[45]:\overline{20}|} = 12.9409\,P.$$

EPV of endowment insurance benefit:

$$100\,000\,A_{[45]:\overline{20}|} = 38\,376.55.$$

EPV of initial and renewal expenses:

$$0.08P + 42 + (0.02P + 8)\ddot{a}_{[45]:\overline{20}|} = 0.3388\,P + 145.53$$

where we have split the initial expenses as $0.1P = 0.08P + 0.02P$ and $50 = 42 + 8$. The equation of value is

$$12.9409\,P = 38\,376.55 + 0.3388\,P + 145.53$$

giving $P = \$3056.80$.

6.7 (a) Let P be the single premium. Then

$$L_0 = \begin{cases} P\,v^{K_{[45]+1}} - P & \text{if } K_{[45]} < 20, \\ 40\,000\left(\ddot{a}_{\overline{K_{[45]+1}|}} - \ddot{a}_{\overline{\min(K_{[45]+1},20)|}}\right) - P & \text{if } K_{[45]} \geq 20. \end{cases}$$

(b) EPV of the death benefit:

$$P\,A^{1}_{[45]:\overline{20}|} = 0.02377\,P.$$

EPV of the deferred annuity:

$$40\,000\,_{20|}\ddot{a}_{[45]} = 195\,113.61.$$

Hence

$$P = 0.02377\,P + 195\,113.61$$

giving $P = \$199\,864.74$.

(c) Let $\hat{P}$ be the new single premium. The EPV of the deferred annuity is now

$$_{20}E_{[45]}\,(\ddot{a}_{\overline{5}|} + {}_5E_{65}\,\ddot{a}_{70}) = 195\,935.36$$

so that the equation of value is

$$\hat{P} = 0.02377\,\hat{P} + 195\,935.36,$$

giving $\hat{P} = \$200\,706.50$.

E6.8 Let P be the annual premium.

EPV of premiums less premium expenses:

$$P\ddot{a}_{[40]:\overline{25}|} \times 0.975 - 0.575\,P.$$

We find $\ddot{a}_{[40]:\overline{25}|} = 14.64954$, so the EPV of premiums less premium related expenses is $13.70830\,P$.

EPV of policy fees:

$$5\left(1 + 1.06\,v\,p_{[40]} + 1.06^2\,v^2\,{}_2p_{[40]} + \cdots + v^{24}\,1.06^{24}\,{}_{24}p_{[40]}\right) = 5\,\ddot{a}_{[40]:\overline{25}|\,i^*}$$

where $i^* = 1.05/1.06 - 1$. We find $\ddot{a}_{[40]:\overline{25}|\,i^*} = 27.66275$ so the EPV of the policy fees is 138.31.

EPV of death benefit:

$$200\,000 \sum_{t=0}^{\infty} v^t\,{}_tp_{[40]}\,1.015^t\,A^{(12)}{}_{[40]+t:\overline{1}|}^{\hspace{1.2em}1}$$

where

$$A^{(12)}{}_{[40]+t:\overline{1}|}^{\hspace{1.2em}1} = \sum_{j=0}^{11} v^{(j+1)/12}\left({}_{j/12}p_{[40]+t} - {}_{(j+1)/12}p_{[40]+t}\right).$$

This EPV is $44\,586.36$.

Equating the EPVs of income and outgo gives $P = \$3262.60$.

E6.9 Let P be the monthly premium. Then

EPV of premiums less premium expenses:

$$0.95 \times 12P\,\ddot{a}^{(12)}_{[40]:\overline{20}|} - 0.15P = 144.65P$$

as $\ddot{a}^{(12)}_{[40]:\overline{20}|} = 12.7019.$

EPV of expenses on death:

$$20\left(q_{[40]}v(1.03) + {}_{1|}q_{[40]}v^2(1.03)^2 + \cdots\right) = 20A_{[40]\,i^*} = 8.33$$

where $i^* = 1.05/1.03 - 1$, and $A_{[40]\,i^*} = 0.416425$.

EPV of other expenses:

$$0.025 \times 50\,000 = 1250.$$

EPV of annuity benefit:

$$50\,000\left({}_{20}p_{[40]}v^{20} + (1.02)v^{21}\,{}_{21}p_{[40]} + (1.02)^2 v^{22}\,{}_{22}p_{[40]} + \cdots\right)$$
$$= 50\,000\,{}_{20}E_{[40]}\,\ddot{a}_{60\,(j)} = 342\,689$$

where $\ddot{a}_{60\,(j)}$ is calculated at rate $j = 1.05/1.02 - 1$, giving $\ddot{a}_{60\,(j)} = 18.6920$. The pure endowment factor ${}_{20}E_{[40]} = 0.366669$ is evaluated at the original rate of 5%.

Equating the EPVs gives a monthly premium of $P = \$2377.75$.

6.10 Let P be the annual premium.

EPV of premiums:

$$P\,\ddot{a}_{[40]:\overline{10|}} = 8.08705\,P.$$

EPV of death benefit:

$$100\,000\,A_{[40]:\overline{20|}}^{\,1} = 1453.58.$$

EPV of taxes and commission:

$$0.09\,P\,\ddot{a}_{[40]:\overline{10|}} + 0.2P = 0.92783\,P.$$

EPV of policy maintenance costs:

$$5\ddot{a}_{[40]:\overline{20|}} + 5 = 69.97.$$

Equate the EPVs of income and outgo to give $P = \$212.81$.

6.11 (a) Let P denote the single premium. Then

$$P = 20\,000\,{}_{30|}\ddot{a}_{[35]} + P\,A_{[35]:\overline{30|}}^{\,1}.$$

We find that

$$_{30|}\ddot{a}_{[35]} = {}_{30}E_{[35]}\,\ddot{a}_{65} = 2.97862$$

and $A_{[35]:\overline{30}|}^{\;\;1} = 0.01848$, giving

$$P = \frac{59\,572.4}{1 - 0.01848} = \$60\,694.00.$$

(b) Because there is an extra benefit, the revised premium will be greater than $\$60\,694.00$. However, the extra benefit, a deferred decreasing term insurance, is unlikely to have much effect on the EPV of the benefits and hence is likely to increase the premium by only a small amount. Assuming that the revised single premium remains less than $\$80\,000$, then the additional death benefit would be payable on death during the first three years of the annuity payout phase of the contract.

So, we let $\tilde{P}$ denote the revised premium and assume, first, that the additional death benefit will apply for three years from age 65 to age 68. Then we have

$$\tilde{P} = 20\,000 \,_{30|}\ddot{a}_{[35]} + \tilde{P} A_{[35]:\overline{30}|}^{\;\;1}$$
$$+ (\tilde{P} - 20\,000)v^{31} \,_{30|}q_{[35]} + (\tilde{P} - 40\,000)v^{32} \,_{31|}q_{[35]}$$
$$+ (\tilde{P} - 60\,000)v^{33} \,_{32|}q_{[35]} \,.$$

That is

$$\tilde{P} = 20\,000 \,_{30|}\ddot{a}_{[35]} + \tilde{P} A_{[35]:\overline{30}|}^{\;\;1} + \tilde{P} \,_{30|}A_{[35]:\overline{3}|}^{\;\;1} - 20\,000 \,_{30|}(IA)_{[35]:\overline{3}|}^{\;\;\;1}$$
$$= 20\,000 \,_{30|}\ddot{a}_{[35]} + \tilde{P} A_{[35]:\overline{33}|}^{\;\;1} - 20\,000 \,_{30|}(IA)_{[35]:\overline{3}|}^{\;\;\;1} \,.$$

That is,

$$\tilde{P} = \frac{59\,572.4 - 160.60}{1 - 0.02242} = \$60\,774.30$$

where the required functions are calculated using the Standard Select Survival Model.

We can see from the answer that we were correct in our assumption that the premium would not increase by a large amount and that the extra death benefit would apply only for three years. Note that, if the premium calculated had been greater than $\$80\,000$, then we would need to change the assumption about the term of the death benefit after the start of the annuity payment period, and repeat the calculations, until the answer is consistent with the assumption used.

6.12 We know that

$$L_0 = v^{K_x+1} - P\ddot{a}_{\overline{K_x+1}|} = v^{K_x+1}(1 + P/d) - P/d$$

and

$$L_0^* = v^{K_x+1} - P^*\ddot{a}_{\overline{K_x+1}|} = v^{K_x+1}(1 + P^*/d) - P^*/d.$$

Hence

$$V[L_0] = (1 + P/d)^2 \, V\left[v^{K_x+1}\right] \quad \text{and} \quad V[L_0^*] = (1 + P^*/d)^2 \, V\left[v^{K_x+1}\right]$$

so that

$$V[L_0^*] = \frac{(1 + P^*/d)^2}{(1 + P/d)^2} V[L_0] = \left(\frac{d + P^*}{d + P}\right)^2 V[L_0].$$

Also

$$E[L_0] = 0 = A_x - P\ddot{a}_x = 1 - (P + d)\ddot{a}_x$$

and

$$E[L_0^*] = -0.5 = A_x - P^*\ddot{a}_x = 1 - (P^* + d)\ddot{a}_x$$

so that

$$\frac{(P + d)\ddot{a}_x}{(P^* + d)\ddot{a}_x} = \frac{1}{1.5} = \frac{P + d}{P^* + d}.$$

Thus

$$V[L_0^*] = 1.5^2 \, V[L_0] = 1.6875.$$

E6.13 Let P^n denote the net annual premium, and P^g denote the gross annual premium.

We calculate the select insurance and annuity functions by constructing the life table for [40]. We calculate the ultimate one-year survival probabilities for ages 40 and over using Makeham's formula, then calculate the select rates using

$$p_{[40]} = 1 - q_{[40]} = 1 - 0.75(1 - p_{40}) = 0.25 + 0.75p_{40}$$

and

$$p_{[40]+1} = 1 - q_{[40]+1} = 1 - 0.9(1 - p_{41}) = 0.1 + 0.9p_{41}.$$

Using this life table in a spreadsheet format, we can calculate all the required functions. We have assumed uniform distribution of deaths; other fractional age assumptions would give very similar results.

EPV of death benefit:

$$20\,000\bar{A}_{[40]} + 80\,000\bar{A}^{\,1}_{[40]:\,\overline{20}|} = 15\,152.74.$$

EPV of net premiums:

$$P^n\ddot{a}_{[40]:\overline{20}|} = 11.2962\,P^n.$$

EPV of gross premiums less premium expenses:

$$0.97\,P^g\ddot{a}_{[40]:\overline{20}|} - 0.27P^g = 10.6874\,P^g.$$

EPV of other expenses:

$$10\,\ddot{a}_{[40]:\,\overline{20}|\,j} = 141.74 \quad \text{where} \quad j = \frac{1.06}{1.03} - 1.$$

Then

$$P^n = \frac{15\,152.74}{11.2962} = \$1341.40$$

and

$$P^g = \frac{15\,152.74 + 141.74}{10.6874} = \$1431.08.$$

6.14 Let P denote the total annual premium.

EPV of premiums less premium expenses:

$$P\left(0.95\,\ddot{a}^{(12)}_{[50]:\overline{10}|} - 0.15\,\ddot{a}^{(12)}_{[50]:\overline{1}|}\right) = 7.33243\,P.$$

Note that the premium related expenses are 20% of all the premiums in the first year, not just the first premium.

EPV of death benefit + claim expenses + other expenses:

$$(100\,000 + 250)\,\bar{A}^{\,1}_{[50]:\overline{10}|}\,v^{\frac{1}{12}} + 100.$$

The $v^{\frac{1}{12}}$ term allows for the one-month delay in paying claims.

Using claims acceleration, we have

$$\bar{A}^{\,1}_{[50]:\,\overline{10}|} = (1+i)^{\frac{1}{2}}\,A^{\,1}_{[50]:\overline{10}|} = 0.01474$$

which gives the EPV of the benefits and non-premium expenses of 1571.91, leading to $P = \$214.38$.

6.15 Let P denote the initial annual premium.

EPV of premiums less premium expenses:

$$\left(P\ddot{a}_{[55]:\overline{10|}} + 0.5P\,_{10|}\ddot{a}_{[55]}\right)0.97 - 0.22P$$
$$= \left(0.5P\,\ddot{a}_{[55]:\overline{10|}} + 0.5P\,\ddot{a}_{[55]}\right)0.97 - 0.22P = 11.4625\,P.$$

EPV of death benefit:

$$50\,000A_{[55]} + 50\,000A_{[55]:\overline{10|}}^{\,1} = 12\,965.63.$$

Hence the initial annual premium is $P = \$1131.13$.

6.16 Let P denote the annual premium. Then

$$P\,\ddot{a}_x = 150\,000A_x.$$

Now

$$L_0^n = 150\,000\,v^{K_x+1} - P\,\ddot{a}_{\overline{K_x+1|}}$$
$$= v^{K_x+1}\left(150\,000 + \frac{P}{d}\right) - \frac{P}{d}$$

so that

$$\mathrm{V}\left[L_0^n\right] = \left(150\,000 + \frac{P}{d}\right)^2 \mathrm{V}\left[v^{K_x+1}\right]$$
$$= \left(150\,000 + \frac{P}{d}\right)^2 \left(^2A_x - (A_x)^2\right)$$
$$= \left(150\,000 + \frac{P}{d}\right)^2 \left(0.0143 - 0.0653^2\right).$$

To find P/d we recall that

$$\ddot{a}_x = \frac{1 - A_x}{d}$$

so we may write the equation of value as

$$\frac{P}{d} = 150\,000\,\frac{A_x}{1 - A_x} = 10\,479.30.$$

Hence

$$\mathrm{V}\left[L_0^n\right] = 258\,460\,863$$

and the standard deviation of L_0^n is $\$16\,076.72$.

6.17 (a) Let P be the single premium. Then

$$P = 30\,000\,a_{[60]} = \$417\,401.93.$$

(b) The present value of profit if death occurs at age $60 + t$ for $t = 1, 2, 3, \ldots$ is

$$P - 30\,000\, a_{\overline{t}|}$$

and this is positive if $a_{\overline{t}|} < 13.9134$, which holds for $t = 1, 2, 3, \ldots, 24$. Thus, the probability that the present value of profit is positive is $1 - {}_{25}p_{[60]} = 0.36641$.

(c) The present value of the profit is

$$P - 30\,000\, a_{\overline{K_{[60]}}|} = P - 30\,000\, (\ddot{a}_{\overline{K_{[60]}+1}|} - 1)$$

and so the variance of the present value of the profit is

$$
30\,000^2\, V\left[\ddot{a}_{\overline{K_{[60]}+1}|}\right] = 30\,000^2\, V\left[\frac{1 - v^{K_{[60]}+1}}{d}\right]
$$

$$
= \frac{30\,000^2}{d^2} V[v^{K_{[60]}+1}]
$$

$$
= \frac{30\,000^2}{d^2}\left({}^2A_{[60]} - (A_{[60]})^2\right).
$$

Hence the standard deviation of the present value of the profit is

$$
\frac{30\,000}{d}\sqrt{{}^2A_{[60]} - (A_{[60]})^2} = \frac{30\,000}{d}\sqrt{0.10781 - 0.28984^2}
$$

$$
= 97\,201.23.
$$

(d) Let X denote the present value of profit on the 1000 policies. By the central limit theorem we have (approximately)

$$X \sim N(1\,000(P - 417\,401.93),\ 1\,000 \times 97\,201.23^2)$$

and so

$$\Pr[X > 0] = \Pr\left[Z > \frac{-1\,000(P - 417\,401.93)}{97\,201.23\,\sqrt{1\,000}}\right]$$

where $Z \sim N(0, 1)$. As $\Pr[Z > -1.6449] = 0.95$ we find $P = \$422\,457.83$.

6.18 We note first that the survival function for the life subject to extra risk is

$$
{}_tp'_x = \exp\left(-\int_0^t \mu'_{x+r}\, dr\right) = \exp\left(-\int_0^t (\mu_{x+r} + \phi)\, dr\right) = {}_tp_x\, e^{-\phi t}
$$

so that

$$\bar{A}'_x = \int_0^\infty v^t \, {}_tp'_x \, \mu'_{x+t} \, dt$$

$$= \int_0^\infty v^t \, {}_tp_x \, e^{-\phi t}(\mu_{x+t} + \phi) dt$$

$$= \int_0^\infty e^{-(\delta+\phi)t} \, {}_tp_x \, \mu_{x+t} dt + \phi \int_0^\infty e^{-(\delta+\phi)t} \, {}_tp_x dt$$

$$= \bar{A}^j_x + \phi \, \bar{a}^j_x$$

where $1 + j = e^{\delta+\phi}$.

E6.19 (a) First, we note that if the policyholder's curtate future lifetime, $K_{[30]}$, is k years, where $k = 0, 1, 2, \ldots, 24$, then the number of bonus additions is k, the death benefit is payable $k + 1$ years from issue, and hence the present value of the death benefit is $250\,000\,(1.025)^{K_{[30]}} v^{K_{[30]}+1}$. However, if the policyholder survives for 25 years, then 25 bonuses are added. Thus the present value of the endowment insurance benefit is $250\,000 Z_1$ where

$$Z_1 = \begin{cases} (1.025)^{K_{[30]}} v^{K_{[30]}+1} & \text{if } K_{[30]} \le 24, \\ (1.025)^{25} v^{25} & \text{if } K_{[30]} \ge 25. \end{cases}$$

As P denotes the annual premium, we have

$$L_0 = 250\,000\,Z_1 + 1200 + 0.39P - 0.99P\ddot{a}_{\overline{\min(K_{[30]}+1,25)|}}$$

$$= 250\,000\,Z_1 + 1200 + 0.39P - 0.99P\,\frac{1 - v^{\min(K_{[30]}+1,25)}}{d}$$

$$= 250\,000\,Z_1 + \frac{0.99P}{d}\,Z_2 + 1200 + 0.39P - \frac{0.99P}{d}$$

where $Z_2 = v^{\min(K_{[30]}+1,25)}$.

(b) We calculate P by taking the expected value of the equation for L_0 in part (a), and setting it equal to 0.

Now

$$E[Z_1] = \left(\frac{1}{1.025} A^{\,1}_{[30]:\,\overline{25}|\,j} + v_j^{25} \, {}_{25}p_{[30]}\right)$$

where j denotes calculation at interest rate $j = (1+i)/1.025 - 1 = 0.02439$. We find $A^{\,1}_{[30]:\,\overline{25}|\,j} = 0.012707$ and so $E[Z_1] = 0.549579$. Also,

$$E[Z_2] = A_{[30]:\,\overline{25}|} = 0.298517 \quad (\text{at } i=5\%).$$

So

$$E[L_0] = 0 \Rightarrow P = \frac{250\,000 \times 0.549579 + 1200}{(0.99/d) \times (1 - 0.298517) - 0.39} = \$9764.44.$$

(c) We have

$$V[L_0] = 250\,000^2\, V[Z_1] + \frac{0.99^2 P^2}{d^2}\, V[Z_2] + 500\,000 \frac{0.99 P}{d} \mathrm{Cov}[Z_1, Z_2].$$

Let us calculate each term in turn. First,

$$Z_1^2 = \begin{cases} ((1.025\, v)^2)^{K_{[30]}+1}/1.025^2 & \text{if } K_{[30]} \leq 24, \\ ((1.025\, v)^2)^{25} & \text{if } K_{[30]} \geq 25. \end{cases}$$

So

$$E[Z_1^2] = \left(\frac{1}{1.025^2} A^{\,1}_{[30]:\,\overline{25}|\,j^*} + v_{j^*}^{25}\,{}_{25}P_{[30]} \right) = 0.302510,$$

where j^* denotes calculation at interest rate $j^* = (1 + j)^2 - 1 = 0.04938$. This gives us $V[Z_1] = 0.00047$. Secondly,

$$E[Z_2^2] = {}^2 A_{[30]:\,\overline{25}|} = 0.090198,$$

giving

$$V[Z_2] = 0.090198 - 0.298517^2 = 0.00109.$$

Thirdly,

$$Z_1 Z_2 = \begin{cases} (1.025\, v^2)^{K_{[30]}+1}/1.025 & \text{if } K_{[30]} \leq 24, \\ (1.025\, v^2)^{25} & \text{if } K_{[30]} \geq 25. \end{cases}$$

So

$$E[Z_1 Z_2] = \frac{1}{1.025} A^{\,1}_{[30]:\,\overline{25}|\,j^\dagger} + v_{j^\dagger}^{25}\,{}_{25}P_{[30]} = 0.16477,$$

where $j^\dagger$ denotes calculation at interest rate $j^\dagger = 1.05^2/1.025 - 1 = 0.07561$. Subtracting $E[Z_1]E[Z_2]$ gives $\mathrm{Cov}[Z_1, Z_2] = 0.00071$. Inserting these values into the formula for $V[L_0]$ gives

$$V[L_0] = 146\,786\,651.$$

(d) Suppose that the benefit is payable at time t years ($t = 1, 2, \ldots, 25$) on account of the policyholder's death. Then the accumulation of premiums less expenses is

$$0.99 P \ddot{s}_{\overline{t}|} - (1\,200 + 0.39 P)(1 + i)^t$$

and the death benefit is $250\,000(1.025)^{t-1}$. Thus, there is a profit at time t years if

$$0.99P\ddot{s}_{\overline{t}|} - (1\,200 + 0.39P)(1 + i)^t - 250\,000(1.025)^{t-1} > 0.$$

A straightforward calculation on a spreadsheet shows that when $t = 24$,

$$0.99P\ddot{s}_{\overline{t}|} - (1\,200 + 0.39P)(1 + i)^t - 250\,000(1.025^{t-1}) = -5603.08$$

and when $t = 25$,

$$0.99P\ddot{s}_{\overline{t}|} - (1\,200 + 0.39P)(1 + i)^t - 250\,000(1.025^{t-1}) = 15\,295.72.$$

Hence there is a profit if the death benefit is payable at time 25. Similarly, there is a profit if the policyholder survives 25 years, the amount of this profit being

$$0.99P\ddot{s}_{\overline{25}|} - (1\,200 + 0.39P)(1 + i)^{25} - 250\,000(1.025^{25}) = 3991.18.$$

Thus, there is a profit if the policyholder survives 24 years and pays the premium at the start of the 25th policy year. Hence the probability of a profit is $_{24}p_{[30]} = 0.98297$.

6.20 (a) Let P be the annual premium. Then

$$P\,\ddot{a}_{[40]:\overline{20}|} = 250\,000A_{[40]:\overline{20}|}$$

gives $P = \$7\,333.84$ since $\ddot{a}_{[40]:\overline{20}|} = 12.9947$ and $A_{[40]:\overline{20}|} = 0.38120$.

(b) We have

$$L_0^n = 250\,000\,v^{\min(K_x+1,20)} - P\,\ddot{a}_{\overline{\min(K_x+1,20)}|}$$

$$= \left(250\,000 + \frac{P}{d}\right)v^{\min(K_x+1,20)} - \frac{P}{d}.$$

Since the premium has been calculated by the equivalence principle, $E[L_0^n] = 0$ and we have

$$V[L_0^n] = \left(250\,000 + \frac{P}{d}\right)^2 V\left[v^{\min(K_x+1,20)}\right]$$

$$= \left(250\,000 + \frac{P}{d}\right)^2 \left(^2A_{[40]:\overline{20}|} - \left(A_{[40]:\overline{20}|}\right)^2\right)$$

$$= 209\,804\,138.$$

Thus, the standard deviation of L_0^n is $\$14\,485$.

(c) The sum of 10 000 independent random variables each having the same distribution as L_0^n has approximately a normal distribution with mean 0 and standard deviation 1 448 500. As the 99th percentile of the standard normal distribution is 2.326, the 99th percentile of the net future loss from the 10 000 policies is

$$2.326 \times 1\,448\,500 = 3\,369\,626.$$

Solutions for Chapter 7

7.1 (a) The annual premium, P, is calculated using the equivalence principle from

$$P\ddot{a}_{[41]:\overline{3}|} = 200\,000\,A^{1}_{[41]:\overline{3}|},$$

giving $P = \$323.59$.

(b) The value of the random variable L_1 depends on whether the policyholder dies in the coming year, dies in the following year or survives for two years. The distribution of L_1 is as follows:

$$L_1 = \begin{cases} 200\,000\,v - P & = & 188\,355.66 & \text{w.p. } q_{[41]+1}, \\ 200\,000\,v^2 - P(1 + v) & = & 177\,370.43 & \text{w.p. } {}_1|q_{[41]+1}, \\ -P(1 + v) & = & -628.85 & \text{w.p. } {}_2p_{[41]+1}. \end{cases}$$

Hence

$$\begin{aligned} E[L_1] &= 188\,355.66 \times 0.001876 + 177\,370.43 \times 0.002197 \\ &\quad - 628.85 \times 0.995927 \\ &= \$116.68, \end{aligned}$$

and

$$\begin{aligned} V[L_1] &= 188\,355.66^2 \times 0.001876 + 177\,370.43^2 \times 0.002197 \\ &\quad + (-628.85)^2 \times 0.995927 - 116.68^2 \\ &= 11\,663.78^2 \end{aligned}$$

so that the standard deviation of L_1 is $\$11\,663.78$.

(c) The sum insured S is calculated using the equivalence principle. As

$$P\ddot{a}_{[41]:\overline{3}|} = SA_{[41]:\overline{3}|}$$

we have $S = \$1090.26$.

(d) For the endowment insurance, the distribution of L_1 is:

$$L_1 = \begin{cases} 1090.26\,v - P & = \$704.96 & \text{w.p. } q_{[41]+1}, \\ 1090.26\,v^2 - P(1+v) & = \$341.47 & \text{w.p. } p_{[41]+1}. \end{cases}$$

Note that the loss is the same whether the policyholder dies between ages 42 and 43 or survives to age 43.

Hence, $E[L_1] = \$342.15$ and $S.D.[L_1] = \$15.73$.

(e) The value of $E[L_1]$ is greater for the endowment insurance than for the term insurance; this is typical, as for endowment insurance a large portion of the premium is needed to fund the maturity benefit. The difference between the standard deviations is more substantial. The value for the term insurance, $\$11\,663.78$, is considerably larger than that for the endowment insurance, $\$15.73$. The future cash flows for the term insurance are much more un-certain than those for the endowment insurance. For the term insurance L_1 takes very different values, $\$177\,370.43$ and $-\$628.85$, depending on whether the policyholder dies between ages 42 and 43 or survives to age 43, whereas for the endowment insurance the value is the same, $\$341.47$. Put more simply, for the endowment insurance the insurer knows that the sum insured will be paid at some time within the next two years, the only uncertainty is over the timing; for the term insurance it is not certain that the sum insured will ever be paid.

7.2 The net annual premium, P, is calculated from

$$P\ddot{a}_{40:\overline{20}|} = 100\,000\,A_{40} - 50\,000\,A^1_{40:\overline{20}|}.$$

The following values have been calculated using the Standard Ultimate Sur-vival Model and an interest rate of 5% per year:

$$A_{40} = 0.12106, \quad A^1_{40:\overline{20}|} = 0.01463, \quad \ddot{a}_{40:\overline{20}|} = 12.99348,$$

so that $P = \$875.38$.

The policy value at duration 10 years, $_{10}V$, is calculated from

$$_{10}V = 100\,000\,A_{50} - 50\,000\,A^1_{50:\overline{10}|} - P\ddot{a}_{50:\overline{10}|}.$$

We have

$$A_{50} = 0.18931, \quad A^1_{50:\overline{10}|} = 0.01461, \quad \ddot{a}_{50:\overline{10}|} = 8.05500,$$

so that $_{10}V = \$11\,149.02$.

7.3 (a) The equation for the gross annual premium, P^g, is

$$0.95P^g \ddot{a}_{[35]} - 0.35P^g = 40\ddot{a}_{[35]} + 85 + 100\,000A_{[35]},$$

which gives $P^g = \$469.81$.

(b) The net premium policy value is calculated using the net premium, P^n, which is calculated as

$$P^n \ddot{a}_{[35]} = 100\,000A_{[35]},$$

giving $P^n = \$391.22$.

The net premium policy value at time $t = 1$, $_1V^n$, is then given by

$$_1V^n = 100\,000A_{[35]+1} - P^n \ddot{a}_{[35]+1} = \$381.39.$$

(c) The gross premium policy value at time $t = 1$ is calculated using the gross premium, $P^g = \$469.81$, and is given by

$$_1V^g = 100\,000A_{[35]+1} + 40\ddot{a}_{[35]+1} - 0.95P^g \ddot{a}_{[35]+1} = \$132.91.$$

(d) Both the net and gross premium policy values value the same future benefits. The difference is that the gross premium policy value includes future expenses, and deducts the value of the future gross premiums, while the net premium policy value does not include future expenses, but only deducts the value of the future net premiums. The expense loading in the gross premium is $P^e = P^g - P^n$. The gross premium policy value is less than the net premium policy value when the expected present value of future expenses is less than the expected present value of future expense loadings. We can write the gross premium policy value as

$$_1V^g = \text{EPV Future Benefits} + \text{EPV Future Expenses}$$
$$- \text{EPV Net Premiums} - \text{EPV Expense Loadings}$$

and the net premium policy value as

$$_1V^n = \text{EPV Future Benefits} - \text{EPV Net Premiums}$$

so the difference, $_1V^n - {_1V^g}$, is

EPV Expense Loadings − EPV Future Expenses.

This is generally greater than zero as the expense loadings include the amortized initial expenses. That is, the gross premium policy value is less than the net premium policy value because it allows for the recovery of the initial expenses from future premiums.

(e) The gross premium policy value uses the original premium, which is $P^g =$ $469.81. Then

$$_1V^g = 100\,000A_{[35]+1} + 40\ddot{a}_{[35]+1} - 0.95\,P^g\ddot{a}_{[35]+1} = \$1125.54.$$

(f) The formula for the asset share at time $t = 1$ is

$$AS_1 = \frac{1.06\,(0.6P^g - 125) - 100\,000q_{[35]}}{P_{[35]}}$$

$$= \$132.91.$$

This is precisely $_1V$, as we know it must be.

(g) In this case the asset share is given by

$$AS_1 = \frac{1.1\,(0.6 \times 469.81 - 125 - 25) - 100\,000 \times 0.0012}{1 - 0.0012} = \$25.10.$$

(h) Per policy issued, the insurer's surplus at the end of the first year will be

$$1.1\,(0.6 \times 469.81 - 125 - 25) - 100\,000 \times 0.0012 - {_1V}(1 - 0.0012)$$
$$= -\$107.67.$$

(i) To calculate the contribution to the surplus from interest, we assume mortality and expenses are as in the premium basis. This gives the actual interest minus the expected interest as

$$(0.1 - 0.06)(0.6P - 125) = \$6.28.$$

The contribution to surplus from mortality is

$$(q_{[35]} - 0.0012)(100\,000 - {_1V}) = -\$86.45.$$

The contribution from expenses, allowing now for the *actual* interest earned, is

$$1.1(125 - 150) = -\$27.50.$$

Note that the total is $-\$107.67$ as required.

7.4 (a) (i) For $t = 0$ and 1 the recursive equation linking successive policy values is

$$1.06(_tV + P) = (1\,000 + {}_{t+1}V)q_{[50]+t} + {}_{t+1}V\,p_{[50]+t}$$
$$= 1\,000q_{[50]+t} + {}_{t+1}V. \tag{7.1}$$

(ii) For $t = 2$ we have

$$_2V = 20\,000A_{52} - P\ddot{a}_{52}. \tag{7.2}$$

(iii) Substituting formula (7.2) into formula (7.1) first for $t = 1$ and then for $t = 0$ gives

$$1.06(_1V + P) = 1\,000q_{[50]+1} + 20\,000A_{52} - P\ddot{a}_{52}$$

so that

$$1.06(1.06(_0V + P) - 1\,000q_{[50]} + P) = 1\,000q_{[50]+1} + 20\,000A_{52} - P\ddot{a}_{52}.$$

Since P is calculated using the equivalence principle, we know that $_0V = 0$ and so the final equation can be solved for P to give $P = \$185.08$. Inserting this value for P into formula (7.2) gives $_2V = \$401.78$.

(b) $_{2.25}V$ is the policy value at time $t = 2.25$ for a policyholder who is alive at that time. We have

$$_{2.25}V = 20\,000\,_{0.75}q_{52.25}\,v^{0.75} + {}_{0.75}p_{52.25}\,v^{0.75}\,_3V$$

where $_3V = 20\,000A_{53} - P\ddot{a}_{53} = \$593.58$, and $_{0.75}p_{52.25} = 0.99888$, so

$$_{2.25}V = \$588.91.$$

7.5 (a) (i) The random variable representing the present value of the deferred annuity benefit can be written as the difference between an immediate whole life annuity and an immediate term annuity, as follows:

$$10\,000\left(\ddot{a}^{(12)}_{\overline{K^{(12)}_{[30]}+\frac{1}{12}|}} - \ddot{a}^{(12)}_{\overline{\min\left(K^{(12)}_{[30]}+\frac{1}{12},30\right)|}}\right).$$

The random variable representing the present value of the return of premiums on death before age 60 is as follows:

$$
\begin{array}{lll}
0 & \text{if} & T_{[30]} \geq 30, \\
T_{[30]}\,P\,v^{T_{[30]}} & \text{if} & T_{[30]} < 10, \\
10P\,v^{T_{[30]}} & \text{if} & 10 \leq T_{[30]} < 30.
\end{array}
$$

This can be written in a single expression using indicator random variables as

$$
T_{[30]}\,P\,v^{T_{[30]}}\,I(T_{[30]} < 10) + 10P\,v^{T_{[30]}}\,I(10 \leq T_{[30]} < 30).
$$

(ii) The loss at issue random variable, L_0, is the present value of the benefits, as in part (i), minus the present value of the premiums. Hence

$$
\begin{aligned}
L_0 = 10\,000 & \left(\ddot{a}^{(12)}_{\overline{K^{(12)}_{[30]} + \frac{1}{12}|}} - \ddot{a}^{(12)}_{\overline{\min\left(K^{(12)}_{[30]} + \frac{1}{12},30\right)|}} \right) \\
& + T_{[30]}\,P\,v^{T_{[30]}}\,I(T_{[30]} < 10) \\
& + 10P\,v^{T_{[30]}}\,I(10 \leq T_{[30]} < 30) - P\ddot{a}_{\overline{\min(T_{[30]},10)|}}.
\end{aligned}
$$

(b) By the equivalence principle, $E[L_0] = 0$. Hence

$$
0 = 10\,000\left(\ddot{a}^{(12)}_{[30]} - \ddot{a}^{(12)}_{[30]:\overline{30}|}\right) + P(\bar{I}\bar{A})^{1}_{[30]:\overline{10}|} + 10P\,_{10}E_{[30]}\,\bar{A}^{1}_{40:\overline{20}|} - P\ddot{a}_{[30]:\overline{10}|}
$$

so that

$$
P = \frac{10\,000(\ddot{a}^{(12)}_{[30]} - \ddot{a}^{(12)}_{[30]:\overline{30}|})}{\ddot{a}_{[30]:\overline{10}|} - (\bar{I}\bar{A})^{1}_{[30]:\overline{30}|} - 10P\,_{10}E_{[30]}\,\bar{A}^{1}_{40:\overline{20}|}}.
$$

(c) When writing down the expression for L_5 we need to be careful to value the return on death before age 60 of the premiums already paid, $5P$, and those yet to be paid. The required expression is

$$
\begin{aligned}
L_5 = 10\,000 & \left(\ddot{a}^{(12)}_{\overline{K^{(12)}_{35} + \frac{1}{12}|}} - \ddot{a}^{(12)}_{\overline{\min\left(K^{(12)}_{35} + \frac{1}{12},25\right)|}} \right) + 5P\,v^{T_{35}}\,I(T_{35} < 25) \\
& + T_{35}\,P\,v^{T_{35}}\,I(T_{35} < 5) + 5P\,v^{T_{35}}\,I(5 \leq T_{35} < 25) - P\ddot{a}_{\overline{\min(T_{35},5)|}}.
\end{aligned}
$$

(d) Recalling that $_5V = E[L_5]$, we have

$$
\begin{aligned}
_5V = 10\,000 & \left(\ddot{a}^{(12)}_{35} - \ddot{a}^{(12)}_{35:\overline{25}|}\right) \\
& + 5P\bar{A}^{1}_{35:\overline{25}|} + P(\bar{I}\bar{A})^{1}_{35:\overline{5}|} + 5P\,_5E_{35}\,\bar{A}^{1}_{40:\overline{20}|} - P\ddot{a}_{35:\overline{5}|}.
\end{aligned}
$$

$^\text{E}$7.6 (a) Let P be the annual premium. Using the equivalence principle, we have

$$0.96 P \ddot{a}_{[35]:\overline{20}|} - 0.11 P = 100\,000 A^{\;\;1}_{[35]:\overline{20}|} + 200$$

so that $P = \$91.37$.

(b) The policy value just *before* the first premium is paid is zero since the premium is calculated using the equivalence principle and the policy value is calculated on the same basis as the premium. The policy value just *after* the first premium is paid is the premium received, $\$91.37$, less the expenses paid, $\$200$ and 0.15×91.37. Hence:

$$_{0+}V = 0 + 91.37 - 200 - 0.15 \times 91.37 = -\$122.33.$$

(c) The policy value just after the first premium is received is negative because the premium is insufficient to cover the initial expenses, as can be seen from the calculation in part (b).

(d) The plot of the policy values is shown as Figure S7.1. It can be seen that the policy value first becomes positive at duration 3+ just after the fourth premium is paid; just before the fifth premium is paid the policy value is negative again, then becomes positive when the fifth premium is paid, and stays positive for the remainder of the contract.

(e) The number of survivors at age $35 + t$, $t = 0, 1, \ldots, k$, is $_t p_{[35]} N$, and the number of deaths between ages $35 + t$ and $35 + t + 1$ is $_t|q_{[35]} N$. These are not *expected* numbers, they are *actual* numbers with probabilities calculated on the premium/policy value basis. Hence, the accumulation of premiums paid up to, but not including, time k is

$$P N \left(1.05^k + 1.05^{k-1}\, p_{[35]} + \cdots + 1.05 \,_{k-1} p_{[35]} \right)$$

$$= P N \, 1.05^k \sum_{t=0}^{k-1} v^t \,_t p_{[35]} \qquad \text{where } v = 1/1.05$$

$$= P N \, 1.05^k \, \ddot{a}_{[35]:\overline{k}|} \, .$$

Similarly, the accumulation of expenses is

$$200 N \times 1.05^k + 0.04 P N \, 1.05^k \, \ddot{a}_{[35]:\overline{k}|} + 0.11 P N \, 1.05^k,$$

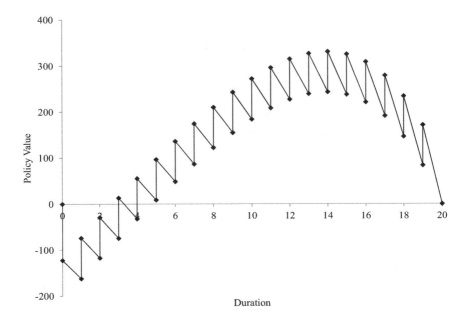

Figure S7.1 Policy values for Exercise 7.6.

and the accumulation of death benefits is

$$100\,000\,N\left(1.05^{k-1}\,q_{[35]} + 1.05^{k-2}\,_1|q_{[35]} + \cdots + \,_{k-1}|q_{[35]}\right)$$

$$= 100\,000\,N\,1.05^k\sum_{t=0}^{k-1}v^{t+1}\,_t|q_{[35]}$$

$$= 100\,000\,N\,1.05^k\,A^{\,1}_{[35]:\overline{k}|}.$$

Hence, the accumulated fund at time k is

$$1.05^k\,N(0.96P\ddot{a}_{[35]:\overline{k}|} - 200 - 0.11P - 100\,000A^{\,1}_{[35]:\overline{k}|}).$$

Since the number of survivors to time k is $_kp_{[35]}N$, the fund per survivor is

$$1.05^k(0.96P\ddot{a}_{[35]:\overline{k}|} - 200 - 0.11P - 100\,000A^{\,1}_{[35]:\overline{k}|})/\,_kp_{[35]}.$$

The equation for the premium can be manipulated as follows, dividing the functions into the first k years and the remaining $20 - k$ years:

$$0.96P\,\ddot{a}_{[35]:\overline{20}|} - 0.11P = 100\,000A^{1}_{[35]:\overline{20}|} + 200$$

$$\implies 0.96P(\ddot{a}_{[35]:\overline{k}|} + 1.05^{-k}\,{}_kp_{[35]}\,\ddot{a}_{[35]+k:\overline{20-k}|}) - 0.11P$$

$$= 100\,000(A^{1}_{[35]:\overline{k}|} + 1.05^{-k}\,{}_kp_{[35]}\,A_{[35]+k:\overline{20-k}|}) + 200$$

$$\implies 0.96P\,\ddot{a}_{[35]:\overline{k}|} - 0.11P - 200 - 100\,000A^{1}_{[35]:\overline{k}|}$$

$$= 1.05^{-k}\,{}_kp_{[35]}(100\,000A^{1}_{[35]+k:\overline{20-k}|} - 0.96P\,\ddot{a}_{[35]+k:\overline{20-k}|})$$

$$\implies 1.05^{k}(0.96P\,\ddot{a}_{[35]:\overline{k}|} - 0.11P - 200 - 100\,000A^{1}_{[35]:\overline{k}|})/\,{}_kp_{[35]}$$

$$= 100\,000A^{1}_{[35]+k:\overline{20-k}|} - 0.96P\,\ddot{a}_{[35]+k:\overline{20-k}|}\,.$$

The left-hand side is the accumulated fund at time k per surviving policy-holder, and the right-hand side is ${}_kV$.

7.7 The contribution to the surplus from mortality is

$$(100\,q_{65} - 1)(100\,000 + 200 - {}_6V) = -\$26\,504.04.$$

Note that this uses the assumed, rather than the actual, expenses.
The contribution from interest is

$$100({}_5V + 0.95 \times 5\,200)(0.065 - 0.05) = \$51\,011.26.$$

The contribution from expenses is

$$100(-0.01)5\,200 \times 1.065 - 250 + 200 = -\$5\,588.00.$$

E7.8 (a) The premium, P, is calculated from

$$P\bar{a}_{[40]:\overline{20}|} = 200\,000\,\bar{A}_{[40]:\overline{20}|}\,,$$

giving $P = \$6\,020.40$.

(b) The policy value at duration 4, ${}_4V$, is calculated as

$${}_4V = 200\,000\,\bar{A}_{44:\overline{16}|} - P\,\bar{a}_{44:\overline{16}|} = \$26\,131.42.$$

(c) The revised values needed for the calculation of the policy value are:

$$\bar{A}_{44:\overline{16}|} = 0.463033 \quad \text{and} \quad \bar{a}_{44:\overline{16}|} = 11.00563.$$

The revised policy value is

$${}_4V = 200\,000 \times 0.463033 - 6\,020.40 \times 11.00563 = \$26\,348.41.$$

(d) The policy value has not changed by very much because, for the age range involved, 44 to 60, mortality is reasonably light. In particular, the change in the mortality basis changes $_{16}p_{44}$ from 0.9751 to 0.9723. Hence, the benefit on survival to the end of the term is the most significant contribution to the EPV of the benefits.

(e) The revised values needed for the calculation of the policy value are:

$$\bar{A}_{44:\overline{16}|} = 0.537698 \quad \text{and} \quad \bar{a}_{44:\overline{16}|} = 11.78720.$$

The revised policy value is

$$_4V = 200\,000 \times 0.537698 - 6\,020.40 \times 11.78720 = \$36\,575.95.$$

(f) Since the benefit is very likely to be paid at the end of the term, the interest earned on the invested premiums matters to a considerable extent. A lower rate of interest, 4% rather than 5%, means that future premiums will accumulate at a lower rate and so more cash is needed now in order to pay for the benefit.

(g) One advantage of using a proportionate paid-up sum insured is that it has an intuitive appeal which can easily be understood by the policyholder.

The policy values and EPV of the proportionate paid-up sum insured are shown in Figure S7.2. It can be seen that the EPV of the proportionate paid-up sum insured is less than the policy value for all durations between 0 and 20, with greater differences for the middle durations. Since $_tV$ represents the value of the investments the insurer should be holding at duration t, adopting the suggestion of a proportionate paid-up sum insured would give the insurer a small profit for each policy becoming paid-up, assuming that experience exactly follows the assumptions. It is generally considered reasonable for the insurer to retain a small profit, on average, as the policyholder has adjusted the terms of the contract.

7.9 (a) We have

$$L_t^n = S\,v^{T_{[x]+t}} - P\,\bar{a}_{\overline{T_{[x]+t}}|}$$

$$= S\,v^{T_{[x]+t}} - P\left(\frac{1 - v^{T_{[x]+t}}}{\delta}\right)$$

$$= -\frac{P}{\delta} + \left(S + \frac{P}{\delta}\right)v^{T_{[x]+t}},$$

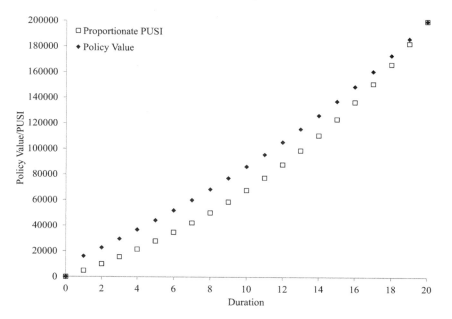

Figure S7.2 Policy values and the EPV of the proportionate paid-up sum insured for Exercise 7.8.

so

$$V[L_t^n] = \left(S + \frac{P}{\delta}\right)^2 V[v^{T_{[x]+t}}]$$
$$= \left(S + \frac{P}{\delta}\right)^2 \left({}^2\bar{A}_{[x]+t} - (\bar{A}_{[x]+t})^2\right).$$

(b) The premium equation is

$$1200\,\bar{a}_{[55]} = S\,\bar{A}_{[55]}.$$

Thus,

$$1200 \times 15.56159 = 0.240747\,S,$$

giving $S = \$77\,566.44$.

(c) The standard deviation of L_t^n is calculated by taking the square root of $V[L_t^n]$, calculated from the formula in part (a). We need the following values, calculated using numerical integration:

$$\bar{A}_{[55]} = 0.240747, \quad {}^2\bar{A}_{[55]} = 0.078216,$$
$$\bar{A}_{60} = 0.297434, \quad {}^2\bar{A}_{60} = 0.113739,$$
$$\bar{A}_{65} = 0.363520, \quad {}^2\bar{A}_{65} = 0.161893.$$

Using these values, we have

$$\text{S.D.}[L_0^n] = \$14\,540.32,$$
$$\text{S.D.}[L_5^n] = \$16\,240.72,$$
$$\text{S.D.}[L_{10}^n] = \$17\,619.98.$$

The values of S.D.$[L_t^n]$ are increasing as t increases from 0 to 10. This is not surprising. As t increases from 0, the time until the sum insured is likely to be paid decreases and so the present value of the loss increases. This will increase the standard deviation of the present value of the loss *provided* there is still considerable uncertainty about when the policyholder is likely to die, as will be the case for the range of values of t being considered here.

7.10 The premium equation is

$$P\ddot{a}_{[x]:\overline{n}|}^{(12)} = SA_{[x]:\overline{n}|}^{(12)}$$

giving

$$P = S\left(\frac{1 - d^{(12)}\ddot{a}_{[x]:\overline{n}|}^{(12)}}{\ddot{a}_{[x]:\overline{n}|}^{(12)}}\right).$$

The policy value *just before* time t, when a monthly premium is due, is

$$
\begin{aligned}
{}_tV &= SA_{[x]+t:\overline{n-t}|}^{(12)} - P\ddot{a}_{[x]+t:\overline{n-t}|}^{(12)} \\
&= S(1 - d^{(12)}\ddot{a}_{[x]+t:\overline{n-t}|}^{(12)}) - S\left(\frac{1 - d^{(12)}\ddot{a}_{[x]:\overline{n}|}^{(12)}}{\ddot{a}_{[x]:\overline{n}|}^{(12)}}\right)\ddot{a}_{[x]+t:\overline{n-t}|}^{(12)} \\
&= S\left(1 - \frac{\ddot{a}_{[x]+t:\overline{n-t}|}^{(12)}}{\ddot{a}_{[x]:\overline{n}|}^{(12)}}\right),
\end{aligned}
$$

as required.

E7.11 (a) The equation for the annual premium, P, is

$$0.95\,P\ddot{a}_{[50]} - 0.17\,P = 90 + 10\,\ddot{a}_{[50]} + 10\,000\,A_{[50]},$$

giving $P = \$144.63$.

(b) For $t = 1, 2, \ldots$, the policy value at time t, just before the premium then due, is

$$_tV = 10\,000\,A_{[50]+t} + 10\,\ddot{a}_{[50]+t} - 0.95\,P\,\ddot{a}_{[50]+t}.$$

An excerpt from the resulting table of values is shown in part (c) below.

(c) Let Pr_t denote the profit at the end of the year $(t - 1, t)$, $t = 1, 2, \ldots$, in respect of a policy in force at time $t - 1$. Then

$$\mathrm{Pr}_1 = 1.055(0.78\,P - 100) - 10\,000\,q_{[50]} - {_1V}\,p_{[50]}$$

and for $t = 2, 3, \ldots$,

$$\mathrm{Pr}_t = 1.055(_{t-1}V + 0.95\,P - 10) - 10\,000\,q_{[50]+t-1} - {_tV}\,p_{[50]+t-1}.$$

For $t = 1, 2, 3, \ldots$ the bonus is $0.9\,\mathrm{Pr}_t / p_{[50]+t-1}$.

We show an excerpt from the full table of calculations.

t	$_tV$	Dividend
0	0.00	0.00
1	3.06	0.12
2	123.84	1.18
3	248.22	2.26
4	376.89	3.39
5	509.93	4.55
$\vdots$	$\vdots$	$\vdots$

(d) The EPV of the bonuses per policy issued can then be written as

$$\sum_{t=1}^{\infty} 0.1\,\mathrm{Pr}_t\,v^t\,_{t-1}p_{[50]} = \$29.26.$$

(e) The policy value on the premium basis at the end of the first year is very small ($_1V = \$3.06$). This is because most of the first year's premium goes to provide the initial expenses. In these circumstances, and since it is the policyholder who has requested that the policy be surrendered, it would be reasonable for the insurer to offer no surrender value.

7.12 (a) The equation for the annual premium, P, is

$$0.95\,P\,\ddot{a}_{[40]:\overline{10|}} = 10\,000\,A_{[40]:\overline{10|}} + 10\,000\,A^{\,1}_{[40]:\overline{10|}},$$

giving $P = \$807.71$.

(b) The fifth premium is paid at duration 4, so that

$$_4V = 20\,000\,A_{44:\overline{6}|} - 10\,000\,A_{44:\overline{6}|}^{\;1} - 0.95\,P\,\ddot{a}_{44:\overline{6}|} = \$3429.68.$$

(c) Let the revised death benefit be S. Then, equating policy values before and after the alteration, we have

$$3\,429.68 = S\,A_{44:\overline{6}|} - 0.5\,S\,A_{44:\overline{6}|}^{\;1} - 0.95 \times 0.5\,P\,\ddot{a}_{44:\overline{6}|}$$

giving $S = \$14\,565.95$.

7.13 (a) The equation for the annual premium, P, is

$$P\,\ddot{a}_{[40]} = 50\,000\,A_{[40]} - 49\,000\,A_{[40]:\overline{3}|}^{\;1},$$

giving $P = \$256.07$.

(b) The formula for the policy value at integer duration $t \geq 3$ is

$$_tV = 50\,000\,A_{40+t} - P\,\ddot{a}_{40+t}.$$

Note that, since the select period for the survival model is two years, the life is no longer select at age $40 + t$ for $t \geq 3$.

(c) We insert the following values into the formula in part (b):

$$P = 256.07, \quad \ddot{a}_{43} = 15.92105, \quad A_{43} = 0.098808.$$

This gives $_3V = \$863.45$.

(d) The recurrence relation for policy values in this case is

$$1.06(_2V + P) = 1\,000\,q_{42} + {_3V}\,p_{42}.$$

Inserting the values for P, $_3V$ and p_{42} ($= 1 - q_{42} = 0.999392$), gives $_2V = \$558.58$.

(e) The total profit for the second year emerging at the end of the year is

$$985 \times 1.055(_2V + P) - 4 \times 1\,000 - 981 \times {_3V} = -\$4476.57.$$

E7.14 (a) Thiele's differential equation for this policy is as follows: for $0 < t < 10$,

$$\frac{d}{dt}\,_tV = \delta_t\,_tV + P - \mu_{[40]+t}(20\,000 - {_tV}),$$

and for $10 < t < 20$,

$$\frac{d}{dt}\,{}_tV = \delta_t\,{}_tV + P.$$

Note that, because the death benefit for $10 < t < 20$ is ${}_tV$, a term $\mu_{40+t}({}_tV - {}_tV)$ should be subtracted from the right-hand side of the second of these equations. Since this term is zero, it has been omitted.

The boundary conditions are

$$\lim_{t\to20-}\,{}_tV = 60\,000, \quad \lim_{t\to10+}\,{}_tV = \lim_{t\to10-}\,{}_tV, \quad \lim_{t\to0+}\,{}_tV = 0.$$

(b) With $h = 0.05$ Thiele's differential equation gives us that, approximately,

$$\frac{{}_{t+h}V - {}_tV}{h} = \delta_t\,{}_tV + P - \mu_{[40]+t}(20\,000 - {}_tV)$$

for $t = 0, h, 2h, \ldots, 10 - h$, and

$$\frac{{}_{t+h}V - {}_tV}{h} = \delta_t\,{}_tV + P,$$

for $t = 10, 10 + h, 10 + 2h, \ldots, 20 - h$. So we have recursive equations

$${}_{t+h}V = {}_tV + h\,\delta_t\,{}_tV + hP - h\,\mu_{[40]+t}(20\,000 - {}_tV)$$

for $t = 0, h, 2h, \ldots, 10 - h$, and

$${}_{t+h}V = {}_tV + h\delta_t\,{}_tV + hP$$

for $t = 10, 10+h, 10+2h, \ldots, 20-h$. Set ${}_0V = 0$, and using Solver in Excel, we set ${}_{20}V = 60\,000$ for the target, and find that $P = \$1810.73$. Note that we could also use a backward recursive approach by setting ${}_{20}V = 60\,000$, with ${}_0V = 0$ for the target.

(c) The graph of ${}_tV$ is shown in Figure S7.3.

7.15 (a) The recurrence relation for $t = 1, 2, 3, \ldots, 19$ is

$$(1 + i)\,{}_tV = q_{[60]+t} + p_{[60]+t}\,{}_{t+1}V.$$

For time 0 we have

$$(1 + i)({}_0V + P) = q_{[60]} + p_{[60]}\,{}_1V,$$

where P is the single premium and ${}_0V = 0$.

For $t = 1, 2, 3, \ldots, 19$ the explanation is as follows: ${}_tV$ represents the expected value (at time t) of the present value (at time t) of the future net cash

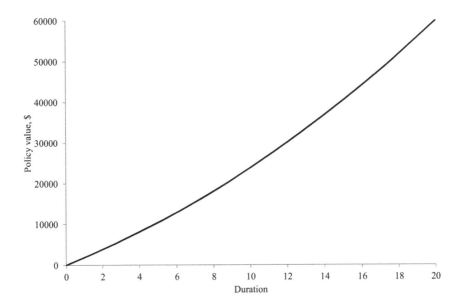

Figure S7.3 Policy values for Exercise 7.14.

flows from the insurer, which in this case are benefits only. The left-hand side gives the accumulated proceeds at time $t + 1$ of the cashflow at time t. The right-hand side gives the expected value of the cashflow required at time $t + 1$, given that the policy is in force at time t. We can calculate this expected value by considering what can happen in the year $(t, t + 1)$. Either the policyholder dies – with probability q_{60+t} – in which case the only future net cash flow is the sum insured, \$1, at time $t + 1$, or the policyholder survives – with probability p_{60+t} – in which case the expected value (at time $t + 1$) of the present value (at time $t + 1$) of the future net cash flows is $_{t+1}V$.

For time 0, the explanation is the same except that the amount we accumulate for one year is the premium rather than the policy value.

(b) In this case the recurrence relation for $t = h, 2h, 3h, \ldots, 20 - h$ is

$$(1 + i)^h \, _tV = \, _hq_{[60]+t} + \, _hp_{[60]+t} \, _{t+h}V$$
$$\Rightarrow (1 + i)^h \, _tV = \, _{t+h}V + \, _hq_{[60]+t} \left(1 - \, _{t+h}V\right). \qquad (7.3)$$

For time 0 we have

$$(1 + i)^h (_0V + P) = {}_hV + {}_hq_{[60]} (1 - {}_hV).$$

(c) First, we will use equation (7.3) to construct an equation for $({}_{t+h}V - {}_tV)/h$. Then, we can take the limit as $h \to 0^+$ to get the differential equation.

Substituting $(1 + i) = e^\delta$ in equation (7.3), and rearranging by first subtracting $_tV$ from each side then dividing throughout by h, we have

$$\frac{t+hV - {}_tV}{h} = \frac{(e^{\delta h} - 1)}{h} {}_tV - \frac{hq_{[60]+t}}{h} (1 - {}_{t+h}V). \tag{7.4}$$

Now,

$$\lim_{h \to 0^+} \frac{(e^{\delta h} - 1)}{h} = \lim_{h \to 0^+} \frac{(1 + \delta h + \delta^2 h^2/2 + \cdots) - 1}{h} = \delta.$$

Also

$$\lim_{h \to 0^+} \frac{hq_y}{h} = \lim_{h \to 0^+} \frac{1}{h} \Pr[T_y \le h] = \mu_y.$$

(See equation (2.6) in AMLCR for the definition of μ_y.)

So, taking $\lim_{h \to 0^+}$ of equation (7.4) we get

$$\frac{d}{dt} {}_tV = \delta {}_tV - \mu_{[60]+t} (1 - {}_tV)$$

$$= (\mu_{[60]+t} + \delta) {}_tV - \mu_{[60]+t}.$$

The boundary conditions are that $\lim_{t \to 0^+} {}_tV = P$ and $\lim_{t \to 20^-} {}_tV = 0$.

(d) To check that

$$_tV = \bar{A} \frac{1}{[60]+t:\overline{20-t}|}$$

is the solution to the differential equation in part (c), we need to check that it satisfies the boundary conditions and that

$$\frac{d}{dt} \bar{A} \frac{1}{[60]+t:\overline{20-t}|} = (\mu_{[60]+t} + \delta) \bar{A} \frac{1}{[60]+t:\overline{20-t}|} - \mu_{[60]+t}. \tag{7.5}$$

To check that the proposed solution satisfies (7.5), we use the arguments from Section 7.5.1 of AMLCR. As

$$\bar{A} \frac{1}{[60]+t:\overline{20-t}|} = \int_t^{20} e^{-\delta(s-t)} {}_{s-t}p_{[60]+t} \, \mu_{[60]+s} \, ds$$

and

$$_{s-t}p_{[60]+t} = {}_sp_{[60]}/{}_tp_{[60]},$$

we have

$$e^{-\delta t}\,{}_tp_{[60]}\,\bar{A}^{\;1}_{[60]+t:\overline{20-t}|} = \int_t^{20} e^{-\delta s}\,{}_sp_{[60]}\,\mu_{[60]+s}\,ds.$$

Differentiating the right-hand side with respect to t we get

$$-e^{-\delta t}\,{}_tp_{[60]}\,\mu_{[60]+t}\,,$$

and differentiating the left-hand side we get

$$\bar{A}^{\;1}_{[60]+t:\overline{20-t}|}\,\frac{d}{dt}\left(e^{-\delta t}\,{}_tp_{[60]}\right) + e^{-\delta t}\,{}_tp_{[60]}\,\frac{d}{dt}\bar{A}^{\;1}_{[60]+t:\overline{20-t}|}\,.$$

As

$$\frac{d}{dt}\left(e^{-\delta t}\,{}_tp_{[60]}\right) = -\delta\,e^{-\delta t}\,{}_tp_{[60]} + e^{-\delta t}\,\frac{d}{dt}\,{}_tp_{[60]}$$

$$= -\delta\,e^{-\delta t}\,{}_tp_{[60]} - e^{-\delta t}\,{}_tp_{[60]}\,\mu_{[60]+t}\,,$$

we have

$$-(\delta\,e^{-\delta t}\,{}_tp_{[60]} + e^{-\delta t}\,{}_tp_{[60]}\,\mu_{[60]+t})\bar{A}^{\;1}_{[60]+t:\overline{20-t}|} + e^{-\delta t}\,{}_tp_{[60]}\,\frac{d}{dt}\bar{A}^{\;1}_{[60]+t:\overline{20-t}|}$$

$$= -e^{-\delta t}\,{}_tp_{[60]}\,\mu_{[60]+t}\,.$$

Dividing throughout by $e^{-\delta t}\,{}_tp_{[60]}$, then rearranging, we obtain

$$\frac{d}{dt}\bar{A}^{\;1}_{[60]+t:\overline{20-t}|} = (\delta + \mu_{[60]+t})\bar{A}^{\;1}_{[60]+t:\overline{20-t}|} - \mu_{[60]+t}\,,$$

as required.

The boundary conditions are clearly satisfied – that is,

$$\lim_{t\to 20^-}\bar{A}^{\;1}_{[60]+t:\overline{20-t}|} = 0 \text{ and } P = \bar{A}^{\;1}_{[60]:\overline{20}|}\,.$$

7.16 (a) The annual premium, P, is calculated from

$$P\,\ddot{a}_{[60]:\overline{10}|} = 50\,000\,A^{\;1}_{[60]:\overline{10}|} + 10\,000\,{}_{10|}\ddot{a}_{[60]}\,,$$

giving $P = \$7909.25$.

(b) The recurrence relations for policy values are

$$1.06(\,{}_tV + P) = 50\,000\,q_{[60]+t} + {}_{t+1}V\,p_{[60]+t} \qquad \text{for } t = 0, 1, \ldots, 9,$$

$$1.06(\,{}_tV - 10\,000) = {}_{t+1}V\,p_{60+t} \qquad\qquad \text{for } t = 10, 11, \ldots$$

(c) The death strain at risk in the third year of the contract, for a policy in force at the start of the third year, is $50\,000 - {}_3V$. We can calculate the policy value at the end of the third year from the recurrence relations in part (b), or using

$$_3V = 50\,000\,A^{\,1}_{63:\overline{7}|} + 10\,000\,{}_{7|}\ddot{a}_{63} = \$26\,328.24.$$

So, the death strain at risk is $50\,000 - 26\,328.24 = \$23\,671.76$.

(d) In the 13th year there is no benefit payable on death. Hence, the death strain at risk is $-{}_{13}V$, which is calculated as

$$- {}_{13}V = -10\,000\,\ddot{a}_{73} = -\$102\,752.83.$$

(e) The mortality profit in the third year is

$$97\,({}_2V + P) \times 1.06 - 3 \times 50\,000 - 94\,{}_3V = -\$61\,294.26.$$

(f) The mortality profit in the 13th year is

$$80\,({}_{12}V - 10\,000) \times 1.06 - 76\,{}_{13}V = \$303\,485.21.$$

E7.17 First note that ${}_0V = 0$ since we are calculating policy values on the premium basis and the premium is calculated using the equivalence principle. Next, we have

$$_1V = 500\,000A_{[50]+1:\overline{19}|} - P\ddot{a}_{[50]+1:\overline{19}|} = \$15\,369.28$$

and

$$_2V = 500\,000A_{52:\overline{18}|} - P\ddot{a}_{52:\overline{18}|} = \$31\,415.28.$$

For $t = 0.1, 0.2, \ldots, 0.9$ the required formula is

$$_tV = 500\,000\,{}_{1-t}q_{[50]+t} + {}_1V\,{}_{1-t}p_{[50]+t}.$$

For $t = 1.1, 1.2, \ldots, 1.9$ the required formula is

$$_tV = 500\,000\,{}_{2-t}q_{[50]+t} + {}_2V\,{}_{2-t}p_{[50]+t}.$$

An excerpt from the table of values is shown below.

t	$_tV$
0.0	0.00
0.1	15 144.56
0.2	15 173.83
$\vdots$	$\vdots$
1.9	31 326.91
2.0	31 415.28

7.18 (a) Let P denote the net single premium. We calculate P as the EPV of the deferred annuity, $50\,000\,{}_{20|}\bar{a}_x$, plus the EPV of the return of the premium. Suppose the premium is returned, with interest, at time s years. The amount refunded will be $P\,(1+i)^s$ and its present value will be $P\,(1+i)^s\,(1+i)^{-s} = P$. The probability that the premium will be refunded is $_{20}q_x$ so that the EPV of the refund is $P\,{}_{20}q_x$. Hence

$$P = 50\,000\,{}_{20|}\bar{a}_x + P\,{}_{20}q_x$$

giving

$$P = 50\,000\,{}_{20|}\bar{a}_x / {}_{20}p_x \, .$$

(i) Using the same argument as above, the EPV at duration t of the return of the premium immediately on death at time s years, measured from the start of the policy, where $t < s < 20$, is $P\,(1+i)^t\,{}_{20-t}q_{x+t}$. Hence, the prospective policy value is

$$_tV = 50\,000\,{}_{20-t|}\bar{a}_{x+t} + P\,(1+i)^t\,{}_{20-t}q_{x+t} \, .$$

(ii) For $t \geq 20$ the prospective policy value at duration t is

$$_tV = 50\,000\,\bar{a}_{x+t} \, .$$

(b) (i) For $t < 20$, the retrospective policy value is given by

$$(P - P\,{}_tq_x)/\,{}_tE_x \, .$$

(ii) For $t \geq 20$, the retrospective policy value is given by

$$(P - P\,{}_{20}q_x - 50\,000\,{}_{20|}\bar{a}_{\overline{x:t-20|}})/\,{}_tE_x \, .$$

(c) The prospective and retrospective net premium policy values are equal without any further conditions since the (net) premium is calculated using the equivalence principle with the same basis as for the policy values. To show that the prospective and retrospective policy values are equal, we start with the equation for the net premium and split the EPVs into values before and after time t.

(i) For $t < 20$ we have

$$P = 50\,000\,_{20|}\bar{a}_x + P\,_{20}q_x$$
$$= 50\,000\,_tE_x\,_{20-t|}\bar{a}_{x+t} + P\,(_tq_x + _tp_x\,_{20-t}p_{x+t})$$
$$= _tE_x(50\,000\,_{20-t|}\bar{a}_{x+t} + P\,(1+i)^t\,_{20-t}q_x) + P\,_tq_x.$$

Rearranging this last formula, we get

$$(P - P\,_tq_x)/\,_tE_x = 50\,000\,_{20-t|}\bar{a}_{x+t} + P\,(1+i)^t\,_{20-t}q_x$$

as required.

(ii) For $t \geq 20$ we have

$$P = 50\,000\,_{20|}\bar{a}_x + P\,_{20}q_x$$
$$= 50\,000(_tE_x\,\bar{a}_{x+t} + _{20|}\bar{a}_{x:\overline{t-20|}}) + P\,_{20}q_x.$$

Rearranging this last formula, we get

$$(P - P\,_{20}q_x - 50\,000\,_{20|}\bar{a}_{x:\overline{t-20|}})/\,_tE_x = 50\,000\,\bar{a}_{x+t}$$

as required.

7.19 (a) Let P^g denote the gross premium payable in the first year. Then

$$0.9 \times 0.5\,P^g \left(\ddot{a}_{[40]:\overline{5|}} + \ddot{a}_{[40]:\overline{20|}}\right) - 0.4\,P^g = 200 + 300\,000 \left(A^{\,1}_{[40]:\overline{5|}} + A^{\,1}_{[40]:\overline{20|}}\right).$$

The following EPVs have been calculated using an interest rate of 5%

$$\ddot{a}_{[40]:\overline{5|}} = 4.541, \quad \ddot{a}_{[40]:\overline{20|}} = 12.995, \quad A^{\,1}_{[40]:\overline{5|}} = 0.00254, \quad A^{\,1}_{[40]:\overline{20|}} = 0.01454.$$

Hence, $P^g = \$710.33$.

(b) Let P^n denote the net premium payable in the first year for the policy. Then

$$P^n = 300\,000 \left(A^{\,1}_{[40]:\overline{5|}} + A^{\,1}_{[40]:\overline{20|}}\right) / \left(0.5 \left(\ddot{a}_{[40]:\overline{5|}} + \ddot{a}_{[40]:\overline{20|}}\right)\right) = \$596.47.$$

Note that the net premium is calculated using an interest rate of 4.5% per year.

Let $_tV^g$, $_tV^n$ and $_tV^{FPT}$ denote the gross premium, net premium and Full Preliminary Term policy values, respectively, at duration t years. Then, using a recursive approach,

$$_0V^g = 200 + 300\,000 \left(A^{\;\;1}_{[40]:\overline{5}|} + A^{\;\;1}_{[40]:\overline{20}|} \right) + 0.4\,P^g$$
$$-0.9 \times 0.5\,P^g \left(\ddot{a}_{[40]:\overline{5}|} + \ddot{a}_{[40]:\overline{20}|} \right),$$
$$_1V^g = ((\,_0V^g - 200 + 0.5\,P^g) \times 1.045 - 600\,000\,q_{[40]})/p_{[40]},$$
$$_2V^g = ((\,_1V^g + 0.9\,P^g) \times 1.045 - 600\,000\,q_{[40]+1})/p_{[40]+1},$$

$$_0V^n = 300\,000 \left(A^{\;\;1}_{[40]:\overline{5}|} + A^{\;\;1}_{[40]:\overline{20}|} \right) - 0.5\,P^n \left(\ddot{a}_{[40]:\overline{5}|} + \ddot{a}_{[40]:\overline{20}|} \right),$$
$$_1V^n = ((\,_0V^n + P^n) \times 1.045 - 600\,000\,q_{[40]})/p_{[40]},$$
$$_2V^n = ((\,_1V^n + P^n) \times 1.045 - 600\,000\,q_{[40]+1})/p_{[40]+1},$$

$$_0V^{FPT} = 300\,000 \left(A^{\;\;1}_{[40]:\overline{5}|} + A^{\;\;1}_{[40]:\overline{20}|} \right) - {_1P_{[40]}}$$
$$-v\,p_{[40]}\,0.5\,P_{[40]+1} \left(\ddot{a}_{[40]+1:\overline{4}|} + \ddot{a}_{[40]+1:\overline{19}|} \right),$$
$$_1V^{FPT} = ((\,_0V^{FPT} + {_1P_{[40]}}) \times 1.045 - 600\,000\,q_{[40]})/p_{[40]},$$
$$_2V^{FPT} = ((\,_1V^{FPT} + P_{[40]+1}) \times 1.045 - 600\,000\,q_{[40]+1})/p_{[40]+1},$$

where $_1P_{[40]}$ is the cost of insurance in the first year and $P_{[40]+1}$ is the net premium payable from duration 1 (and halving from duration 5), so that

$$_1P_{[40]} = 600\,000\,v\,q_{[40]} = 258.74$$

and

$$P_{[40]+1} = 300\,000 \left(A^{\;\;1}_{[40]+1:\overline{4}|} + A^{\;\;1}_{[40]+1:\overline{19}|} \right) / \left(0.5 \left(\ddot{a}_{[40]+1:\overline{4}|} + \ddot{a}_{[40]+1:\overline{19}|} \right) \right)$$
$$= 638.47.$$

Note that all EPVs are calculated using an interest rate of 4.5% per year.

The table below shows the policy values at durations 0, 1 and 2 years.

t	$_tV^g$	$_tV^n$	$_tV^{FPT}$
0	96.93	0	0
1	−6.95	353.08	0
2	338.85	670.50	345.25

Note that

$$_0V^n = 0 = {}_0V^{FPT} = {}_1V^{FPT}$$

as must be the case from the definitions of these policy values. However, $_0V^g \neq 0$ since the gross premium, \$710.33, was calculated using an interest rate of 5%, not 4.5%, per year.

(c) The rationale for the FPT approach is explained in Section 7.9 of AMLCR. In brief, it is intended to combine the computational advantages of a net premium policy value calculation, in other words, simplicity, with the advantages of the gross premium policy value calculation. To be effective, the FTP policy value should approximate reasonably closely the gross premium policy value. In this example $_tV^n$ is closer to $_tV^g$ than $_tV^{FPT}$ is to $_tV^g$, at least for $t = 0, 1, 2$, so the FPT approach is not effective here.

7.20 (a) The modified premiums are calculated as

$$_1P_{[50]} = 100\,000\,v\,q_{[50]} = \$99.36$$

and

$$\begin{aligned} P_{[50]+1} &= (100\,000\,A_{[50]} - {}_1P_{[50]})/(v\,p_{[50]}\,\ddot{a}_{[50]+1:\overline{19}|}) \\ &= 100\,000\,A_{[50]+1}/\ddot{a}_{[50]+1:\overline{19}|} \\ &= \$1980.39. \end{aligned}$$

Here, $_1P_{[50]}$ is the premium for the first year and $P_{[50]+1}$ is the premium for the remaining 19 years.

(b) The net and gross premiums, P^n and P^g, respectively, are calculated as

$$P^n = 100\,000\,A_{[50]}/\ddot{a}_{[50]:\overline{20}|} = \$1844.68$$

and

$$\begin{aligned} P^g &= (100\,000\,A_{[50]} + 225 + 25\,\ddot{a}_{[50]:\overline{20}|})/(0.97\,\ddot{a}_{[50]:\overline{20}|} - 0.47) \\ &= \$2014.67. \end{aligned}$$

The gross premium, net premium and Full Preliminary Term policy values at duration t years, $_tV^g$, $_tV^n$ and $_tV^{FPT}$, respectively, are calculated as

$$_0V^g = 100\,000\,A_{[50]} + 225 + 0.47\,P^g - (0.97\,P^g - 25)\,\ddot{a}_{[50]:\overline{20}|},$$

$$_tV^g = 100\,000\,A_{[50]+t} - (0.97\,P^g - 25)\,\ddot{a}_{[50]+t:\overline{20-t}|} \quad \text{for } t = 1, 2, 10,$$

$$_0V^n = 100\,000\,A_{[50]} - P^n\,\ddot{a}_{[50]:\overline{20}|},$$

$$_tV^n = 100\,000\,A_{[50]+t} - P^g\,\ddot{a}_{[50]+t:\overline{20-t}|} \quad \text{for } t = 1, 2, 10,$$

$$_0V^{FPT} = 100\,000\,A_{[50]} - {}_1P_{[50]} - v\,p_{[50]}\,P_{[50]+1}\,\ddot{a}_{[50]+1:\overline{19}|},$$

$$_tV^{FPT} = 100\,000\,A_{[50]+t} - P_{[50]+1}\,\ddot{a}_{[50]+t:\overline{20-t}|} \quad \text{for } t = 1, 2, 10.$$

Numerical values are shown in the table below.

t	$_tV^g$	$_tV^n$	$_tV^{FPT}$
0	0	0	0
1	685.01	1 817.02	0
2	2 595.64	3 686.39	1 935.61
10	20 338.41	21 037.88	19 915.15

Solutions for Chapter 8

8.1 The EPV of the death benefit is

$$100\,000 \int_0^{10} e^{-\delta t} (\,_t p_{50}^{00} \mu_{50+t}^{02} + \,_t p_{50}^{01} \mu_{50+t}^{12}) \, dt,$$

and the EPV of the bonus is $10\,000 \,_{10} p_{50}^{\overline{00}}$ which is the same as

$$10\,000 \exp \left\{ - \int_0^{10} (\mu_{50+t}^{01} + \mu_{50+t}^{02}) \, dt \right\}.$$

8.2 (a) The EPV of the benefit is

$$100\,000 \int_0^5 e^{-\delta t} \,_t p_{60}^{00} (\mu_{60+t}^{01} + \mu_{60+t}^{02}) \, dt.$$

(b) First,

$$\begin{aligned}
\,_t p_{60}^{00} &= \exp \left\{ - \int_0^t (\mu_{60+s}^{01} + \mu_{60+s}^{02}) \, ds \right\} \\
&= \exp \left\{ - \int_0^t 0.025 \, ds \right\} \\
&= \exp\{-0.025t\},
\end{aligned}$$

so that the EPV of the benefit is

$$100\,000 \int_0^5 e^{-0.05t} e^{-0.025t} \, 0.025 \, dt = 2\,500 \int_0^5 e^{-0.075t} \, dt$$
$$= 10\,423.69.$$

8.3 Let P be the total premium per year. Then the equation of value is

$$P \int_0^2 e^{-0.05t} \, _t p_{50}^{00} \, dt = 60\,000 \int_0^2 e^{-0.05t} \, _t p_{50}^{01} \, dt.$$

We have

$$\int_0^2 e^{-0.05t} \, _t p_{50}^{00} \, dt = \int_0^2 e^{-0.05t} \left(\frac{2}{3} e^{-0.015t} + \frac{1}{3} e^{-0.01t} \right) dt$$

$$= \frac{2}{3} \int_0^2 e^{-0.065t} \, dt + \frac{1}{3} \int_0^2 e^{-0.06t} \, dt$$

$$= 1.87852,$$

and as

$$_t p_{50}^{01} = 1 - \, _t p_{50}^{00} - \, _t p_{50}^{02} = \frac{2}{3} \left(e^{-0.01t} - e^{-0.015t} \right)$$

we have

$$\int_0^2 e^{-0.05t} \, _t p_{50}^{01} \, dt = \int_0^2 e^{-0.05t} \frac{2}{3} \left(e^{-0.011t} - e^{-0.015t} \right) dt$$

$$= \frac{2}{3} \left(\int_0^2 e^{-0.06t} \, dt - \int_0^2 e^{-0.065t} \, dt \right)$$

$$= 0.00614.$$

Hence $P = \$195.99$.

8.4 (a) The policy value in state 1 at time t is $_t V^{(1)}$ where

$$\frac{d}{dt} \, _t V^{(1)} = \delta \, _t V^{(1)} - 50\,000 - \mu_{50+t}^{10} \left(_t V^{(0)} - \, _t V^{(1)} \right) - \mu_{50+t}^{12} \left(200\,000 - \, _t V^{(1)} \right).$$

(b) Let P be the total premium per year. Then the equation of value is

$$P \bar{a}_{50}^{00} = 50\,000 \, \bar{a}_{50}^{01} + 200\,000 \, \bar{A}_{50}^{02}$$

which gives $P = \$11\,413.99$.

(c) At time 10 years, the policy value in state 1 is

$$_{10} V^{(1)} = 50\,000 \, \bar{a}_{60}^{11} + 200\,000 \, \bar{A}_{60}^{12} - P \, \bar{a}_{60}^{10}$$

$$= 450\,155.85.$$

8.5 (a) Kolmogorov's forward equations for this model are

$$\frac{d}{dt}\,{}_tp_x^{00} = {}_tp_x^{01}\,\mu_{x+t}^{10} - {}_tp_x^{00}\,(\mu_{x+t}^{01} + \mu_{x+t}^{02}),$$

$$\frac{d}{dt}\,{}_tp_x^{01} = {}_tp_x^{00}\,\mu_{x+t}^{01} - {}_tp_x^{01}\,(\mu_{x+t}^{10} + \mu_{x+t}^{12}),$$

$$\frac{d}{dt}\,{}_tp_x^{02} = {}_tp_x^{00}\,\mu_{x+t}^{02} + {}_tp_x^{01}\,\mu_{x+t}^{12}.$$

(b) $\bar{a}_{x:\overline{n}|}^{01}$ is the EPV of a benefit of 1 per year, payable continuously for a maximum of n years to a life who is now aged x and in state 0 (healthy), as long as the life is in state 1 (sick). We have

$$\bar{a}_{x:\overline{n}|}^{01} = \int_0^n v^t\,{}_tp_x^{01}\,dt.$$

$\bar{A}_{x:\overline{n}|}^{02}$ is the EPV of a benefit of 1 payable on the death before time n years of a life who is now aged x and in state 0. The benefit is payable should death occur from either live state. We have

$$\bar{A}_{x:\overline{n}|}^{02} = \int_0^n v^t({}_tp_x^{00}\,\mu_{x+t}^{02} + {}_tp_x^{01}\,\mu_{x+t}^{12})\,dt.$$

(c) The policy value in state 1 at time t is

$$_tV^{(1)} = B\,\bar{a}^{11}_{40+t:\overline{20-t}|} + S\,\bar{A}^{12}_{40+t:\overline{20-t}|} - P\,\bar{a}^{10}_{40+t:\overline{20-t}|}.$$

(d)   (i) We use the approximations

$$_{t+h}p_{40}^{00} \approx {}_tp_{40}^{00}(1 - h\,(\mu_{40+t}^{01} + \mu_{40+t}^{02})) + {}_tp_{40}^{01}\,h\,\mu_{40+t}^{10}$$

and

$$_{t+h}p_{40}^{01} \approx {}_tp_{40}^{01}(1 - h\,(\mu_{40+t}^{10} + \mu_{40+t}^{12})) + {}_tp_{40}^{00}\,h\,\mu_{40+t}^{01}$$

with $h = 0.1$, $_0p_{40}^{00} = 1$ and $_0p_{40}^{01} = 0$. These give

$$_{0.1}p_{40}^{00} \approx 1 - 0.1(0.01074 + 0.00328) = 0.99860,$$

$$_{0.1}p_{40}^{01} \approx 0.1 \times 0.01074 = 0.00107,$$

$$_{0.2}p_{40}^{00} \approx 0.99860(1 - 0.1(0.01094 + 0.00330))$$
$$+0.00107 \times 0.1 \times 0.09003$$
$$= 0.99719,$$

$$_{0.2}p_{40}^{01} \approx 0.00107(1 - 0.1(0.09003 + 0.00719))$$
$$+0.99860 \times 0.1 \times 0.01094$$
$$= 0.00216.$$

(ii) Thiele's differential equations are

$$\frac{d}{dt}\,_tV^{(0)} = \delta\,_tV^{(0)} + P - \mu^{01}_{40+t}(\,_tV^{(1)} - \,_tV^{(0)}) - \mu^{02}_{40+t}(S - \,_tV^{(0)})$$

and

$$\frac{d}{dt}\,_tV^{(1)} = \delta\,_tV^{(1)} - B - \mu^{10}_{40+t}(\,_tV^{(0)} - \,_tV^{(1)}) - \mu^{12}_{40+t}(S - \,_tV^{(1)}).$$

(iii) Using the approximation

$$\frac{d}{dt}\,_tV^{(i)} \approx \frac{1}{h}(\,_tV^{(i)} - \,_{t-h}V^{(i)})$$

for $i = 1, 2$ we have

$$_tV^{(0)} \approx \,_{t-h}V^{(0)} + h\left(\delta\,_tV^{(0)} + P - \mu^{01}_{40+t}(\,_tV^{(1)} - \,_tV^{(0)}) - \mu^{02}_{40+t}(S - \,_tV^{(0)})\right)$$

and

$$_tV^{(1)} \approx \,_{t-h}V^{(1)} + h\left(\delta\,_tV^{(1)} - B - \mu^{10}_{40+t}(\,_tV^{(0)} - \,_tV^{(1)}) - \mu^{12}_{40+t}(S - \,_tV^{(1)})\right),$$

with $_{20}V^{(0)} = \,_{20}V^{(1)} = 0$. Setting $h = 0.1$ these equations give

$$_{19.9}V^{(0)} = -h\,(P - \mu^{02}_{60}\,S) = -427,$$

$$_{19.9}V^{(1)} = -h\,(-B - \mu^{12}_{60}\,S) = 2594.$$

^{E}8.6 (a) (i) We have

$$_{10}p^{00}_{30} = \exp\left\{-\int_0^{10}(\mu^{01}_{30+t} + \mu^{02}_{30+t})\,dt\right\}$$

$$= \exp\left\{-10^{-4} - \int_0^{10}(A + Bc^{30+t})\,dt\right\}$$

$$= \exp\{-10^{-4}\}\,s^{10}\,g^{c^{30}(c^{10}-1)}$$

where

$$s = \exp\{-A\} = 0.999490, \quad g = \exp\{-B/\log c\} = 0.999118.$$

Hence $_{10}p^{00}_{30} = 0.979122$.

(ii) The formula for this probability is

$$_{10}p^{01}_{30} = \int_0^{10} \,_{10}p^{00}_{30}\,\mu^{01}_{30+t}\,dt$$

which can be evaluated by numerical integration, giving

$$_{10}p^{01}_{30} = 0.020779.$$

(iii) This probability is

$$_{10}p_{30}^{02} = 1 - {_{10}p_{30}^{00}} - {_{10}p_{30}^{01}} = 0.000099.$$

(b) (i) The EPV for the premium, P per year payable continuously, is

$$P\bar{a}_{30:\overline{10}|}^{00} = P \int_0^{10} v^t \, {_tp_{30}^{00}} \, dt.$$

The EPV of the death benefit is

$$100\,000\,\bar{A}_{30:\overline{10}|}^{02} + 200\,000\bar{A}_{30:\overline{10}|}^{01}$$

$$= 100\,000 \int_0^{10} v^t \, {_tp_{30}^{00}} \, (\mu_{30+t}^{02} + 2\mu_{30+t}^{01}) \, dt.$$

The integrals can be evaluated using numerical integration, giving

$$P = \$206.28.$$

(ii) The policy value at time 5 (in state 0) is given by

$$_5V^{(0)} = 100\,000\bar{A}_{35:\overline{5}|}^{02} + 200\,000\bar{A}_{35:\overline{5}|}^{01} - P\bar{a}_{35:\overline{5}|}^{00} = \$167.15.$$

^{E}8.7 (a) Kolmogorov's equations, discretized, in this case give us

$$_{t+h}p_{30}^{00} = {_tp_{30}^{00}} - {_tp_{30}^{00}} \, h \, (\mu_{30+t}^{01} + \mu_{30+t}^{02} + \mu_{30+t}^{03}) + {_tp_{30}^{01}} \, h \, \mu_{30+t}^{10}$$

and

$$_{t+h}p_{30}^{01} = {_tp_{30}^{01}} - {_tp_{30}^{01}} \, h \, (\mu_{30+t}^{10} + \mu_{30+t}^{12} + \mu_{30+t}^{13}) + {_tp_{30}^{00}} \, h \, \mu_{30+t}^{01}.$$

Setting $h = \frac{1}{12}$ and using the starting values $_0p_{30}^{00} = 1$ and $_0p_{30}^{01} = 0$, we can use these two (approximate) equations to calculate successively

$$_hp_{30}^{00}, \, _hp_{30}^{01}, \, _{2h}p_{30}^{00}, \, _{2h}p_{30}^{01}, \ldots, \, _{35}p_{30}^{00}.$$

(b) (i) The EPV of the premiums of P per year payable monthly is

$$P\ddot{a}_{30:\overline{35}|}^{00(12)} = P \sum_{k=0}^{419} v^{\frac{k}{12}} \, {_{\frac{k}{12}}p_{30}^{00}} = 15.58544P.$$

The EPV of the death and critical illness benefits is

$$100\,000 \int_0^{35} v^t \, ({_tp_{30}^{00}} (\mu_{30+t}^{02} + \mu_{30+t}^{03}) + {_tp_{30}^{01}} (\mu_{30+t}^{12} + \mu_{30+t}^{13})) \, dt$$

$$= \$8971.30.$$

The EPV of the disability income, paid continuously, is

$$75\,000\,\bar{a}^{01}_{\overline{30:35|}} = 75\,000 \int_0^{35} v^t \,_t p^{01}_{30}\, dt = \$29\,660.94.$$

Hence, the monthly premium, $P/12$, is given by

$$P/12 = (8\,971.30 + 29\,660.94)/(12 \times 15.58544) = \$206.56.$$

(ii) With a premium P per year payable continuously, Thiele's differential equations for $_tV^{(0)}$ and $_tV^{(1)}$ are

$$\frac{d}{dt}\,_tV^{(0)} = \delta\,_tV^{(0)} + P - \mu^{01}_{30+t}(_tV^{(1)} - _tV^{(0)})$$
$$- (\mu^{02}_{30+t} + \mu^{03}_{30+t})(100\,000 - _tV^{(0)})$$

and

$$\frac{d}{dt}\,_tV^{(1)} = \delta\,_tV^{(1)} - 75\,000 - \mu^{10}_{30+t}(_tV^{(0)} - _tV^{(1)})$$
$$- (\mu^{12}_{30+t} + \mu^{13}_{30+t})(100\,000 - _tV^{(1)}).$$

Using Euler's method with a step size $h = \frac{1}{12}$, we have the following (approximate) equations:

$$_tV^{(0)} - _{t-\frac{1}{12}}V^{(0)} = \frac{1}{12}\Big(\delta\,_tV^{(0)} + P - \mu^{01}_{30+t}(_tV^{(1)} - _tV^{(0)})$$
$$- (\mu^{02}_{30+t} + \mu^{03}_{30+t})(100\,000 - _tV^{(0)})\Big)$$

giving

$$_{t-\frac{1}{12}}V^{(0)} = _tV^{(0)} - \frac{1}{12}\Big(\delta\,_tV^{(0)} + P - \mu^{01}_{30+t}(_tV^{(1)} - _tV^{(0)})$$
$$- (\mu^{02}_{30+t} + \mu^{03}_{30+t})(100\,000 - _tV^{(0)})\Big),$$

and

$$_tV^{(1)} - _{t-\frac{1}{12}}V^{(1)} = \frac{1}{12}\Big(\delta\,_tV^{(1)} - 75\,000 - \mu^{10}_{30+t}(_tV^{(0)} - _tV^{(1)})$$
$$- (\mu^{12}_{30+t} + \mu^{13}_{30+t})(100\,000 - _tV^{(1)})\Big)$$

giving

$$_{t-\frac{1}{12}}V^{(1)} = _tV^{(1)} - \frac{1}{12}\Big(\delta\,_tV^{(1)} - 75\,000 - \mu^{10}_{30+t}(_tV^{(0)} - _tV^{(1)})$$
$$- (\mu^{12}_{30+t} + \mu^{13}_{30+t})(100\,000 - _tV^{(1)})\Big).$$

The boundary conditions are

$$_{35}V^{(0)} = \, _{35}V^{(1)} = 0.$$

These equations can be solved, in terms of the unknown P, successively for $t = 35, 35 - \frac{1}{12}, 35 - \frac{2}{12}, \ldots, \frac{1}{12}, 0$. Requiring $_0V^{(0)}$ to be equal to 0 gives $P = \$2\,498.07$.

(iii) The value of $_{10}V^{(0)}$ is calculated as part of the recursive scheme in part (ii), $_{10}V^{(0)} = \$16\,925.88$.

8.8 (a) First note that

$$v(t + s)/v(t) = \exp\left\{-\int_t^{t+s} \delta_u \, du\right\},$$

so that $v(t + s)/v(t)$ represents the present value at time t of a unit amount payable at time $t + s$.

The left-hand side of the formula, $_tV^{(i)}$, is the EPV of all future net cash flows from the insurer from time t, given that the life is in state i at time t. Suppose that the first transition out of state i occurs in the time interval $(t + s, t+s+ds)$, where ds is small, and is to state j, where $j = 0, 1, \ldots, n$, $j \neq i$; the probability that this happens is (approximately)

$$_sp_{x+t}^{\overline{ii}} \, \mu_{x+t+s}^{ij} \, ds.$$

Given that it does happen, there will be a net single payment at that time of amount $S_{t+s}^{(ij)}$ and the EPV of all future net cash flows from time $t + s$ is $_{t+s}V^{(j)}$. The EPV at time t of these future cash flows is

$$\frac{v(t + s)}{v(t)} \left(S_{t+s}^{(ij)} + \, _{t+s}V^{(j)}\right) \, _sp_{x+t}^{\overline{ii}} \, \mu_{x+t+s}^{ij} \, ds.$$

Summing, that is, integrating, over all possible values for s, $s = 0 \to \infty$, and summing over all possible future states j gives the first term on the right-hand side.

The second term on the right-hand side is the EPV of a continuous stream of payments at rate $B_{t+s}^{(i)}$ while the life remains in state i.

(b) Following the approach in Section 7.5.1 of AMLCR, we change the variable of integration to $r = s + t$, so that

$$
{}_tV^{(i)} = \sum_{j=0, j\neq i}^{n} \int_t^\infty \frac{v(r)}{v(t)} \left(S_r^{(ij)} + {}_rV^{(j)} \right) \frac{{}_rp_x^{\overline{ii}}}{{}_tp_x^{\overline{ii}}} \mu_{x+r}^{ij} \, dr
$$
$$
+ \int_t^\infty \frac{v(r)}{v(t)} B_r^{(i)} \frac{{}_rp_x^{\overline{ii}}}{{}_tp_x^{\overline{ii}}} \, dr \, .
$$

Next, note that

$$
\frac{d}{dt}\left[\frac{1}{v(t)\,{}_tp_x^{\overline{ii}}}\right] = \frac{d}{dt}\left[\exp\left\{\int_0^t \left(\delta_s + \sum_{j=0, j\neq i}^{n} \mu_{x+s}^{ij}\right) ds \right\}\right]
$$
$$
= \left(\delta_t + \sum_{j=0, j\neq i}^{n} \mu_{x+t}^{ij}\right) \exp\left\{\int_0^t \left(\delta_s + \sum_{j=0, j\neq i}^{n} \mu_{x+s}^{ij}\right) ds\right\}
$$
$$
= \left(\delta_t + \sum_{j=0, j\neq i}^{n} \mu_{x+t}^{ij}\right) \Big/ \left(v(t)\,{}_tp_x^{\overline{ii}}\right).
$$

Finally, note that for any function of two variables, $g(r, t)$,

$$
\frac{d}{dt}\left[\int_t^\infty g(r, t) \, dr\right] = -g(t, t) + \int_t^\infty \frac{d}{dt}[g(t, r)] \, dr.
$$

Putting these pieces together, we have

$$
\frac{d}{dt}\,{}_tV^{(i)} = -\sum_{j=0, j\neq i}^{n} \frac{v(t)}{v(t)} \left(S_t^{(ij)} + {}_tV^{(j)} \right) \frac{{}_tp_x^{\overline{ii}}}{{}_tp_x^{\overline{ii}}} \mu_{x+t}^{ij}
$$
$$
+ \left(\delta_t + \sum_{j=0, j\neq i}^{n} \mu_{x+t}^{ij}\right) \sum_{j=0, j\neq i}^{n} \int_t^\infty \frac{v(r)}{v(t)} \left(S_r^{(ij)} + {}_rV^{(j)} \right) \frac{{}_rp_x^{\overline{ii}}}{{}_tp_x^{\overline{ii}}} \mu_{x+r}^{ij} \, dr
$$
$$
- \frac{v(t)}{v(t)} B_t^{(i)} \frac{{}_tp_x^{\overline{ii}}}{{}_tp_x^{\overline{ii}}} + \left(\delta_t + \sum_{j=0, j\neq i}^{n} \mu_{x+t}^{ij}\right) \int_t^\infty \frac{v(r)}{v(t)} B_r^{(i)} \frac{{}_rp_x^{\overline{ii}}}{{}_tp_x^{\overline{ii}}} \, dr
$$
$$
= \left(\delta_t + \sum_{j=0, j\neq i}^{n} \mu_{x+t}^{ij}\right) {}_tV^{(i)} - B_t^{(i)} - \sum_{j=0, j\neq i}^{n} \left(S_t^{(ij)} + {}_tV^{(j)} \right) \mu_{x+t}^{ij}
$$
$$
= \delta_t\, {}_tV^{(i)} - B_t^{(i)} - \sum_{j=0, j\neq i}^{n} \left(S_t^{(ij)} + {}_tV^{(j)} - {}_tV^{(i)} \right) \mu_{x+t}^{ij}
$$

which is Thiele's differential equation.

8.9 (a) We have

$$
{}_t p_x^{00} \, {}_{n-t} p_{x+t}^{11} = \exp\left\{-\int_0^t (\mu_{x+s}^{01} + \mu_{x+s}^{02}) ds\right\} \exp\left\{-\int_0^{n-t} \mu_{x+t+r}^{12} \, dr\right\}
$$

$$
= \exp\left\{-\int_0^t (\mu_{x+s}^{01} + \mu_{x+s}^{02}) ds\right\} \exp\left\{-\int_t^n \mu_{x+r}^{12} \, dr\right\}
$$

$$
= \exp\left\{-\int_0^t \mu_{x+s}^{01} \, ds\right\} \exp\left\{-\int_0^n \mu_{x+s}^{02} \, ds\right\}
$$

since $\mu_x^{02} = \mu_x^{12}$ for all x.

(b) We have

$$
{}_n p_x^{01} = \int_0^n {}_t p_x^{00} \, \mu_{x+t}^{01} \, {}_{n-t} p_{x+t}^{11} \, dt
$$

$$
= \int_0^n \exp\left\{-\int_0^t \mu_{x+s}^{01} \, ds\right\} \mu_{x+t}^{01} \, \exp\left\{-\int_0^n \mu_{x+s}^{02} \, ds\right\} dt
$$

$$
= \exp\left\{-\int_0^n \mu_{x+s}^{02} \, ds\right\} \int_0^n \exp\left\{-\int_0^t \mu_{x+s}^{01} \, ds\right\} \mu_{x+t}^{01} \, dt.
$$

Noting that

$$
\frac{d}{dt} \exp\left\{-\int_0^t \mu_{x+s}^{01} \, ds\right\} = -\mu_{x+t}^{01} \exp\left\{-\int_0^t \mu_{x+s}^{01} \, ds\right\}
$$

we get

$$
{}_n p_x^{01} = \exp\left\{-\int_0^n \mu_{x+s}^{02} \, ds\right\} \int_0^n \left(-\frac{d}{dt} \exp\left\{-\int_0^t \mu_{x+s}^{01} \, ds\right\}\right) dt
$$

$$
= \exp\left\{-\int_0^n \mu_{x+s}^{02} \, ds\right\} \left(1 - \exp\left\{-\int_0^n \mu_{x+s}^{01} \, ds\right\}\right).
$$

8.10 (a) The models under consideration are shown in Figures S8.1 and S8.2.

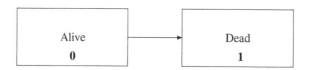

Figure S8.1 The alive–dead model.

Consider the Kolmogorov equations for the mortality probability for the two models; let μ_x denote the transition intensity in the two-state model,

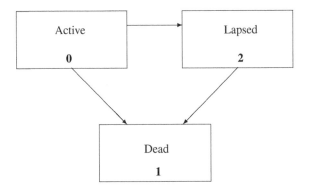

Figure S8.2 The active / lapsed / dead model.

and for both possible mortality transitions in the three-state model, so that in Figure S8.2 $\mu_x = \mu_x^{01} = \mu_x^{21}$ for all x.

For the alive–dead model, the Kolmogorov equation for the mortality probability is

$$\frac{d}{dt}\, _tq_x = {}_tp_x\, \mu_{x+t} = \mu_{x+t}\,(1 - {}_tq_x).$$

(Note that we have used the notation of Chapter 2 here to distinguish equations for this model from those for the three-state model.) For the three-state model, the Kolmogorov equation for the mortality probability, for a life in state 0 at age x, is

$$\frac{d}{dt}\, _tp_x^{01} = {}_tp_x^{00}\, \mu_{x+t} + {}_tp_x^{02}\, \mu_{x+t}$$
$$= \mu_{x+t}\left(1 - {}_tp_x^{01}\right).$$

We note that the differential equations for $_tq_x$ and $_tp_x^{01}$ are identical in form, and also that both functions have the same value at $t = 0$, $_0q_x = {}_0p_x^{01} = 0$, hence the two functions are the same for all $t \geq 0$.

(b) The result is intuitively obvious because the intensity of dying, $\mu_x^{01} \equiv \mu_x^{21}$, does not depend on whether the individual has lapsed or not. We can reconsider the model in Figure S8.2. The life is alive when the process is in state 0 or state 2. The transitions out of these states happen with force μ_x.

The two-state model is the same as the three-state model under which the two alive states are merged.

E8.11 Let P be the monthly premium. The premium equation is

$$P\ddot{a}^{00(12)}_{30:\overline{20}|} = 50\,000\bar{A}^{01}_{30:\overline{20}|} + 75\,000\bar{A}^{02}_{30:\overline{20}|}$$

where

$$\ddot{a}^{00(12)}_{30:\overline{20}|} = \sum_{k=0}^{239} v^{\frac{k}{12}}\,{}_{\frac{k}{12}}p^{00}_{30},$$

$$\bar{A}^{01}_{30:\overline{20}|} = \int_0^{20} v^t\,{}_t p^{00}_{30}\,\mu^{01}_{30+t}\,dt, \quad \bar{A}^{02}_{30:\overline{20}|} = \int_0^{20} v^t\,{}_t p^{00}_{30}\,\mu^{02}_{30+t}\,dt.$$

To calculate ${}_t p^{00}_{30}$, we have

$$\begin{aligned}{}_t p^{00}_{30} &= \exp\left\{-\int_0^t (\mu^{01}_{30+s} + \mu^{02}_{30+s})\,ds\right\}\\ &= \exp\left\{-\int_0^t 1.05\,\mu^{01}_{30+s}\,ds\right\}\\ &= \left(\exp\left\{-\int_0^t \mu^{01}_{30+s}\,ds\right\}\right)^{1.05}\\ &= \left(s^t\,g^{c^{30}(c^t-1)}\right)^{1.05}\end{aligned}$$

where $s = \exp\{-A\}$ and $g = \exp\{-B/\log c\}$. Using numerical integration, we find that

$$\ddot{a}^{00(12)}_{30:\overline{20}|} = 13.2535, \quad \bar{A}^{01}_{30:\overline{20}|} = 0.08288 \quad \text{and} \quad \bar{A}^{02}_{30:\overline{20}|} = 0.00414,$$

which gives a monthly premium of $P = \$28.01$.

E8.12 First note that

$$\begin{aligned}{}_t p^{00}_x &= \exp\left\{-\int_0^t (\mu^{01}_{x+s} + \mu^{02}_{x+s} + \mu^{03}_{x+s})\,ds\right\}\\ &= \exp\{-0.0005((x+t)^2 - x^2)\}\,\exp\{-0.01t\}\,s^t\,g^{c^x(c^t-1)}\end{aligned}$$

where $s = \exp\{-A\}$ and $g = \exp\{-B/\log c\}$. So ${}_t p^{00}_x$ can be evaluated for any values of x and t.

(a) (i) The required probability can be written as

$$2p^{01}_{25} = \int_0^2 {}_t p^{00}_{25}\,\mu^{01}_{25+t}\,dt = 0.050002,$$

evaluated by numerical integration.

(ii) The required probability is

$$2p_{25}^{00}\,p_{27}^{03} = 2p_{25}^{00} \int_0^1 {}_tp_{27}^{00}\,\mu_{25+t}^{03}\,dt = 0.003234.$$

(iii) The required probability is

$$3p_{25}^{00} = 0.887168.$$

(b) Let L denote the levy payable by each individual in active service on the first and second anniversaries of joining. The EPV (at the time of joining) of the levies payable by an individual is

$$L(v\,{}_1p_{25}^{00} + v^2\,{}_2p_{25}^{00}).$$

The EPV of the lump sum payment on transfer is

$$10\,000\,\bar{A}_{25:\overline{3}|}^{01} = 10\,000 \int_0^3 v^t\,{}_tp_{25}^{00}\,\mu_{25+t}^{01}\,dt.$$

Equating these two EPVs gives

$$L = \$397.24.$$

(c) We now expand the model to incorporate transitions after transfer. The model is now:

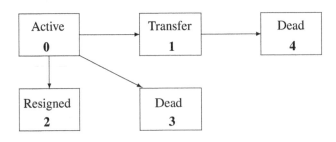

We require

$$3p_{25}^{04} = \int_0^3 {}_tp_{25}^{00}\,\mu_{25+t}^{01}\,{}_{3-t}p_{25+t}^{14}\,dt.$$

Now, once the life has transferred to state 1, the survival probability is a two-state Makeham survival probability, with parameters $1.5A$, $1.5B$ and c, so that

$$_{3-t}p^{11}_{25+t} = \exp\left\{-\left(1.5A(3-t) + \frac{1.5B}{\log c}\left(c^{28} - c^{25+t}\right)\right)\right\}.$$

Numerical integration gives

$$_3p^{04}_{25} = 0.000586.$$

E8.13 Let $_t p_{19}$ denote the probability that a student, currently aged 19, will be alive at age $19 + t$. Then, for example,

$$_{0.5}p_{19} = \exp\{-0.5 \times 5 \times 19 \times 10^{-5}\} = 0.999525,$$
$$_{1}p_{19} = \exp\{-5 \times 19 \times 10^{-5}\} = 0.999050,$$
$$_{3.5}p_{19} = {}_3p_{19}\exp\{-0.5 \times 5 \times 22 \times 10^{-5}\} = 0.996456.$$

Let $_t p^*_{19}$ denote the probability that a student, currently aged 19, will be alive at age $19 + t$ and still be at university. Then, for example,

$$_{0.5+}p^*_{19} = 0.85\,_{0.5}p_{19},$$
$$_{1+}p^*_{19} = 0.85^2\,_1p_{19},$$
$$_{3.5+}p^*_{19} = 0.85^2 \times 0.9^2 \times 0.95^2 \times 0.98^2\,_{3.5}p_{19}.$$

The EPV of the tuition fees is

$$10\,000 \sum_{k=0}^{7} 1.02^{\frac{k}{2}}\,v^{\frac{k}{2}}\,_{\frac{k}{2}+}p^*_{19} = \$53\,285.18.$$

E8.14 Let $_t p_{50}$ denote the probability that the policyholder, currently aged 50, will still be alive at age $50 + t$. Then

$$_t p_{50} = s^t\,g^{c^{50}(c^t - 1)}$$

where $s = \exp\{-A\}$, and $g = \exp\{-B/\log c\}$. Let $_t p^{00}_{50}$ denote the probability that the policyholder, currently aged 50, will still be alive at age $50 + t$ and will not have lapsed the policy. Then

$$_t p^{00}_{50} = \begin{cases} _t p_{50} & \text{for } 0 \leq t < 1, \\ 0.98\,_t p_{50} & \text{for } 1 \leq t < 2, \\ 0.98^2\,_t p_{50} & \text{for } 2 \leq t \leq 10. \end{cases}$$

Let P denote the monthly premium. The EPV of the premiums is

$$12\,P\,\ddot{a}^{00(12)}_{50:\overline{10|}} = 12\,P\sum_{k=0}^{119} v^{\frac{k}{12}} {}_{\frac{k}{12}} p^{00}_{50}.$$

Let $\bar{A}^{1*}_{50:\overline{10|}}$ denote the EPV of a payment of 1 on death before lapsation. Then the EPV of the sum insured is

$$100\,000\bar{A}^{1*}_{50:\overline{10|}}$$

where, under the assumption of UDD,

$$\bar{A}^{1*}_{50:\overline{10|}} \approx \frac{i}{\delta}A^{1*}_{50:\overline{10|}}$$

$$= \frac{i}{\delta}\left(A^{*}_{50:\overline{10|}} - v^{10}\,{}_{10}p^{00}_{50}\right)$$

$$= \frac{i}{\delta}\left(1 - d\,\ddot{a}^{00}_{50:\overline{10|}} - v^{10}\,{}_{10}p^{00}_{50}\right).$$

The premium equation is

$$0.975 \times 12\,P\,\ddot{a}^{00(12)}_{50:\overline{10|}} = 100\,000\,\bar{A}^{1*}_{50:\overline{10|}} + 200$$

giving $P = \$225.95$.

8.15 (a) ${}_3p^{01}_{60} = (d^{(1)}_{60} + d^{(1)}_{61} + d^{(1)}_{62})/l_{60} = 0.109$.

(b) As $l_{63} = 8\,945 - 380 - 110 - 70 = 8\,385$ we get

$$ {}_2p^{00}_{61} = l_{63}/l_{61} = 0.8850.$$

(c) The EPV at 5% per year is

$$10\,000\,(v\,d^{(3)}_{60} + v^2\,d^{(3)}_{61} + v^3\,d^{(3)}_{62})/l_{60} = 125.09.$$

(d) The EPV at 5% per year is

$$1\,000\,(l_{60} + v\,l_{61} + v^2\,l_{62})/l_{60} = 2\,738.74.$$

(e) Let μ^{0j} denote the (assumed) constant transition intensity from state 0 to state j at age 62, for $j = 1, 2, 3$, and let

$$\mu^{0\bullet} = \mu^{01} + \mu^{02} + \mu^{03}.$$

Then for $0 < t \le 1$,

$$ {}_tp^{00}_{62} = \exp\left\{-\int_0^t (\mu^{01} + \mu^{02} + \mu^{03})\,ds\right\} = \exp\{-\mu^{0\bullet}t\},$$

with $p_{62}^{00} = \exp\{-\mu^{0\bullet}\} = 8\,385/8\,945 = 0.93740$. Further,

$$p_{62}^{01} = \int_0^1 {}_t p_{62}^{00} \mu^{01} dt$$

$$= \mu^{01} \int_0^1 \exp\{-\mu^{0\bullet}t\} dt$$

$$= \frac{\mu^{01}}{\mu^{0\bullet}} \left(1 - \exp\{-\mu^{0\bullet}\}\right)$$

$$= 0.04248.$$

Hence $\mu^{01} = 0.04387$ and so $q_{62}^{*(1)} = 1 - \exp\{-\mu^{01}\} = 0.04292$.

(f) Under the constant force assumption,

$$q_{62}^{*(1)} = 0.1 = 1 - \exp\{-\mu^{01}\},$$

giving $\mu^{01} = 0.10536$. Using the same approach as in part (e), we get $\mu^{02} = 0.01270$ and $\mu^{03} = 0.00808$, so $\mu^{0\bullet} = 0.012614$. Then

$$p_{62}^{01} = \int_0^1 \exp\{-\mu^{0\bullet}t\} \mu^{01} dt$$

$$= \frac{0.10536}{0.12614}(1 - \exp\{-0.12614\})$$

$$= 0.09899.$$

Similarly, $p_{62}^{02} = 0.01193$ and $p_{63}^{03} = 0.00759$, and so

$$d_{62}^{(1)} = 885.4, \quad d_{62}^{(2)} = 106.7, \quad d_{62}^{(3)} = 67.9.$$

To use the UDD assumption in the single decrement models, we first calculate $q_{62}^{*(2)} = 0.01262$ and $q_{62}^{*(3)} = 0.00805$, using the same approach as in part (e). Then

$$p_{62}^{01} = q_{62}^{*(1)} \left(1 - \frac{1}{2}(q_{62}^{*(2)} + q_{62}^{*(3)}) + \frac{1}{3} q_{62}^{*(2)} q_{62}^{*(3)}\right) = 0.09897,$$

and similarly $p_{62}^{02} = 0.01194$ and $p_{62}^{03} = 0.00760$, giving

$$d_{62}^{(1)} = 885.3, \quad d_{62}^{(2)} = 106.8, \quad d_{62}^{(3)} = 68.0.$$

8.16 (a) The independent probabilities of death are

$$q_{39}^{*(1)} = 0.00049, \quad q_{40}^{*(1)} = 0.00053, \quad q_{41}^{*(1)} = 0.00057.$$

For $x = 39, 40+, 41$, where $40+$ indicates age 40 after resignations at that age we calculate

$$p_x^{01} = q_x^{*(1)}\left(1 - \tfrac{1}{2}q_x^{*(2)}\right) \quad \text{and} \quad p_x^{02} = q_x^{*(2)}\left(1 - \tfrac{1}{2}q_x^{*(1)}\right),$$

giving the following values:

x	p_x^{01}	p_x^{02}
39	0.00047	0.08998
40+	0.00050	0.09997
41	0.00053	0.10997

For these values of x we can then calculate $d_x^{(j)}$ as $l_x \, p_x^{0j}$ for $j = 1, 2$, with $d_{40}^{(3)} = 0.2 \, l_{40}$. We get the following values:

x	l_x	$d_x^{(1)}$	$d_x^{(2)}$	$d_x^{(3)}$
39	100 000.0	47.1	8 997.8	
40	90 955.1			1 8191.0
40+	72 764.1	36.4	7 274.5	
41	65 453.2	35.0	7 197.8	

(b) The probability that an employee aged 39 is still employed at age 42 is l_{42}/l_{39}, and from the above multiple decrement table we find $l_{42} = 58\,220.4$, so the probability is 0.58220.

(c) The probability that an employee aged 39 transfers between ages 41 and 42 is $d_{41}^{(2)}/l_{39} = 0.07198$.

(d) Let D be the annual deposit. Then the EPV of deposits is

$$D\left(1 + v \, l_{40+} + v^2 \, l_{41}\right)/l_{39} = 2.2349\,D$$

and, assuming that transfers take place mid-way through the year of age, the EPV of the grant is

$$10\,000\left(v^{1/2}\, d_{39}^{(2)} + v^{3/2}\, d_{40}^{(2)} + v^{5/2}\, d_{41}^{(2)}\right)/l_{39} = 2\,107.75.$$

Equating these EPVs gives $D = \$943.11$.

8.17 (a) Assume a uniform distribution of decrements in the single decrement tables. Then

$$p_{40}^{01} = \frac{2\,400}{15\,490} = q_{40}^{*(1)}\left(1 - \tfrac{1}{2}q_{40}^{*(2)}\right)$$

and

$$p_{40}^{02} = \frac{51}{15\,490} = q_{40}^{*(2)} \left(1 - \tfrac{1}{2} q_{40}^{*(1)}\right).$$

Now write the first equation as

$$q_{40}^{*(1)} = \frac{p_{40}^{01}}{1 - \tfrac{1}{2} q_{40}^{*(2)}}$$

and substitute into the second equation to get

$$p_{40}^{02} = q_{40}^{*(2)} \left(1 - \tfrac{1}{2} \frac{p_{40}^{01}}{1 - \tfrac{1}{2} q_{40}^{*(2)}}\right).$$

Multiplying throughout by $1 - \tfrac{1}{2} q_{40}^{*(2)}$ leads to the quadratic equation

$$\left(q_{40}^{*(2)}\right)^2 - q_{40}^{*(2)} \left(2 + p_{40}^{02} - p_{40}^{01}\right) + 2\, p_{40}^{02} = 0,$$

which gives $q_{40}^{*(2)} = 0.00357$.

Alternatively, if we assume constant transition intensities at age 40, denoted μ^{01} and μ^{02}, then

$$p_{40}^{01} = \frac{2400}{15\,490} = \frac{\mu^{01}}{\mu^{01} + \mu^{02}} \left(1 - \exp\{-(\mu^{01} + \mu^{02})\}\right)$$

and

$$p_{40}^{02} = \frac{51}{15\,490} = \frac{\mu^{02}}{\mu^{01} + \mu^{02}} \left(1 - \exp\{-(\mu^{01} + \mu^{02})\}\right)$$

so that

$$\mu^{01} = \frac{2400}{51} \mu^{02},$$

and hence

$$p_{40}^{00} = \frac{13\,039}{15\,490} = \exp\left\{-\left(\frac{2400}{51} + 1\right)\mu^{02}\right\},$$

giving $\mu^{02} = 0.003584$. Hence

$$q_{40}^{*(2)} = 1 - \exp\{-\mu^{02}\} = 0.00358.$$

(b) If withdrawals take place at exact age 40, then

$$l_{40+} = 15\,490 - 2400 = 13\,090$$

and $q_{40}^{*(2)} = 51/13\,090 = 0.00390$.

8.18 First, note that $\bar{A}_x$, the EPV of a unit payment immediately on the death of a life now aged x, does not depend on whether this individual is still an employee, has withdrawn or has retired. This is because the intensity of mortality is the same from states 0, 1 and 2 in our model.

We calculate probabilities by breaking the probability up into the part before the specified age, the part relating to transition at the specified age, and the part after. For example, the probability of surviving in employment to just before age 60 from age 40 is, say, $_{20^-}p_{40}^{00}$, where

$$_{20^-}p_{40}^{00} = \exp\left\{-\int_0^{20} (\mu^{02} + \mu_{40+t}^{03})\, dt\right\}$$

$$= \exp\left\{-\int_0^{20} \mu_{40+t}\, dt\right\} e^{-20\,\mu^{02}}$$

$$= {}_{20}p_{40}\, e^{-20\mu^{02}}.$$

At exact age 60, 40% of the survivors retire, so the probability of surviving to just after age 60, $_{20^+}p_{40}^{00}$ say, can be written

$$_{20^+}p_{40}^{00} = 0.6\, {}_{20^-}p_{40}^{00}.$$

Between ages 60 and 61 the only cause of decrement is mortality. So, the probability of surviving in employment from age 40 to just before age 61 is

$$_{21^-}p_{40}^{00} = {}_{20^+}p_{40}^{00}\, p_{60}.$$

Then at age 61, another 40% exit, so the probability of being in employment just after age 61 is

$$_{21^+}p_{40}^{00} = 0.6\, {}_{21^-}p_{40}^{00} = 0.6^2\, {}_{21}p_{40}\, e^{-20\mu^{02}},$$

and so on.

Consider the benefit on death after retirement. Retirement can take place only at exact ages $60, 61, 62, \ldots, 65$. If the employee retires at age x, the EPV of the benefit from that age is

$$150\,000\, \bar{A}_x.$$

The probability that an employee currently aged 40 will retire at 60 is

$$_{20^-}p_{40}^{00} \times 0.4 = 0.4\, {}_{20}p_{40}\, e^{-20\mu_{02}}.$$

Hence the EPV at age 40 of the retirement benefit from age 60 is

$$150\,000\,\bar{A}_{60}\,e^{-20\delta}\,0.4\,_{20}p_{40}\,e^{-20\mu_{02}} = 150\,000\,e^{-20\mu^{02}}\,0.4\,_{20}p_{40}\,e^{-20\delta}\,\bar{A}_{60}\,.$$

The probability of retiring at age 61 is the product of the probabilities of the following events:

(i) surviving in employment to age 60^{-},

(ii) not retiring at age 60,

(iii) surviving from age 60^{+} to age 61^{-}, and

(iv) retiring at age 61.

This probability is equal to

$$_{20^{-}}p_{40}^{00} \times 0.6 \times {}_1p_{60} \times 0.4 = {}_{21}p_{60}e^{-20\mu^{02}}\,(0.6 \times 0.4).$$

Continuing in this way, the probability that the 40-year old employee retires at age 65 is

$$_{20^{-}}p_{40}^{00} \times 0.6 \times {}_1p_{60} \times 0.6 \times {}_1p_{61} \times 0.6 \times {}_1p_{62} \times 0.6 \times {}_1p_{63} \times 0.6 \times {}_1p_{64}$$
$$= {}_{25}p_{40}\,e^{-20\mu^{02}}\,0.6^5.$$

Hence the EPV of the benefit payable on death after retirement is

$$150\,000\,\exp\{-20\mu^{02}\}\Bigg(\sum_{k=0}^{4} 0.6^k \times 0.4\,\exp\left\{-\int_0^{20+k}\mu_{40+t}^{03}\,dt\right\}e^{-(20+k)\delta}\,\bar{A}_{60+k}$$
$$+\,0.6^5\,\exp\left\{-\int_0^{25}\mu_{40+t}^{03}\,dt\right\}e^{-25\delta}\,\bar{A}_{65}\Bigg)$$
$$= 150\,000\,_{20}E_{40}\,e^{-20\mu^{02}}\Bigg(0.4\sum_{k=0}^{4} 0.6^k\,{}_k|\bar{A}_{60} + 0.6^5\,{}_5|\bar{A}_{60}\Bigg).$$

The EPV of the lump sum payable on death as an employee can be expressed as the sum of the EPV of any benefit payable before age 60, the EPV of any benefit payable between 60 and 61, and so on up to the value of any benefit payable between 64 and 65. As with the death after retirement benefit, we need to split the probabilities after age 60 into up to, at and after the year-end exits. Recalling that, in this example, the probability of surviving in employment between exact age retirements is the ordinary survival probability $_1p_x$, the EPV is

$$200\,000\Bigg(\int_0^{20} e^{-\delta t}\, _tp_{40}^{00}\, \mu_{40+t}^{03}\, dt + e^{-20\delta}\, _{20^-}p_{40}^{00} \times 0.6 \int_0^1 e^{-\delta t}\, _tp_{60^+}^{00}\, \mu_{60+t}^{03}\, dt$$

$$+ e^{-21\delta}\, _{20^-}p_{40}^{00} \times 0.6 \times\, _1p_{60} \times 0.6 \int_0^1 e^{-\delta t}\, _tp_{61^+}^{00}\, \mu_{61+t}^{03}\, dt$$

$$+ \cdots$$

$$+ e^{-24\delta}\, _{20^-}p_{40}^{00} \times 0.6 \times\, _1p_{60} \times 0.6 \times\, _1p_{61} \times 0.6 \times\, _1p_{62} \times 0.6$$

$$\times\, _1p_{63} \times 0.6 \int_0^1 e^{-\delta t}\, _tp_{64^+}^{00}\, \mu_{64+t}^{03}\, dt \Bigg)$$

which can be written more neatly as

$$200\,000\left(\bar{A}_{40:\overline{20}|}^{\,1} + {}_{20}E_{40}\, e^{-20\mu^{02}}\left(\sum_{k=1}^5 0.6^k\, _{k-1|}\bar{A}_{60:\overline{1}|}^{\,1} \right) \right).$$

^{E}8.19 The EPV of the contributions is

$$10\,000 \sum_{k=0}^{34} v^k\, _{k+}p_{30}^{00}.$$

For $k = 0, 1, \ldots, 29$,

$$_{k+}p_{30}^{00} = s^k\, g^{c^{30}(c^k-1)} \exp\{-k\,\mu^{02}\}$$

where $s = \exp\{-A\}$, and $g = \exp\{-B/\log c\}$, and for $k = 30, 31, \ldots, 34$,

$$_{k+}p_{30}^{00} = s^k\, g^{c^{30}(c^k-1)} \exp\{-30\,\mu^{02}\}(0.6^{k-29}).$$

The EPV is $\$125\,489.33$.

8.20 Let P denote the annual premium. Then the EPV of premium income is

$$P(1 + v\, p_{58}^{00}) = 1.94762\,P.$$

Note that if the life is in state 0 at the start of a year and is in state 2 (i.e. dead) at the end of that year, then $\$100\,000$ will be the benefit amount at the year end since either (i) the life has died without making a transition to state 1, and so the benefit is a death benefit of $\$100\,000$, or (ii) the life moves from state 0 to state 1, and then to state 2, meaning that both the permanent disability benefit of $\$75\,000$ and the death benefit of $\$25\,000$ are payable. Thus, the EPV of the benefits is

$$(100\,000\,p_{58}^{02} + 75\,000\,p_{58}^{01})\,v$$
$$+ p_{58}^{00}\,(100\,000\,p_{59}^{02} + 75\,000\,p_{59}^{01})\,v^2$$
$$+ p_{58}^{01}\,(25\,000\,p_{59}^{12})\,v^2$$
$$= 993.08.$$

Equating this with the EPV of the premium income gives $P = \$509.90$.

Solutions for Chapter 9

9.1 (a) $_{10}p_{60} \times {_{10}}p_{70} = 0.7802.$

(b) $_{10}p_{60} \, (1 - {_{10}}p_{70}) + {_{10}}p_{70} \, (1 - {_{10}}p_{60}) + {_{10}}p_{60} \times {_{10}}p_{70} = 0.9898.$

(c) $_{10}p_{60} \, (1 - {_{10}}p_{70}) + {_{10}}p_{70} \, (1 - {_{10}}p_{60}) = 0.2096.$

(d) $1 - {_{10}}p_{60} \times {_{10}}p_{70} = 0.2198.$

(e) $(1 - {_{10}}p_{60})(1 - {_{10}}p_{70}) = 0.0102.$

E9.2 First note that for each life

$$_{t}p_{x} = s^{t} \, g^{c^{x}(c^{t}-1)}$$

where $s = \exp\{-A\}$ and $g = \exp\{-B/\log c\}$.

(a) Since the lives are independent, we have

$$_{10}p_{30:40} = {_{10}}p_{30} \, {_{10}}p_{40} = 0.886962.$$

(b) We can evaluate this probability as follows:

$$_{10}q^{1}_{30:40} = \int_{0}^{10} {_{t}}p_{30:40} \, \mu_{30+t} \, dt = 0.037257.$$

(c) We can evaluate this probability as follows:

$$_{10}q^{2}_{30:40} = \int_{0}^{10} {_{t}}p_{30} \, (1 - {_{t}}p_{40}) \, \mu_{30+t} \, dt = {_{10}}q_{30} - {_{10}} \, q^{1}_{30:40} = 0.001505.$$

(d) Finally,

$$_{10}p_{\overline{30:40}} = {_{10}p_{30}} + {_{10}p_{40}} - {_{10}p_{30:40}} = 0.997005.$$

E9.3 The probability that Jones dies before age 50 and before Smith is, in the obvious notation,

$$\int_0^{20} {_t p_{30}^{(J)}} \, \mu_{30+t}^{(J)} \, {_t p_{30}^{(S)}} \, dt.$$

Note that

$$_t p_{30}^{(J)} = g^{c^{30}(c^t-1)}$$

where $g = \exp\{-B/\log c\}$ and

$$_t p_{30}^{(S)} = g^{c^{30}(c^t-1)} \exp\{-0.039221\,t\}.$$

The integral expression for the probability can be evaluated numerically to give 0.567376.

E9.4 First note that since the lives are independent

$$_t p_{25:30} = {_t p_{25}} \, {_t p_{30}}.$$

(a) The EPV is calculated as follows:

$$\ddot{a}_{25:30} = \sum_{k=0}^{\infty} v^k \, {_k p_{25:30}} = \sum_{k=0}^{\infty} v^k \, {_k p_{25}} \, {_k p_{30}} = 15.8901.$$

(b) The EPV is calculated as follows:

$$\ddot{a}_{\overline{25:30}} = \sum_{k=0}^{\infty} v^k \, {_k p_{\overline{25:30}}}$$

$$= \sum_{k=0}^{\infty} v^k \left({_k p_{25}} + {_k p_{30}} - {_k p_{25:30}} \right)$$

$$= 18.9670.$$

(c) The EPV of the reversionary annuity is calculated as follows:

$$\ddot{a}_{25|30} = \sum_{k=0}^{\infty} v^k \left({_k p_{30}} - {_k p_{25:30}} \right) = 1.2013.$$

(d) The EPV of the insurance is calculated as follows:

$$\bar{A}_{25:30} = \int_0^{\infty} v^t \, {_t p_{25:30}} (\mu_{25+t} + \mu_{30+t}) \, dt = 0.2493.$$

(e) The EPV of the insurance is calculated as follows:

$$\bar{A}^{\,1}_{25:30:\overline{10}|} = \int_0^{10} v^t \,_t p_{25:30} \,\mu_{25+t} \, dt = 0.0208.$$

(f) The EPV of the insurance is calculated as follows:

$$\bar{A}^{\,2}_{25:30} = \int_0^\infty v^t \,(1 - \,_t p_{25}) \,_t p_{30} \,\mu_{30+t} \, dt = 0.0440.$$

9.5 (a) The EPV of the annuity is

$$20\,000 \sum_{t=1}^\infty v^t \left(\,_t p_{60}\,(1 - \,_t p_{70}) + \,_t p_{70}\,(1 - \,_t p_{60}) + \,_t p_{60:70}\right)$$

$$= 20\,000 \,(a_{60} + a_{70} - a_{60:70})$$

$$= 293\,808.37.$$

(b) The EPV of the annuity is

$$30\,000 \sum_{t=0}^9 v^t \,_t p_{60:70} = \ddot{a}_{60:70:\overline{10}|} = 225\,329.46.$$

(c) The EPV of the annuity is

$$25\,000 \sum_{t=1}^\infty v^t \,_t p_{60}\,(1 - \,_t p_{70}) = 25\,000\,(a_{60} - a_{60:70})$$

$$= 92\,052.87.$$

9.6 (a) Since the lives are independent, we have

$$\,_t p_{xy} = \,_t p_x \,_t p_y$$
$$= g^{c^x(c^t - 1)} \, g^{c^y(c^t - 1)}$$
$$= g^{(c^x + c^y)(c^t - 1)}$$
$$= g^{c^w(c^t - 1)}$$
$$= \,_t p_w$$

where $c^w = (c^x + c^y)$ so that

$$w = \frac{\log\,(c^x + c^y)}{\log c}.$$

(b) The insurance function can be written as

$$A^1_{x:y} = \sum_{k=0}^{\infty} v^{k+1} {}_kp_{xy} \, q^1_{x+k:y+k} = \sum_{k=0}^{\infty} v^{k+1} {}_kp_w \, q^1_{x+k:y+k} .$$

Now

$$q^1_{x+k:y+k} = \int_0^1 {}_tp_{x+k:y+k} \, \mu_{x+k+t} \, dt$$

$$= \int_0^1 {}_tp_{w+k} \, B \, c^{x+k+t} \, dt$$

$$= \int_0^1 {}_tp_{w+k} \, B \, c^{w+k+t} \, \frac{c^x}{c^w} \, dt$$

$$= q_{w+k} \, \frac{c^x}{c^w} .$$

So

$$A^1_{x:y} = \frac{c^x}{c^w} \sum_{k=0}^{\infty} v^{k+1} {}_kp_w \, q_{w+k}$$

$$= \frac{c^x}{c^w} A_w$$

as required.

9.7 Let Y denote the present value random variable for the reversionary annuity. Then

$$Y = \begin{cases} \bar{a}_{\overline{T_y}} - \bar{a}_{\overline{T_x}} & \text{if } T_y > T_x , \\ 0 & \text{if } T_y \le T_x , \end{cases}$$

$$\Rightarrow Y = \begin{cases} \bar{a}_{\overline{T_y}} - \bar{a}_{\overline{T_x}} & \text{if } T_y > T_x , \\ \bar{a}_{\overline{T_y}} - \bar{a}_{\overline{T_y}} & \text{if } T_y \le T_x . \end{cases}$$

Now, if $T_y > T_x$ then $T_x = T_{xy}$, and, similarly, if $T_y \le T_x$ then $T_y = T_{xy}$, so

$$Y = \begin{cases} \bar{a}_{\overline{T_y}} - \bar{a}_{\overline{T_{xy}}} & \text{if } T_y > T_x , \\ \bar{a}_{\overline{T_y}} - \bar{a}_{\overline{T_{xy}}} & \text{if } T_y \le T_x , \end{cases}$$

giving $Y = \bar{a}_{\overline{T_y}} - \bar{a}_{\overline{T_{xy}}}$.

9.8 (a) Let $F_{T_{xy}}$ denote the distribution function of T_{xy}. Then

$$1 - F_{T_{xy}}(t) = \Pr(T_{xy} > t) = \Pr(T_x > t \text{ and } T_y > t).$$

By independence,

$$\Pr(T_x > t \text{ and } T_y > t) = \Pr(T_x > t) \Pr(T_y > t) = {}_tp_x \, {}_tp_y \, .$$

Hence $F_{T_{xy}}(t) = 1 - {}_tp_x \, {}_tp_y$ and so

$$f_{T_{xy}}(t) = \frac{d}{dt} F_{T_{xy}}(t)$$

$$= -{}_tp_x \frac{d}{dt} {}_tp_y - {}_tp_y \frac{d}{dt} {}_tp_x$$

$$= {}_tp_{xy} \, (\mu_{x+t} + \mu_{y+t})$$

using formula (2.17) of AMLCR.

(b) Let f_x and f_y be the probability density functions of T_x and T_y respectively. As T_x and T_y are independent, the joint probability density function of (T_x, T_y) is the product of f_x and f_y.

We have $\bar{A}_{xy}^1 = \mathrm{E}\left[v^{T_x} I(T_x < T_y)\right]$, and writing this expectation in integral form we have

$$\bar{A}_{xy}^1 = \int_{t=0}^{\infty} \int_{s=0}^{\infty} v^t \, f_x(t) \, f_y(s) \, I(t < s) \, ds \, dt$$

$$= \int_{t=0}^{\infty} \int_{s=t}^{\infty} v^t \, f_x(t) \, f_y(s) \, ds \, dt$$

$$= \int_{t=0}^{\infty} v^t \, f_x(t) \int_{s=t}^{\infty} f_y(s) \, ds.$$

As $f_x(t) = {}_tp_x \, \mu_{x+t}$ and

$$\int_{t}^{\infty} f_y(s) \, ds = \Pr(T_y > t) = {}_tp_y \, ,$$

we get

$$\bar{A}_{xy}^1 = \int_0^{\infty} {}_tp_x \, \mu_{x+t} \, {}_tp_y \, dt = \int_0^{\infty} {}_tp_{xy} \, \mu_{x+t} \, dt.$$

(c) We now have $\bar{A}_{xy}^2 = \mathrm{E}\left[v^{T_x} I(T_x > T_y)\right]$. The argument in part (b) now yields

$$\bar{A}_{xy}^2 = \int_{t=0}^{\infty} \int_{s=0}^{t} v^t \, f_x(t) \, f_y(s) \, ds \, dt$$

$$= \int_0^{\infty} {}_tp_x \, (1 - {}_tp_y) \, \mu_{x+t} \, dt$$

$$= \bar{A}_x - \bar{A}_{xy}^1 \, .$$

Rearranging this result we see that

$$\bar{A}_x = \bar{A}^1_{xy} + \bar{A}^2_{xy}.$$

The result follows as (x) must die either before or after (y). If (x) were to effect two contracts, one paying \$1 on death before (y), the other paying \$1 on death after (y), then the total payout under these contracts is \$1 on the death of (x).

9.9 (a) Let P denote the annual premium. The EPV of the premiums is

$$P\ddot{a}_{25} = P \sum_{k=0}^{\infty} v^k {}_k p_{25}.$$

To find the EPV of the death benefit, we initially use letters as subscripts. In an obvious notation, the EPV of the death benefit is

$$100\,000 A^2_{B:M}.$$

We have

$$A_B = A^1_{B:M} + A^2_{B:M}$$

so that

$$A^2_{B:M} = A_B - A^1_{B:M}.$$

Replacing B and M by age 25 and noting (by symmetry) that

$$A^1_{25:25} = \frac{1}{2} A_{25:25},$$

we see that the EPV of the death benefit is

$$100\,000 \left(A_{25} - \frac{1}{2} A_{25:25} \right),$$

where we can calculate $A_{25:25}$ from $A_{25:25} = 1 - d\ddot{a}_{25:25}$. Equating this EPV to the EPV of the premiums gives $P = \$243.16$.

(b) (i) If only Bob is alive, the policy value at time 10 is

$$\begin{aligned}
_{10}V &= 100\,000 A_{35} - P\ddot{a}_{35} \\
&= 100\,000 \sum_{k=0}^{\infty} v^{k+1} {}_k p_{35}\, q_{35+k} - P \sum_{k=0}^{\infty} v^k {}_k p_{35} \\
&= \$18\,269.42.
\end{aligned}$$

(ii) If both are alive at time 10, the policy value at time 10 is

$$_{10}V = 100\,000(A_{35} - \frac{1}{2}A_{35:35}) - P\ddot{a}_{35} = \$2817.95.$$

E9.10 (a) The EPV is $\$100\,000\,\ddot{a}_{65}^{(12)}$, using Ryan's mortality, which is $\$802\,693$.

(b) Recall the joint and last survivor model, Figure 9.2 in AMLCR. We will use that figure to reference the states involved in the annuity payments. The annuity calculated in (a) corresponds to

$$\ddot{a}_{x:y}^{00(12)} + \ddot{a}_{x:y}^{01(12)}$$

where x denotes Ryan and y denotes Lindsay. The new annuity is found by equating the value of the benefits with the EPV of the single life annuity in (a), so the equation of value for an annual starting benefit of B per year is

$$802\,693 = B\,\ddot{a}_{x:y}^{00(12)} + B\,\ddot{a}_{x:y}^{01(12)} + 0.6B\,\ddot{a}_{x:y}^{02(12)}.$$

We can calculate $\ddot{a}_{x:y}^{02(12)}$ using the approach of Section 8.6 of AMLCR, summing the product of the appropriate probability and discount function at each month end. For $_t p_{x:y}^{02}$ we calculate recursively, starting from $_0 p_{x:y}^{02} = 0$, using

$$_{t+h}p_{xy}^{02} = {}_t p_{xy}^{02}\,{}_h p_{y+t}^{22} + {}_t p_{x:y}^{00}\,{}_h p_{x+t:y+t}^{02}$$

where $h = \frac{1}{12}$. Let m denote male mortality, fm denote female married mortality and fw denote female widowed mortality. Then

$$_t p_{x:y}^{00} = {}_t p_x^m\,{}_t p_y^{fm} \quad \text{and} \quad {}_h p_{y+t}^{22} = {}_h p_{y+t}^{fw}.$$

Now

$$_h p_{x+t:y+t}^{02} = \int_0^h {}_r p_{x+t:y+t}^{00}\,\mu_{x+t+r:y+t+r}^{02}\,{}_{h-r}p_{y+t+r}^{fw}\,dr.$$

We can approximate this using the trapezium rule as

$$\frac{h}{2}\left(\mu_{x+t:y+t}^{02}\,{}_h p_{y+t}^{fw} + {}_h p_{x+t:y+t}^{00}\,\mu_{x+t+h:y+t+h}^{02}\right).$$

Alternatively, if we assume Ryan's death occurs half-way through the interval from t to $t + h$ we obtain the approximation

$$_h p_{x+t:y+t}^{02} \approx {}_h q_{x+t}^m \times {}_{h/2}p_{y+t}^{fm} \times {}_{h/2}p_{y+t+h/2}^{fw}.$$

We find that $\ddot{a}_{x:y}^{02(12)} = 4.0307$, so that the revised benefit while both partners survive is $\$76\,846$.

(c) The equation of value for a starting benefit of B per year is now

$$802\,693 = B\,\ddot{a}_{x:y}^{00(12)} + 100\,000\,\ddot{a}_{x:y}^{01(12)} + 0.6B\,\ddot{a}_{x:y}^{02(12)}$$

which gives a revised starting benefit of \$73 942.

E9.11 Let P denote the monthly premium. Let superscript f denote the female survival model, and superscript m denote the male survival model. The equation of value for the premium is

$$0.97 \times 12P\,\ddot{a}_{24:28:\overline{25}|}^{(12)} = 100\,000\,\bar{A}_{24:28} + 250$$

where

$$\ddot{a}_{24:28:\overline{25}|}^{(12)} = \frac{1}{12}\sum_{k=0}^{299} {}_{\frac{k}{12}}p_{28}^{m}\,{}_{\frac{k}{12}}p_{24}^{f}\,v^{\frac{k}{12}} = 13.3266$$

and

$$\bar{A}_{24:28} = \int_0^\infty v^t\,{}_tp_{28}^m\,{}_tp_{24}^f\left(\mu_{28+t}^m + \mu_{24+t}^f\right)dt = 0.24846,$$

from which we calculate that $P = \$161.78$.

9.12 (a) The discount factor, $v^{t/m}$, is the present value of a unit amount payable at time t/m in the future. The term ${}_{(t-1)/m}p_{xy} - {}_{t/m}p_{xy}$ is the probability that x and y are both alive at time $(t-1)/m$ but are not both alive at time t/m. Hence

$$\sum_{t=1}^{m} v^{t/m}\left({}_{(t-1)/m}p_{xy} - {}_{t/m}p_{xy}\right)$$

is the EPV of a payment of 1 at the end of the $\frac{1}{m}$th of a year in which the first death of x and y occurs, provided this is within one year from now.

(b) Using the result from part (a), we can write

$$A_{xy}^{(m)} = \sum_{k=0}^{\infty} v^k\,{}_kp_{xy}\sum_{t=1}^{m} v^{t/m}\left({}_{(t-1)/m}p_{x+k:y+k} - {}_{t/m}p_{x+k:y+k}\right).$$

(c) Since the lives are independent, we can write the joint life probabilities in terms of single life probabilities, as follows:

$$_{(t-1)/m}p_{xy} - {}_{t/m}p_{xy}$$

$$= {}_{(t-1)/m}p_x \, {}_{(t-1)/m}p_y - {}_{t/m}p_x \, {}_{t/m}p_y$$

$$= (1 - {}_{(t-1)/m}q_x)(1 - {}_{(t-1)/m}q_y) - (1 - {}_{t/m}q_x)(1 - {}_{t/m}q_y)$$

$$= \left(1 - \frac{t-1}{m}q_x\right)\left(1 - \frac{t-1}{m}q_y\right) - \left(1 - \frac{t}{m}q_x\right)\left(1 - \frac{t}{m}q_y\right)$$

using UDD

$$= \frac{1}{m}(q_x + q_y) + \frac{1 - 2t}{m^2}q_x q_y$$

$$= \frac{1}{m}(q_x + q_y - q_x q_y) + \frac{m + 1 - 2t}{m^2}q_x q_y$$

$$= \frac{1}{m}(1 - p_{xy}) + \frac{m - 2t + 1}{m^2}q_x q_y$$

as required.

Using this formula, we have

$$\sum_{t=1}^{m} v^{t/m}\left({}_{(t-1)/m}p_{xy} - {}_{t/m}p_{xy}\right)$$

$$= (1 - p_{xy})\sum_{t=1}^{m} \frac{v^{t/m}}{m} + q_x q_y \sum_{t=1}^{m} v^{t/m}\frac{m - 2t + 1}{m^2}.$$

The result follows since

$$\sum_{t=1}^{m} \frac{v^{t/m}}{m} = \frac{1}{m}v^{1/m}\frac{1 - v}{1 - v^{1/m}}$$

$$= \frac{1}{m}\frac{1 - v}{((1 + i)^{1/m} - 1)}$$

$$= \frac{iv}{i^{(m)}}.$$

(d) Compare the two parts of the expression in part (c) for

$$\sum_{t=1}^{m} v^{t/m}\left({}_{(t-1)/m}p_{xy} - {}_{t/m}p_{xy}\right).$$

Since, for most ages, q_x and q_y are likely to be small, $1 - p_{xy}$ is likely to be much larger than $q_x q_y$. Hence, the first term is likely to be much larger than the second term. Ignoring the second term in the expression for $A_{xy}^{(m)}$

in part (c), we have

$$A_{xy}^{(m)} \approx \sum_{k=0}^{\infty} v^k \, {}_kp_{xy}(1 - p_{x+k:y+k}) \frac{iv}{i^{(m)}}$$

$$= \frac{i}{i^{(m)}} \sum_{k=0}^{\infty} v^{k+1} \, {}_kp_{xy}(1 - p_{x+k:y+k})$$

$$= \frac{i}{i^{(m)}} A_{xy}.$$

9.13 (a) First, note that

$$\frac{d}{dt} \, {}_tp_x = - \, {}_tp_x \, \mu_{x+t}.$$

Then we have

$$\frac{d}{dt} \left(v^t \, {}_tp_x \, {}_tp_y \right) = -\delta \, v^t \, {}_tp_x \, {}_tp_y - v^t \, {}_tp_x \, \mu_{x+t} \, {}_tp_y - v^t \, {}_tp_x \, {}_tp_y \, \mu_{y+t}$$

$$= -\delta \, v^t \, {}_tp_x \, {}_tp_y - v^t \, {}_tp_x \, {}_tp_y \, \mu_{x+t:y+t}.$$

(b) Apply formula (B.4) in Appendix B.2 of AMLCR, with $f(u) = v^u \, {}_up_x \, {}_up_y$ and $n = \infty$, so that, using the result in part (a),

$$f(0) = 1, \quad f(n) = 0, \quad f'(0) = -(\delta + \mu_{xy}), \quad f'(n) = 0.$$

This gives

$$\frac{1}{m} \sum_{k=0}^{\infty} v^{\frac{k}{m}} \, {}_{\frac{k}{m}}p_x \, {}_{\frac{k}{m}}p_y \approx \sum_{k=0}^{\infty} v^k \, {}_kp_x \, {}_kp_y - \frac{m-1}{2m} - \frac{m^2-1}{12m}(\delta + \mu_{xy}),$$

i.e.

$$\ddot{a}_{xy}^{(m)} \approx \ddot{a}_{xy} - \frac{m-1}{2m} - \frac{m^2-1}{12m}(\delta + \mu_{xy}).$$

9.14 We have

$$\mathrm{Cov}(v^{T_{\overline{xy}}}, v^{T_{xy}}) = \mathrm{E}[v^{T_{\overline{xy}}} v^{T_{xy}}] - \mathrm{E}[v^{T_{\overline{xy}}}] \, \mathrm{E}[v^{T_{xy}}]$$

$$= \mathrm{E}[v^{T_{\overline{xy}} + T_{xy}}] - \bar{A}_{\overline{xy}} \bar{A}_{xy}$$

$$= \mathrm{E}[v^{T_x + T_y}] - \bar{A}_{\overline{xy}} \bar{A}_{xy} \quad \text{using part (b)}$$

$$= \mathrm{E}[v^{T_x}] \, \mathrm{E}[v^{T_y}] - \bar{A}_{\overline{xy}} \bar{A}_{xy} \quad \text{using independence}$$

$$= \bar{A}_x \bar{A}_y - \bar{A}_{\overline{xy}} \bar{A}_{xy}$$

$$= \bar{A}_x \bar{A}_y - (\bar{A}_x + \bar{A}_y - \bar{A}_{xy}) \bar{A}_{xy} \quad \text{using formula (9.5)}$$

$$= (\bar{A}_x - \bar{A}_{xy})(\bar{A}_y - \bar{A}_{xy}).$$

^{E}9.15 First note that we can evaluate $_tp^{00}_{28:27}$ as follows:

$$_tp^{00}_{28:27} = \exp\left\{-\int_0^t (\mu^{01}_{28+t:27+t} + \mu^{02}_{28+t:27+t} + \mu^{03}_{28+t:27+t})\,dt\right\}$$

$$= s^t\, g_1^{c^{28}(c^t-1)}\, s^t\, g_2^{c^{27}(c^t-1)}\, \exp\{-(5\times 10^{-5})t\}$$

where

$$s = \exp\{-A\}, \quad g_1 = \exp\{-B/\log c\}, \quad g_2 = \exp\{-D/\log c\}.$$

The formula for the annual premium, P, is

$$P\ddot{a}^{00}_{28:27:\overline{30|}} = 500\,000 \int_0^\infty v^t\, _tp^{00}_{28:27}(\mu^{02}_{28+t:27+t} + \mu^{03}_{28+t:27+t})\,dt$$

where

$$\ddot{a}^{00}_{28:27:\overline{30|}} = \sum_{k=0}^{29} v^k\, _kp^{00}_{28:27}.$$

The integral can be evaluated by numerical integration, giving $P = \$4948.24$.

9.16 (a) We can value the lump sum death benefits as $1000 payable on the death of each life plus an extra $9000 payable on the first death. The EPV of these benefits is

$$1000(\bar{A}_{65} + \bar{A}_{60}) + 9000\bar{A}_{65:60} = \$5440.32.$$

(b) There is a reversionary annuity to each of the lives so that the EPV is

$$5000(\bar{a}_{65} - \bar{a}_{65:60} + \bar{a}_{60} - \bar{a}_{65:60})$$
$$= 5000\left(\frac{1-\bar{A}_{65}}{\delta} + \frac{1-\bar{A}_{60}}{\delta} - 2\frac{1-\bar{A}_{65:60}}{\delta}\right)$$
$$= \$25\,262.16.$$

(c) Let P be the annual rate of premium. The equation for P is

$$P\bar{a}_{65:60} = 5440.32 + 25\,262.16$$

so that

$$P = (5440.32 + 25\,262.16)/((1-\bar{A}_{65:60})/\delta)$$

giving $P = \$2470.55$.

(d) Using the labelling of states in Figure 9.2, the policy values required in parts (i) and (ii) are denoted $_{10}V^{(0)}$ and $_{10}V^{(2)}$, respectively.

(i) The policy value is given by

$$_{10}V^{(0)} = 5000(\bar{a}_{75} + \bar{a}_{70} - 2\bar{a}_{75:70}) + 1000(\bar{A}_{75} + \bar{A}_{70})$$
$$+ 9000\bar{A}_{75:70} - P\bar{a}_{75:70}.$$

(ii) The policy value is given by

$$_{10}V^{(2)} = 5000\,\bar{a}_{70} + 1000\,\bar{A}_{70}.$$

(iii) Thiele's differential equation at policy duration t in these two cases is

(1) $\dfrac{d}{dt}\,_tV^{(0)} = \delta\,_tV^{(0)} + P - \mu^{02}_{65+t:60+t}(\,_tV^{(2)} + 10\,000 - \,_tV^{(0)})$

$\qquad\qquad\qquad - \mu^{01}_{65+t:60+t}(\,_tV^{(1)} + 10\,000 - \,_tV^{(0)}),$

(2) $\dfrac{d}{dt}\,_tV^{(2)} = \delta\,_tV^{(2)} - 5000 - \mu^{23}_{60+t}(1000 - \,_tV^{(2)}).$

Solutions for Chapter 10

10.1 Assuming that each month is one-twelfth of a year, the member's age at the valuation date is 46.75 years. The member's expected earnings in 2008 are thus

$$75\,000\frac{s_{46.75}}{s_{46.25}}$$

since 75 000 is the rate of salary at age 46.75 and so represents expected earnings from age 46.25 to 47.25.

Using linear interpolation between $s_{46} = 2.637$ and $s_{47} = 2.730$ we have

$$s_{46.25} = \frac{1}{4}(3 \times 2.637 + 2.730) = 2.660$$

(to three decimal places) and

$$s_{46.75} = \frac{1}{4}(2.637 + 3 \times 2.730) = 2.707,$$

so that the expected earnings are

$$75\,000\frac{2.707}{2.660} = \$76\,311.$$

10.2 (a) The member's expected final average salary is

$$75\,000\frac{s_{56} + s_{57} + s_{58} + s_{59}}{4\,s_{34}} = \$185\,265.$$

(b) The expected average salary earned in the two years prior to retirement is

$$100\,000\frac{s_{63} + s_{64}}{2\,s_{54.5}} = \$114\,346.$$

10.3 (a) The probability that the employee dies in service before age 60 is

$$(d_{55} + d_{56} + \cdots + d_{59})/l_{55} = 0.01171.$$

(b) The EPV of the death benefit is

$$200\,000 \sum_{t=0}^{4} 1.06^{-(t+1/2)} \frac{d_{55+t}}{l_{55}} = \$2011.21.$$

(c) The EPV of the death benefit is now

$$2 \times 85\,000 \sum_{t=0}^{4} 1.06^{-(t+1/2)} \frac{s_{55+t}}{s_{54.5}} \frac{d_{55+t}}{l_{55}} = \$1776.02.$$

^{E}10.4 We can work per unit of salary at age 35 since contributions and benefits are both salary dependent. Thus, the EPV of the member's contributions is

$$0.04 \sum_{t=0}^{29} v^{t+1/2} \frac{s_{35+t}}{s_{35}} \frac{l_{35+t+1/2}}{l_{35}} + 0.01 \sum_{t=15}^{29} v^{t+1/2} \frac{s_{35+t}}{s_{35}} \frac{l_{35+t+1/2}}{l_{35}} = 0.7557,$$

where $v = 1/1.04$.

Define $z_y = (s_{y-3} + s_{y-2} + s_{y-1})/3$. Then the EPV of the retirement benefit is

$$v^{25} \frac{z_{60}}{s_{35}} \frac{r_{60^-}}{l_{35}} \frac{25}{60} \ddot{a}_{60}^{(12)} + \sum_{t=25}^{29} v^{t+1/2} \frac{z_{35+t+1/2}}{s_{35}} \frac{r_{35+t}}{l_{35}} \frac{t+1/2}{60} \ddot{a}_{35+t+1/2}^{(12)}$$

$$+ v^{30} \frac{z_{65}}{s_{35}} \frac{r_{65}}{l_{35}} \frac{30}{60} \ddot{a}_{65}^{(12)}$$

$$= 2.3807.$$

If the employer contributes a multiple m of the member's contribution, then

$$0.7557 (1 + m) = 2.3807$$

giving $m = 2.15$.

10.5 (a) The accumulation to time 35 years of 1% of salary over the first 20 years is

$$\frac{40\,000}{100} \int_{0}^{20} 1.07^{t} \, 1.07^{35-t} \, dt = 400 \times 20 \times 1.07^{35} = \$85\,412.65.$$

The accumulation to time 35 years of 1% of salary over the last 15 years is

$$\frac{40\,000}{100} \int_0^{15} 1.07^{20}\, 1.04^t\, 1.07^{15-t}\, dt$$

$$= 400 \times 1.07^{35} \int_0^{15} \left(\frac{1.04}{1.07}\right)^t dt$$

$$= 400 \times 1.07^{35} \frac{1 - (1.04/1.07)^{15}}{\log(1.07/1.04)}$$

$$= \$52\,148.63.$$

Hence the total accumulation at age 60 of 1% of salary is $137\,561.28. The employee's projected salary earned between ages 59 and 60 is

$$40\,000 \times 1.07^{20} \times 1.04^{14} \int_0^1 1.04^t\, dt$$

$$= 40\,000 \times 1.07^{20} \times 1.04^{14} \frac{0.04}{\log 1.04}$$

$$= \$273\,367.45$$

which means that, using a replacement ratio of 70%, the pension in the first year is

$$0.7 \times 273367.45 = \$191\,357.21.$$

Hence the EPV (at age 60 and with $i = 5\%$) of the pension benefit is

$$191\,357.21 \left(\ddot{a}_{\overline{10}|}^{(12)} + v^{10}\, {}_{10}p_{60}\, \ddot{a}_{70}^{(12)} \right) = \$2\,795\,692.86.$$

Setting the contribution rate c, such that the accumulated contributions at age 60 are equal to the EPV of the pension benefit at age 60, under the assumptions given, we find that

$$c = (2\,795\,962.86/137\,561.28)\,\% = 20.3\%.$$

(b) Now the accumulation to time 35 years of contributions of 20.3% of salary is

$$0.203 \times 40\,000 \int_0^{35} 1.05^t\, 1.06^{35-t}\, dt$$

$$= 0.203 \times 40\,000 \times 1.06^{35} \frac{1 - (1.05/1.06)^{35}}{\log(1.06/1.05)}$$

$$= \$1\,861\,128.98.$$

Her projected salary earned between ages 59 and 60 is now

$$40\,000 \times 1.05^{34} \int_0^1 1.05^t \, dt$$

$$= 40\,000 \times 1.05^{34} \frac{0.05}{\log 1.05}$$

$$= \$215\,344.55.$$

The expression for the EPV of the pension benefits is unchanged from part (a), but it is calculated with $i = 4.5\%$. The EPV of a pension of $\$X$ per year is $15.4068X$. Setting this EPV equal to the accumulation of contributions, we find that $X = 120\,798.93$. Dividing X by the salary earned between ages 59 and 60 gives the replacement ratio as 56.1%.

10.6 At age 61, the EPV of the death benefit is

$$5000 \times 35 \sum_{t=0}^{3} v^{t+1/2} \frac{s_{61+t}}{s_{60}} \frac{d_{61+t}}{l_{61}} = \$2351.48.$$

If the member survives to age 62, the EPV of the death benefit at that age is

$$5000 \times 36 \sum_{t=0}^{2} v^{t+1/2} \frac{s_{62+t}}{s_{60}} \frac{d_{62+t}}{l_{62}} = \$2094.46.$$

The EPV at age 61 of benefits payable due to a mid-year death is

$$5000 \times 35.5 \, v^{1/2} \frac{s_{61}}{s_{60}} \frac{d_{61}}{l_{61}} = \$630.47.$$

Hence the normal contribution, C, for the death in service benefit is such that

$$2351.48 + C = v \frac{l_{62}}{l_{61}} \times 2094.46 + 630.47$$

giving $C = \$58.31$.

10.7 (a) The annual rate of pension from age 65 is B, say, where

$$B = 0.016 \times 40 \times 50\,000 \times 1.05^{39} = \$214\,552.$$

(b) As we have a new member, the value at time 0 (i.e. the date of entry) of the accrued benefits is 0. If the member survives to age 26, the value at that time of the accrued benefits is

$$0.016 \times S_{Fin} \times v^{39} \, _{39}p_{26} \, \ddot{a}_{65}^{(12)}$$

where $S_{Fin} = 50\,000 \times 1.05^{39}$, so the value at time 0 is

$$0.016 \times S_{Fin} \times v^{40} \,_{40}p_{25} \, \ddot{a}_{65}^{(12)} = 5363.80 \times 1.06^{-40} \times 0.8 \times 11 = 4589.03.$$

As there are no exits other than by death (and there is no death benefit), the funding equation gives the contribution as this amount, and hence the contribution is 9.18% of salary.

(c) Assuming contributions are made mid-year, the accumulation of contributions to the retirement date is

$$0.12 \times 50\,000 \sum_{t=0}^{39} 1.05^t \, 1.08^{39.5-t} = \frac{0.12 \times 50\,000}{1.08^{0.5}} \frac{1.08^{40} - 1.05^{40}}{(1 - 1.05/1.08)}$$
$$= \$3052\,123.$$

At the retirement date, the EPV of a pension of B per year is $11\,B$, and setting this equal to the accumulated amount of contributions gives $B = \$277\,466$.

(d) The defined benefit plan offers a pension that is known in the sense that it is expressed in terms of her final salary. The amount of the pension does not depend on the financial performance of the underlying assets. If, for example, the underlying assets provide a lower level of accumulation than expected, the replacement ratio would be reduced under a defined contribution plan, but not under a defined benefit plan.

(e) From the employer's point of view, the defined contribution plan leads to a known level of contributions, which is desirable from the point of view of setting a company's budget. By contrast, with a defined benefit plan, the employer's contribution rate could vary. For example, if the underlying assets do not perform strongly, the employer may have to increase its contributions to the fund to ensure that benefits can be paid.

10.8 Let B_x denote the pension accrued up to age x. The pension is payable from age 65 without actuarial reduction, or at age x with the reduction factor applied. For retirement at age 55 we set

$$(1 - 120k)\,B_{55}\,\ddot{a}_{55}^{(12)} = v^{10}\,B_{55}\,\ddot{a}_{65}^{(12)}$$

since the reduced pension is payable 10 years (120 months) early. This identity yields $k = 0.43\%$.

Similarly, for retirement at age 60 we set

$$(1 - 60k)\,B_{60}\,\ddot{a}_{60}^{(12)} = v^5\,B_{60}\,\ddot{a}_{65}^{(12)}$$

which gives $k = 0.53\%$.

E10.9 With $i = 0.06$, the accrued liability at time 0 is

$$_0V = 5 \times 350\left(v^{25}\frac{r_{60^-}}{l_{35}}\ddot{a}_{60}^{(12)} + v^{25.5}\frac{r_{60}}{l_{35}}\ddot{a}_{60.5}^{(12)} + \cdots + v^{29.5}\frac{r_{64}}{l_{35}}\ddot{a}_{64.5}^{(12)} + v^{30}\frac{r_{65}}{l_{35}}\ddot{a}_{65}^{(12)}\right)$$
$$= 1842.26,$$

and this is the actuarial liability.

The accrued liability at time 1 if the member is alive then is

$$_1V = 6 \times 350\left(v^{24}\frac{r_{60^-}}{l_{36}}\ddot{a}_{60}^{(12)} + v^{24.5}\frac{r_{60}}{l_{36}}\ddot{a}_{60.5}^{(12)} + \cdots + v^{28.5}\frac{r_{64}}{l_{36}}\ddot{a}_{64.5}^{(12)} + v^{29}\frac{r_{65}}{l_{36}}\ddot{a}_{65}^{(12)}\right)$$

so that

$$v\frac{l_{36}}{l_{35}}\,_1V = \frac{6}{5}\,_0V,$$

and as there is no mid-year retirement at age 35 the funding equation for the contribution C is

$$_0V + C = v\frac{l_{36}}{l_{35}}\,_1V = \frac{6}{5}\,_0V,$$

giving

$$C = \frac{1}{5}\,_0V = \$368.45.$$

E10.10 The accrued pension benefit at time 0 is

$$0.025 \times 5 \times \frac{175\,000}{5} = \$4375.$$

With $i = 0.06$ this has expected present value

$$_0V = 4375\left(v^{25}\frac{r_{60^-}}{l_{35}}\ddot{a}_{60}^{(12)} + v^{25.5}\frac{r_{60}}{l_{35}}\ddot{a}_{60.5}^{(12)} + \cdots + v^{29.5}\frac{r_{64}}{l_{35}}\ddot{a}_{64.5}^{(12)} + v^{30}\frac{r_{65}}{l_{35}}\ddot{a}_{65}^{(12)}\right)$$
$$= 4605.65,$$

and this is the actuarial liability.

The accrued liability at time 1 if the member is alive then is based on the projected career average salary at age 36, $(175\,000 + 40\,000)/6 = 35\,833.33$, giving a projected accrued pension at the year end of \$5375. The expected present value at time 1 of this pension benefit is

$$_1V = 5375\left(v^{24}\frac{r_{60^-}}{l_{36}}\ddot{a}_{60}^{(12)} + v^{24.5}\frac{r_{60}}{l_{36}}\ddot{a}_{60.5}^{(12)} + \cdots + v^{28.5}\frac{r_{64}}{l_{36}}\ddot{a}_{64.5}^{(12)} + v^{29}\frac{r_{65}}{l_{36}}\ddot{a}_{65}^{(12)}\right),$$

so that

$$v\frac{l_{36}}{l_{35}}\,_1V = \frac{5375}{4375}\,_0V,$$

and as there is no mid-year retirement at age 35 the funding equation for the contribution C is

$$_0V + C = v\frac{l_{36}}{l_{35}}\,_1V = \frac{5375}{4375}\,_0V,$$

giving

$$C = \$1052.72.$$

10.11 (a) On retirement at age 60.5, the pension is

$$0.015 \times 30.5 \times FAS_{60.5} \times (1 - 18 \times 0.005) = \$58\,615.08,$$

where $FAS_{60.5} = 100\,000\,z_{60.5}/s_{44}$ and $z_x = (s_{x-1} + s_{x-2})/2$. Her salary in the year prior to retirement is

$$100\,000\frac{s_{59.5}}{s_{44}} = \$141\,837.57$$

and so the replacement ratio is 41.3%.

On retirement at age exact 62, the pension is

$$0.015 \times 32 \times FAS_{62} = \$69\,105.82,$$

and her salary in the year prior to retirement is

$$100\,000\frac{s_{61}}{s_{44}} = \$145\,036.92,$$

and so the replacement ratio is 47.6%.

On retirement at age exact 65, the pension is

$$0.015 \times 35 \times FAS_{65} = \$79\,040.71$$

where $FAS_{65} = 100\,000z_{65}/s_{44}$. Her salary in the year prior to retirement is

$$100\,000\frac{s_{64}}{s_{44}} = \$151\,681.71$$

and so the replacement ratio is 52.1%.

(b) For retirement at age x, the EPV of the pension is

$$v^{x-45}\,_{x-45}p_{45}\,B_x\,\ddot{a}_x^{(12)}$$

where B_x is the pension calculated in part (a). With $i = 0.05$, values are as follows:

$$x = 60.5: \quad \text{EPV} = 383\,700,$$
$$x = 62: \quad \text{EPV} = 406\,686,$$
$$x = 65: \quad \text{EPV} = 372\,321.$$

(c) The EPV of the withdrawal benefit is

$$0.015 \times 15 \times 93\,000\,v^{17}\,{}_{17}p_{45}\,\ddot{a}^{(12)}_{62} = \$123\,143.$$

10.12 There is no actuarial liability for the active members aged 25 since they have no past service. For the active members aged 35 the actuarial liability is

$$3 \times 10 \times 300\,v^{25}\,{}_{25}p_{35}\,\bar{a}^r_{60} = 26\,565.77$$

where

$$\bar{a}^r_{60} = \bar{a}_{\overline{5}|} + v^5\,{}_5p_{60}\,\bar{a}_{65} = 13.0517.$$

For the active member aged 45 the actuarial liability is

$$15 \times 300\,v^{15}\,{}_{15}p_{45}\,\bar{a}^r_{60} = 23\,913.20;$$

for the active member aged 55 the actuarial liability is

$$25 \times 300\,v^5\,{}_5p_{55}\,\bar{a}^r_{60} = 72\,241.24;$$

for the deferred pensioner the actuarial liability is

$$7 \times 300\,v^{25}\,{}_{25}p_{35}\,\bar{a}^r_{60} = 6198.68;$$

and for the pensioner aged 75 the actuarial liability is

$$25 \times 300\,\bar{a}_{75} = 68\,771.71.$$

Summing these, the total actuarial liability is $\$197\,691$.

To calculate the normal contribution for the three members aged 25, we have ${}_0V = 0$ and

$$v\frac{l_{26}}{l_{25}}\,{}_1V = 3 \times 300\,v^{25}\frac{l_{60}}{l_{25}}\,\bar{a}^r_{60} = \$1478.75.$$

This is the normal contribution for these three members.

For the three members aged 35, we have ${}_0V = 26\,565.77$ and if they all survive to age 36,

$$_1V = 3 \times 11 \times 300\,v^{24}\,{}_{24}p_{36}\,\bar{a}^r_{60}$$

so that

$$v \frac{l_{36}}{l_{35}} \, {}_1V = \frac{11}{10} \, {}_0V,$$

and hence the funding equation for the contributions from these three members, C_{35} say, is

$$26\,565.77 + C_{35} = \frac{11}{10}\,26\,565.77,$$

so that $C_{35} = \$2656.58$. The same argument gives the contributions for the members aged 45 and 55 as

$$C_{45} = \frac{1}{15}\,23\,913.20 = \$1594.21$$

and

$$C_{55} = \frac{1}{25}\,72\,241.24 = \$2889.65.$$

Hence the total of the normal contributions is $\$8619$.

10.13 (a) (i) For Giles, the final salary is $FS_G = 40\,000 s_{64}/s_{35} = \$101\,245.72$, and the actuarial liability (assuming no exit before age 65) is

$$_0V_G = v^{30} \times 0.02 \times 5 \times FS_G \times \ddot{a}^{(12)}_{65} = \$44\,990.14.$$

For Faith, the final salary is $FS_F = 50\,000 s_{64}/s_{60} = \$53\,071.18$, and the actuarial liability is

$$_0V_F = v^5 \times 0.02 \times 30 \times FS_F \times \ddot{a}^{(12)}_{65} = \$377\,210.84.$$

Hence the total actuarial liability is $\$422\,201$.

(ii) The funding equation for Giles' contribution (C_G) is

$$_0V_G + C_G = v^{30} \times 0.02 \times 6 \times FS_G \times \ddot{a}^{(12)}_{65}$$

(since we are ignoring pre-retirement mortality and other modes of exit) so that $C_G = {}_0V_G/5 = \$8998.03$, which is 22.5% of salary.

The funding equation for Faith's contribution (C_F) is

$$_0V_F + C_F = v^5 \times 0.02 \times 31 \times FS_F \times \ddot{a}^{(12)}_{65}$$

so that $C_F = {}_0V_F/30 = \$12\,573.69$, which is 25.1% of salary.

(b) (i) For Giles, the final salary is now $\$38\,000$ and the actuarial liability is

$$_0V_G = v^{30} \times 0.02 \times 5 \times 38\,000 \times \ddot{a}^{(12)}_{65} = \$16\,885.90.$$

For Faith, the final salary is now $47\,000$ and the actuarial liability is

$$_0V_F = v^5 \times 0.02 \times 30 \times 47\,000 \times \ddot{a}^{(12)}_{65} = \$334\,059.06.$$

Hence the total actuarial liability is $\$350\,945$.

(ii) For Giles' contribution, the funding equation is

$$_0V_G + C_G = v^{30} \times 0.02 \times 6 \times 40\,000 \times \ddot{a}^{(12)}_{65} = \frac{24}{19}\,_0V_G$$

so that $C_G = \frac{5}{19}\,_0V_G = \$4443.66$, which is 11.1% of salary.

For Faith's contribution, the funding equation is

$$_0V_F + C_F = v^5 \times 0.02 \times 31 \times 50\,000 \times \ddot{a}^{(12)}_{65} = \frac{155}{141}\,_0V_F$$

so that $C_F = \frac{14}{141}\,_0V_F = \$33\,168.98$, which is 66.3% of salary.

(c) Under the PUC method, the projected impact of future salary increases on the accrued benefits is included in the actuarial liability. The normal contribution pays for the increase in benefit arising solely from the impact of additional service. Under the TUC method, future salary increases are not included in the actuarial liability, and the normal contribution must fund both the impact of the additional service and the impact of salary increases on the whole accrued benefit. Because the PUC pre-funds the projected salary increases, the actuarial liability is always higher than for the TUC, but the values must converge at the retirement age. We see that, in this case, the actuarial liability for Giles is much lower under the TUC method than under the PUC method, because he is a long way from retirement. Faith is close to retirement, so the difference is smaller.

To build up the higher early actuarial liability, the contributions under the PUC method start out higher than under the TUC method, as the benefit funded under the PUC method is based on the higher, projected final salary. Later, the contribution under the TUC method becomes higher; the TUC contributions pay for the additional year of accrued benefit each year, and also pay for the entire past accrued benefit to be adjusted for the projected one-year salary increase. The cost of increasing the accrued benefits in line with salaries becomes very high as the employee moves closer to retirement, as the accrued benefit becomes larger. In this case, Giles' contribution under the TUC method is still substantially below that under the PUC method, as his accrued benefit is still fairly small. Faith's accrued benefit is large, and the cost of paying for the salary increase in the TUC contribution is very significant.

Solutions for Chapter 11

11.1 (a) The spot rate for time t is calculated as

$$y_t = \left(\frac{P(t)}{100}\right)^{-1/t} - 1.$$

Thus, for example,

$$y_3 = \left(\frac{84.45}{100}\right)^{-1/3} - 1 = 0.05795.$$

The other values are $y_1 = 0.05988$, $y_2 = 0.05881$, $y_4 = 0.05754$ and $y_5 = 0.05701$.

(b) The one-year forward rate at time 0 is just y_1. For all other values of t, the one-year forward rate is calculated as

$$\frac{P(t)}{P(t+1)} - 1.$$

Thus, for example, the one-year forward rate for $t = 4$ is

$$\frac{79.95}{75.79} - 1 = 0.05489.$$

Similar calculations give the one-year forward rates for $t = 1, 2$ and 3 as 0.05774, 0.05625 and 0.05629.

(c) The EPV of the five-year term annuity-due is

$$1000\left(1 + \sum_{t=1}^{4} \frac{P(t)}{100} 0.99^t\right) = \$4395.73.$$

135

^{E}11.2 (a) Let P denote the net premium, and let $v(t) = (1 + y_t)^{-t}$ for $t = 1, 2, 3, \ldots$, with $v(0) = 1$. Then the equation of value is

$$P \sum_{t=0}^{14} v(t)\,{}_tp_{45} = 100\,000 \left(\sum_{t=0}^{14} v(t+1)\,{}_t|q_{45} + v(15)\,{}_{15}p_{45} \right),$$

which gives $P = \$4207.77$.

(b) Now let $\hat{P}$ denote the net premium. Then the equation of value is, using standard actuarial notation,

$$\hat{P}\ddot{a}_{45:\overline{15}|} = 100\,000 A_{45:\overline{15}|}$$

at an effective interest rate of $i = y_{15}$ per year, giving $\hat{P} = \$4319.50$. The change in the interest rate basis has resulted in a 2.7% increase in the premium.

(c) The policy value is

$$_3V = 100\,000 \left(\sum_{t=0}^{11} \frac{v(t+4)}{v(3)}\,{}_t|q_{48} + \frac{v(15)}{v(3)}\,{}_{12}p_{48} \right) - P \sum_{t=0}^{11} \frac{v(t+3)}{v(3)}\,{}_tp_{48}.$$

Thus, $_3V = \$13\,548$.

11.3 (a) Let Z denote the present value of the benefit payment under a randomly selected policy. Then, treating the sum insured as a random variable, S, which is equally likely to be $10\,000$ or $100\,000$, we have

$$E[Z|S] = S\bar{A}^1_{75:\overline{5}|}$$

and

$$\begin{aligned}
E[Z] &= E[E[Z|S]] \\
&= \frac{1}{2}\,10\,000\,\bar{A}^1_{75:\overline{5}|} + \frac{1}{2}\,100\,000\,\bar{A}^1_{75:\overline{5}|} \\
&= \frac{1}{2}\left(10^4 + 10^5\right)\bar{A}^1_{75:\overline{5}|} \\
&= \$5286.49
\end{aligned}$$

since $\bar{A}^1_{75:\overline{5}|} = 0.096118$.

Similarly,

$$E[Z^2] = \frac{1}{2}\left(10^8 + 10^{10}\right){}^2\bar{A}^1_{75:\overline{5}|}$$

where the superscript 2 indicates that the term insurance function is evaluated using an effective interest rate of $1.06^2 - 1 = 0.1236$ per year. As

$^2\bar{A}^{\,1}_{75:\overline{5}|} = 0.083041$ we have $E[Z^2] = 419\,354\,543$ and hence the standard deviation of Z is $\$19\,784$.

(b) Consider a policy with sum insured S. The variance of the present value of the benefit is

$$S^2\left(^2\bar{A}^{\,1}_{75:\overline{5}|} - \left(\bar{A}^{\,1}_{75:\overline{5}|}\right)^2\right).$$

There are 50 policies for which $S = 10\,000$ and 50 for which $S = 100\,000$. By the independence of the policyholders, the variance of the present value of benefits from the portfolio is

$$50\left(10^8 + 10^{10}\right)\left(^2\bar{A}^{\,1}_{75:\overline{5}|} - \left(\bar{A}^{\,1}_{75:\overline{5}|}\right)^2\right) = 37\,269\,931\,272,$$

and hence the standard deviation is $\$193\,054$.

(c) Now let X_i denote the present value of the benefit payment under the ith policy in a portfolio of size N in which half the policies have sum insured $10\,000$ and the other half have sum insured $100\,000$. For the case $N = 100$,

$$\frac{\sqrt{V\left[\sum_{i=1}^{N} X_i\right]}}{N} = \frac{193\,054}{100} = 1930.54,$$

while in the case $N = 100\,000$,

$$\frac{\sqrt{V\left[\sum_{i=1}^{N} X_i\right]}}{N} = \frac{\sqrt{1\,000} \times 193\,054}{100\,000} = \frac{193\,054}{100\,\sqrt{1\,000}} = 61.05.$$

This result follows since the variance in the case $N = 100\,000$ is 1000 times the variance in the case $N = 100$. For the risk to be fully diversifiable we require

$$\lim_{N\to\infty} \frac{\sqrt{V\left[\sum_{i=1}^{N} X_i\right]}}{N} = 0$$

and we can see that this will be the case. If we set $N = 100n$,

$$\frac{\sqrt{V\left[\sum_{i=1}^{N} X_i\right]}}{N} = \frac{193\,054}{100\,\sqrt{n}}$$

and this quantity goes to 0 as $n \to \infty$ (and hence as $N \to \infty$).

11.4 (a) For a portfolio of N insurance policies the coefficient of variation (CV_N) is

$$\frac{\sqrt{V\left[\sum_{i=1}^{N} X_i\right]}}{E\left[\sum_{i=1}^{N} X_i\right]}.$$

For a diversifiable risk we know that

$$\lim_{N\to\infty} \frac{\sqrt{V\left[\sum_{i=1}^{N} X_i\right]}}{N} = 0.$$

As $E[X_i] = \mu$ for $i = 1, 2, \ldots, N$, we have $E\left[\sum_{i=1}^{N} X_i\right] = N\mu$, where $\mu > 0$, so that

$$CV_N = \frac{\sqrt{V\left[\sum_{i=1}^{N} X_i\right]}}{N\mu} = \frac{1}{\mu}\frac{\sqrt{V\left[\sum_{i=1}^{N} X_i\right]}}{N}.$$

Taking limits of both sides, we have

$$\lim_{N\to\infty} CV_N = \frac{1}{\mu}\lim_{N\to\infty} \frac{\sqrt{V\left[\sum_{i=1}^{N} X_i\right]}}{N} = 0.$$

(b) (i) We treat the parameter c of Makeham's law as a random variable, which we denote $\mathbf{c}$. Then

$$Pr[\mathbf{c} = 1.124] = 0.75 = 1 - Pr[\mathbf{c} = 1.114].$$

Let Z denote the present value of the benefit from an individual policy. Then

$$E[Z] = E[E[Z|\mathbf{c}]]$$
$$= 0.75 \times 100\,000 A^{\,1}_{65:\overline{15}|} + 0.25 \times 100\,000 A^{\,1\,*}_{65:\overline{15}|}$$

where the unstarred function is calculated using the Standard Ultimate Survival Model and the starred function is calculated using Makeham's law with $c = 1.114$. We find that

$$A^{\,1}_{65:\overline{15}|} = 0.11642 \quad \text{and} \quad A^{\,1\,*}_{65:\overline{15}|} = 0.06410$$

giving $E[Z] = 10^5 \times 0.10334$.

Next,

$$V[Z] = E[V[Z|\mathbf{c}]] + V[E[Z|\mathbf{c}]].$$

Now

$$V[Z|c = 1.124] = 100\,000^2 \left({}^2A\,{}^1_{65:\overline{15|}} - \left(A\,{}^1_{65:\overline{15|}} \right)^2 \right)$$
$$= 10^{10} \left(0.07202 - 0.11642^2 \right)$$
$$= 10^{10} \times 0.05846$$

where the superscript 2 indicates calculation using an effective interest rate of $1.06^2 - 1 = 0.1236$ per year. Similarly,

$$V[Z|c = 1.114] = 10^{10} \times 0.03570,$$

giving

$$E[V[Z|c]] = 0.75 \times 10^{10} \times 0.05846 + 0.25 \times 10^{10} \times 0.03570$$
$$= 10^{10} \times 0.05277.$$

Finally,

$$V[E[Z|c]] = 0.75 \times \left(10^5 A\,{}^1_{65:\overline{15|}} \right)^2 + 0.25 \times \left(10^5 A\,{}^{1*}_{65:\overline{15|}} \right)^2 - E[Z^2]$$
$$= 10^{10} \times 0.00051,$$

giving $V[Z] = 10^{10} \times 0.05328$. Thus, the coefficient of variation of Z is

$$\frac{\sqrt{V[Z]}}{E[Z]} = \frac{\sqrt{0.05328}}{0.10334} = 2.2337.$$

(ii) Let Z_n denote the total present value of benefits from a portfolio of n policies, and let Z be as in part (i) above, so that $Z \equiv Z_1$. Then

$$E[Z_n] = n\,E[Z] = 10^5 \times 0.10334\,n$$

and

$$V[Z_n] = E[V[Z_n|c]] + V[E[Z_n|c]].$$

Now

$$E[V[Z_n|c]] = n\,E[V[Z|c]] = 10^{10} \times 0.05277\,n$$

and

$$V[E[Z_n|c]] = V[n\,E[Z|c]] = 10^{10} \times 0.00051n^2$$

giving

$$V[Z_n] = 10^{10} \left(0.05277\,n + 0.00051n^2 \right).$$

Hence for $n = 10\,000$ we have

$$E[Z_n] = 10^9 \times 0.10334 \quad \text{and} \quad V[Z_n] = 10^{14} \times 5.18584$$

so that the coefficient of variation in this case is 0.2204.

(iii) For a general number of policies, n, we have

$$\lim_{n\to\infty} \frac{\sqrt{V[Z_n]}}{n} = \lim_{n\to\infty} \sqrt{10^{10}\,(0.05277\,n^{-1} + 0.00051)}$$
$$= 10^5 \times \sqrt{0.00051} > 0,$$

which means that the mortality risk is not fully diversifiable. The limiting value of the coefficient of variation is

$$\lim_{n\to\infty} \frac{\sqrt{V[Z_n]}}{E[Z_n]} = \lim_{n\to\infty} \frac{\sqrt{10^{10}\,(0.05277\,n + 0.00051\,n^2)}}{10^5 \times 0.10334\,n}$$
$$= \frac{10^5 \times \sqrt{0.00051}}{10^5 \times 0.10334}$$
$$= 0.2192.$$

^{E}11.5 (a) Let P denote the net annual premium. Then

$$P\,\bar{a}_{40:\overline{25}|} = 100\,000\,\bar{A}_{40:\overline{25}|}$$

at 7%, giving $P = \$1608.13$.

(b) The mean rate of interest is

$$0.5 \times 5\% + 0.25 \times 7\% + 0.25 \times 11\% = 7\%.$$

As this is the interest rate used to calculate P in part (a), the EPV of the net future loss is 0.

(c) The modal interest rate is 5% and the EPV of the net future loss is

$$100\,000\,\bar{A}_{40:\overline{25}|} - 1\,608.13\,\bar{a}_{40:\overline{25}|}$$

at 5%, giving the EPV as \$7325.40.

(d) The present value (*PV*) of the net future loss given $\mathbf{i} = i$ is

$$PV = 100\,000\,v^{\min(T_{40},25)} - P\frac{1 - v^{\min(T_{40},25)}}{\delta}$$
$$= \left(100\,000 + \frac{P}{\delta}\right)v^{\min(T_{40},25)} - \frac{P}{\delta}.$$

Thus,

$$
\begin{aligned}
\mathrm{E}[PV | \mathbf{i} = i] &= \left(100\,000 + \frac{P}{\delta}\right) \mathrm{E}\left[v^{\min(T_{40},\,25)}\right] - \frac{P}{\delta} \\
&= \left(100\,000 + \frac{P}{\delta}\right) \bar{A}_{40:\overline{25}|} - \frac{P}{\delta}\,,
\end{aligned}
$$

and

$$
\begin{aligned}
\mathrm{V}[PV | \mathbf{i} = i] &= \left(100\,000 + \frac{P}{\delta}\right)^2 \mathrm{V}\left[v^{\min(T_{40},\,25)}\right] \\
&= \left(100\,000 + \frac{P}{\delta}\right)^2 \left({}^2\bar{A}_{40:\overline{25}|} - \left(\bar{A}_{40:\overline{25}|}\right)^2\right)
\end{aligned}
$$

where the superscript 2 indicates calculation using an effective interest rate of $(1 + i)^2 - 1$ per year.

Then

$$
\begin{aligned}
\mathrm{E}[PV] &= 0.5\,\mathrm{E}[PV | \mathbf{i} = 0.05] + 0.25\,\mathrm{E}[PV | \mathbf{i} = 0.07] \\
&\quad + 0.25\,\mathrm{E}[PV | \mathbf{i} = 0.11] \\
&= \$2129.80.
\end{aligned}
$$

Note from part (b) that $\mathrm{E}[PV | \mathbf{i} = 0.07] = 0$.

Next,

$$
\mathrm{V}[PV] = \mathrm{E}[\mathrm{V}[PV | \mathbf{i}\,]] + \mathrm{V}[\mathrm{E}[PV | \mathbf{i}\,]]
$$

where

$$
\begin{aligned}
\mathrm{E}[\mathrm{V}[PV | \mathbf{i}\,]] &= 0.5\,\mathrm{V}[PV | \mathbf{i} = 0.05] + 0.25\,\mathrm{V}[PV | \mathbf{i} = 0.07] \\
&\quad + 0.25\,\mathrm{V}[PV | \mathbf{i} = 0.11] \\
&= 40\,371\,859,
\end{aligned}
$$

and

$$
\begin{aligned}
\mathrm{V}[\mathrm{E}[PV | \mathbf{i}\,]] &= 0.5\,\mathrm{E}[PV | \mathbf{i} = 0.05]^2 + 0.25\,\mathrm{E}[PV | \mathbf{i} = 0.11]^2 - \mathrm{E}[PV]^2 \\
&= 31\,693\,915,
\end{aligned}
$$

(using the fact that $\mathrm{E}[PV | \mathbf{i} = 0.07] = 0$), which leads to

$$
\mathrm{V}[PV] = 72\,065\,775,
$$

and hence the standard deviation is $8489.16.

(e) It is common to use a deterministic approach to premium calculation. Using the expected interest rate, 7%, and using the equivalence principle to calculate the premium, generates a high risk (50%) of significant losses ($7325.40) from interest rate risk alone.

This risk is not compensated by the up-side potential, allowing for the possibility of profits if $i = 11\%$. Using the mean rate of interest in the deterministic premium calculation generates an expected loss of $2129.80 on each policy.

The significant uncertainty about the profitability of the contract is demonstrated by the variance of the present value of the net future loss. We may compare the overall standard deviation, which allows for mortality and interest rate risk, with the standard deviation that would apply if the interest rate were fixed at, say, 7%. The overall standard deviation of present value of losses is $8489.16 from (d) above. If the interest rate of 7% could be locked in, leaving only mortality risk, the standard deviation would be $6468.27.

^{E}11.6 (a) We have

$$\Pr[T_{50} \le t] = 1 - {}_tp_{50} = 1 - g^{c^x(c^t-1)}$$

where $g = \exp\{-B/\log c\}$. Using the inverse transform method, if u is a random drawing from the $U(0, 1)$ distribution, we find the simulated value of future lifetime, t, by setting

$$u = 1 - g^{c^x(c^t-1)}.$$

Algebraic manipulation gives

$$t = \log\left(1 + \frac{\log(1-u)}{c^{50}\log g}\right) \div \log c$$

$$= \log\left(1 - \frac{\log(1-u)}{B\,c^{50}/\log c}\right) \div \log c.$$

If $t > 15$, no death benefit is payable and so the simulated value of the future loss is

$$-550\,\ddot{a}_{\overline{15}|}.$$

If $t \le 15$, the simulated value of the future loss is

$$200\,000v^t - 550\,\ddot{a}_{\overline{t}|}.$$

For example, with $u = 0.013$, the simulated value of future lifetime is $t = 7.513$ and the simulated value of future loss is $135\,162$.

(b) The answers will depend on the random uniform variates used.

(c) Let $\bar{x}$ and s^2 denote the sample mean and variance from 1000 simulations of the future loss. If the true mean and variance are denoted by μ and σ^2, then the sample mean is approximately normally distributed with mean μ and variance $\sigma^2/1000$. We approximate σ^2 by s^2, to get an estimated 90% confidence interval estimate for μ of

$$\bar{x} \pm 1.645 \, \frac{s}{\sqrt{1000}}.$$

For example, if for one set of 1000 simulated values for the loss, we have $\bar{x} = -795$ and $s = 25\,267$, then the 90% confidence interval for μ would be

$$-795 \pm 1.645 \frac{25\,267}{\sqrt{1000}} = (-2109,\ 519).$$

(d) The true value of the mean future loss is

$$200\,000\,\bar{A}^{\,1}_{50:\overline{15}|} - 550\,\bar{a}_{50:\overline{15}|} = -\$184.07.$$

This value does lie in the confidence interval calculated in part (c).

(e) The answer here will depend on your simulations. See (f) below.

(f) By the nature of a 90% confidence interval, we would expect that 10% of the sets of simulations would produce a confidence interval that does not contain the (true) mean future loss. Thus, the answer to part (e) above is expected to be 2.

(g) Under this interest rate model, $E[I] = 0.05$, which is the deterministic rate used in the calculations in part (a). To simulate values of the interest rate, we can simulate from the $N(0.0485, 0.0241^2)$ distribution in Excel. Suppose a simulated value is y. Then the simulated value of $1 + I$ is e^y. For each simulated value of I the calculation of the simulated value of future loss proceeds exactly as in part (a), using the same future lifetimes as in part (a). So, for the jth simulation, $j = 1, 2, \ldots, 1000$, the procedure is

1. Generate a simulated future lifetime, as in part (a), t_j, say.

2. Generate a simulated $N(0.0485, 0.0241^2)$ variate, y_j.

3. Set the interest rate for the simulation as $i_j = \exp\{y_j\} - 1$.

4. Calculate the present value of the future loss at this simulated rate of interest as

$$L_j = \begin{cases} 200\,000(1+i_j)^{-t_j} - 550\,\bar{a}_{\overline{t_j}|} & \text{if } t_j \le 15, \\ -550\,\bar{a}_{\overline{15}|} & \text{if } t_j > 15. \end{cases}$$

Note that allowing for interest rate uncertainty, in addition to mortality uncertainty, does not increase the standard deviation of the future loss by very much. This is because term insurance is not very sensitive to the interest rate assumption. However, in this question there is no uncertainty about the parameters of the survival model, so that the mortality risk is diversifiable whereas the interest rate risk is non-diversifiable. Hence, for a large portfolio of identical policies the interest rate risk will be relatively more significant.

11.7 (a) Intuitively, pandemic risk is a non-diversifiable risk, since all lives in a portfolio will be affected if a single life is affected. To illustrate that it is not a diversifiable risk, consider a portfolio consisting of n one-year term insurance policies, each with sum insured S, issued to independent lives who are the same age. Let q denote the normal mortality rate, and let $\hat{q} = 1.25q$. Let X denote the total amount of claims in the portfolio in the next year. Let Q be a random variable denoting the mortality rate with

$$\Pr[Q = q] = 0.99 = 1 - \Pr[Q = \hat{q}].$$

Then

$$E[X] = E[E[X|Q]] = 0.99\,S\,n\,q + 0.01\,S\,n\,\hat{q},$$

and

$$V[X] = E[V[X|Q]] + V[E[X|Q]],$$

where

$$E[V[X|Q]] = 0.99\,S^2\,n\,q\,(1-q) + 0.01\,S^2\,n\,\hat{q}\,(1-\hat{q})$$

and

$$V[E[X|Q]] = 0.99\,S^2\,n^2\,q^2 + 0.01\,S^2\,n^2\,\hat{q}^2 - (0.99\,S\,n\,q + 0.01\,S\,n\,\hat{q})^2.$$

The risk is fully diversifiable if

$$\lim_{n\to\infty} \frac{\sqrt{V[X]}}{n} = 0,$$

and as

$$\frac{V[X]}{n^2} = 0.99\, S^2\, n^{-1}\, q\, (1-q) + 0.01\, S^2\, n^{-1}\, \hat{q}\, (1-\hat{q})$$
$$+ 0.99\, S^2\, q^2 + 0.01\, S^2\, \hat{q}^2 - (0.99\, S\, q + 0.01\, S\, \hat{q})^2,$$

we see that

$$\lim_{n\to\infty} \frac{\sqrt{V[X]}}{n} = \sqrt{0.99\, S^2\, q^2 + 0.01\, S^2\, \hat{q}^2 - (0.99\, S\, q + 0.01\, S\, \hat{q})^2} > 0,$$

meaning that the risk is not fully diversifiable.

(b) The actuary would be able to calculate the distribution of the present value of future loss from the portfolio assuming no pandemic risk. To asses the impact of pandemic risk, the most suitable approach would be to simulate the losses assuming an appropriate model for the incidence of pandemic risk for each year that the portfolio is in force. The simulations could be used to re-evaluate the moments of the loss distribution, to quantify the impact of pandemic risk on this portfolio.

In addition to considering the impact of pandemic risk on the mean and variance of the future losses, the actuary might try stress testing the portfolio, to ensure that if a pandemic arose at any point in the near future, the insurer would have sufficient capital available to meet the extra costs. Stress testing involves assuming a deterministic path which is adverse, to assess the most important vulnerabilities of a portfolio.

Solutions for Chapter 12

12.1 The surplus emerging at the end of the tenth policy year, per policy in force at the start of that year, is the accumulation of the reserve at the start of the year plus the premium (P) minus expenses, less the expected cost of the death benefit and expenses, less the expected cost of setting up the year-end reserve. Thus, the emerging surplus is

$$1.06 \, (_9V + 0.985 \, P) - 150\,060 \, q_{49} - {}_{10}V \, p_{49} = 15.36,$$

since $q_{49} = 0.0019$, $P = 270$ and $_9V = {}_{10}V = 300$.

12.2 (a) Following the same logic as in the previous solution, the surplus emerging at the end of the tenth policy year, per policy in force at the start of that year, is

$$1.05 \, (_9V + 0.975 \, P) - 250\,040 \, q_{54} - {}_{10}V \, p_{54} = 773.86,$$

where $P = \$8400$ is the annual premium, and $q_{54} = 0.0024$.

(b) As there is certain to be a claim (on death or maturity), the surplus emerging at the end of the twentieth policy year, per policy in force at the start of that year, is

$$1.05 \, (_{19}V + 0.975 \, P) - 250\,040 = 2172.10.$$

12.3 (a) Let P denote the annual premium. The surplus emerging at the end of the first policy year, per policy in force at the start of that year, is

$$1.05 \, P - {}_1V \, p_{45} = 580.70,$$

since $p_{45} = 0.99923$ and $P = 26\,100$. Note that there are no expenses in the first year, as initial expenses are deemed to be paid at time 0.

146

The surplus emerging at the end of the second policy year, per policy in force at the start of that year, is

$$1.05\,({}_1V + P - 25) - {}_2V\,p_{46} = 688.11,$$

since $p_{46} = 0.99916$.

As the initial expenses are $5220,

$$NPV(2) = -5220 + 580.70\,v + 688.11\,v^2\,p_{45} = -4067.02,$$

where the risk discount rate is 10% per year.

(b) At time 29 years, the annuity payment is $50\,000\,(1.02^9)$. Hence, the surplus emerging at the end of the 30th policy year, per policy in force at the start of that year, is

$$1.05\,({}_{29}V - 40 - 50\,000\,(1.02^9)) - {}_{30}V\,p_{74} = 3503.74,$$

where $p_{74} = 0.98356$ and the total expenses at the start of the year are $25 + 15 = 40$.

12.4 (a) We calculate survival probabilities ${}_t p_x$ for $t = 1, 2, 3$ and 4 from

$$_t p_x = \prod_{r=0}^{t-1} (1 - q_{x+r}).$$

The tth element of the profit signature is then calculated as $\Pi_t = \Pr_t \times {}_{t-1}p_x$, for $t = 1, 2, \ldots, 5$, with $\Pi_0 = \Pr_0$. Thus, the profit signature is

$$(-360.98,\ 149.66,\ 14.62,\ 268.43,\ 377.66,\ 388.29)'.$$

(b) The NPV using a risk discount rate of 10% per year is

$$\sum_{t=0}^{5} 1.1^{-t}\,\Pi_t = 487.88.$$

(c) The NPV using a risk discount rate of 15% per year is

$$\sum_{t=0}^{5} 1.15^{-t}\,\Pi_t = 365.69.$$

(d) A higher risk discount rate generates a lower NPV. However, both the 10% and 15% rates indicate a positive NPV for this profit vector.

(e) The IRR, say j per year, satisfies

$$\sum_{t=0}^{5} (1 + j)^{-t}\, \Pi_t = 0.$$

The solution is $j = 42.72\%$.

E12.5 Assume that the insurer holds no reserves for this contract.

We show here an excerpt from the profit test table, and explain the entries in more detail below.

t	P_t	E_t	I_t	EB_t	Pr_t
(1)	(2)	(3)	(4)	(5)	(6)
0		550			−550.00
$\frac{1}{12}$	100	0	0.49	31.76	68.73
$\frac{2}{12}$	100	5	0.46	32.04	63.43
$\frac{3}{12}$	100	5	0.46	32.31	63.15
⋮	⋮	⋮	⋮	⋮	⋮
10	100	5	0.46	93.18	2.28

Column (1) shows the time at which the cash flows are valued; the first row accounts for the initial expenses, incurred at time $t = 0$.

All other rows accumulate the cash flows to the end of each month (i.e. time t). For each row, the cash flows are determined assuming that the policy is in force at the start of the month (i.e. at time $t - \frac{1}{12}$).

Column (2) shows the premium income at the start of each month.

Column (3) shows the expenses incurred; the initial expenses in the first row include all first-month expenses, which is why there are no further expenses in the second row (which shows cash flows during the first month of the contract).

Column (4) shows the interest earned during the month on the beginning-month cash flows, i.e. $(1.06^{1/12} - 1)(P_t - E_t)$.

Column (5) shows the expected benefit outgo for the month for a policy in force at the beginning of the month, accumulated to the end of the month. We assume that, on average, the death benefit is paid half-way through the month of death, so that

$$EB_t = 200\,000\ {}_{\frac{1}{12}}q_{55+t-\frac{1}{12}}\,(1.06^{1/24}).$$

Column (6) shows the profit vector, which is the expected profit at time t for each policy in force at time $t - \frac{1}{12}$, where

$$\text{Pr}_t = P_t - E_t + I_t - EB_t .$$

Mortality probabilities are calculated from Makeham's formula.

^{E}12.6 (a) We show the profit test table, and explain below how the entries are calculated.

t	$_{t-1}V$	P_t	E_t	I_t	EB_t	EV_t	Pr_t
(1)	(2)	(3)	(4)	(5)	(6)	(7)	(8)
0			330				−330.00
1		1100	0	88.00	800.48	327.36	60.16
2	330	1100	22	112.64	900.54	327.03	293.07
3	330	1100	22	112.64	1000.60	326.70	193.34
4	330	1100	22	112.64	1200.72	0	319.92

In column (1) of the table, t refers to the cash flow date.

The first row deals with the initial expenses, assumed incurred at time $t = 0$. We assume that the insurer does not establish a reserve for the policy until the end of the first year, so that the initial expenses represent the only outgo at inception.

Column (2) is for the reserve brought forward from the previous year; the reserve is set at $_{t-1}V = \$330$ for $t = 2, 3, 4$.

Column (3) is the premium, $P_t = \$1100$, collected at the start of each year.

Column (4) shows the renewal expenses, E_t.

Column (5) shows the interest earned through the year,

$$I_t = 0.08(_{t-1}V + P_t - E_t).$$

Column (6) is the expected cost of the death benefit, \$100 000, and claim expenses, \$60, for a policy in force at the start of the year; that is, for $t = 1, 2, 3, 4$,

$$EB_t = q_{60+t-1}\, 100\,060.$$

Column (7) is the expected cost of the year-end reserve for policies which are continuing, given that the policy is in force at the start of the year; that is, for $t = 1, 2, 3$,

$$EV_t = p_{60+t-1} \, 330.$$

Column (8) is the profit vector:

$$\text{Pr}_0 = -330$$

and for $t = 1, 2, 3, 4$,

$$\text{Pr}_t = {}_{t-1}V + P_t - E_t + I_t - EB_t - EV_t .$$

(b) We have $\Pi_0 = \text{Pr}_0$, and for $t = 1, 2, 3$ and 4,

$$\Pi_t = {}_{t-1}p_{60} \, \text{Pr}_t .$$

So

$$\Pi = (-330.00, \ 60.16, \ 290.73, \ 190.07, \ 311.36)' .$$

(c) The NPV, using a risk discount rate of 12% per year, is

$$\sum_{t=0}^{4} 1.12^{-t} \, \Pi_t = \$288.64.$$

(d) The EPV of premium income, at 12% per year interest, is

$$1100 \sum_{t=0}^{3} 1.12^{-t} \, {}_{t}p_{60} = 3698.36$$

and so the profit margin is

$$\frac{323.19}{3698.36} = 7.8\%.$$

(e) The discounted payback period is the least integer t such that the partial NPV up to time t, denoted NPV_t, is greater than or equal to 0, that is, where

$$NPV_t = \sum_{k=0}^{t} 1.12^{-k} \, \Pi_k \geq 0.$$

In this case we have

t	Π_t	NPV_t
0	−330.00	−330.00
1	60.16	−276.29
2	290.73	−44.52
3	190.07	90.76
4	311.36	288.64

We see the partial NPV changes sign when $t = 3$, so the discounted payback period is three years.

(f) To calculate the IRR we find j such that

$$\sum_{t=0}^{4} (1 + j)^{-t} \, \Pi_t = 0.$$

The solution is $j = 41.9\%$, which is less than 50% per year.

(g) As the IRR exceeds the hurdle rate of 15% per year, the contract is satisfactory.

E12.7 There are some preliminary calculations to be carried out to establish the net premium and the net premium reserves. Let P^n denote the net premium. Recall that for net premium policy values, the net premium is always calculated on the policy value basis, and is not affected by changes in the gross premium. Then

$$P^n \, \ddot{a}_{55:\overline{10|}} = 100\,000 \, A_{55:\overline{20|}}.$$

We have

$$\ddot{a}_{55:\overline{10|}} = 7.71822 \qquad \text{and} \qquad A_{55:\overline{20|}} = 0.33236,$$

giving $P^n = \$4306.23$.

Next, we can calculate the net premium reserves recursively as $_0V = 0$, and for $t = 0, 1, 2, \ldots, 9,$

$$(_tV + P^n)(1.06) = 100\,000 \, q_{55+t} + p_{55+t} \,_{t+1}V$$

and for $t = 10, 11, 12, \ldots, 18$, after premiums cease,

$$_tV (1.06) = 100\,000 \, q_{55+t} + p_{55+t} \,_{t+1}V .$$

The approach to calculating the premium is to set up a spreadsheet calculation with an arbitrary, but realistic, guess at the gross premium entered in a particular cell. The net premium calculated above would be a good starting value. The NPV, and hence the profit margin, are calculated using this value of the premium and then the premium is adjusted until the profit margin is 15%. Solver in Excel will do this automatically.

Given the premium P we set up the profit test table as usual. The first four rows and last two rows of the profit test are shown here, using the net premium in place of the gross premium.

Profit test using first guess premium. Rounded for presentation.

t	$_{t-1}V$	P_t	E_t	I_t	EB_t	EV_t	Pr_t
(1)	(2)	(3)	(4)	(5)	(6)	(7)	(8)
0			300				−300.00
1	0	4306	0	323	199	4 365	64.59
2	4 374	4306	108	643	221	8 980	14.47
3	9 000	4306	108	990	246	13 858	83.86
⋮	⋮	⋮	⋮	⋮	⋮	⋮	⋮
19	89 078	0	0	6681	1 466	92 956	1336.17
20	94 340	0	0	7075	100 000	0	1415.09

As usual, the first row accounts for the initial expenses and each row from $t = 1$ to $t = 20$ considers the cash flows for that year, accumulated to the year end, assuming the policy is in force at the start of the year.

Column (1) is the time to which the year's cash flows are accumulated.

Column (2) shows the reserve brought forward in the tth year, $_{t-1}V$, calculated from the above net premium recursion.

Column (3) shows the premium, $P_t = P$, for $t = 1, 2, \ldots, 10$, and 0 thereafter.

Column (4) shows the expenses, E_t.

Column (5) shows the interest earned during the year on the start-year cash flows,

$$I_t = 0.075 \left(_{t-1}V + P_t - E_t \right).$$

Column (6) shows the expected cost of benefits at year end, given that the policy is in force at the start of the year, EB_t. For $t = 1, 2, \ldots, 19$, this is the expected death benefit, and in the final year, if the policyholder survives to the start of the year, the full benefit is payable at the year end on death or survival, so

$$EB_t = 100\,000\, q_{55+t-1} \text{ for } t = 1, 2, \ldots, 19 \text{ and } EB_{20} = 100\,000.$$

Column (7) shows the expected cost of the reserve for continuing policies,

$$EV_t = p_{55+t-1}\, {}_tV.$$

Column (8) shows the profit vector

$$Pr_t = {}_{t-1}V + P_t - E_t + I_t - EB_t - EV_t.$$

The net present value of the policy using a risk discount rate of 12% per year is

$$Pr_0 + \sum_{t=1}^{20} 1.12^{-t}\, {}_{t-1}p_{55}\, Pr_t.$$

To obtain the profit margin, we divide this by the EPV of the premiums, i.e. by

$$P \sum_{t=0}^{9} 1.12^{-t}\, {}_t p_{55}.$$

Using Solver in Excel, with a target profit margin of 15%, we find that the required value of P is \$4553.75.

The updated profit test using this premium is shown below.

Profit test using the correct premium.

t	${}_{t-1}V$	P_t	E_t	I_t	EB_t	EV_t	Pr_t
(1)	(2)	(3)	(4)	(5)	(6)	(7)	(8)
0			300				-300.00
1	0	4554	0	342	199	4 365	330.68
2	4 374	4554	114	661	221	8 980	273.91
3	9 000	4554	114	1008	246	13 858	343.29
⋮	⋮	⋮	⋮	⋮	⋮	⋮	⋮
19	89 078	0	0	6681	1 466	92 956	1336.17
20	94 340	0	0	7075	100 000	0	1415.09

^{E}12.8 The approach to this question is virtually identical to the previous one. There are changes to the detail of the calculations, most notably that the time unit for the profit test is a month rather than a year.

Once again we start with calculations relating to the net premium reserve. Now let P^n denote the total net premium in a year. Then

$$P^n \ddot{a}^{(12)}_{55:\overline{10}|} = 100\,000\,\bar{A}_{55:\overline{20}|}.$$

We have

$$\ddot{a}^{(12)}_{55:\overline{10}|} = 7.50515 \quad \text{and} \quad \bar{A}_{55:\overline{20}|} = 0.33414$$

resulting in $P^n = \$4452.16$ or $\$371.01$ per month.

Next, we calculate the net premium reserves recursively. The death benefit is payable immediately on death, and we approximate the cost of this by assuming that it is payable in the middle of the month of death, which means that the end of month cost has an extra half-month accumulation. We have $_0V = 0$, and for $t = 0, \frac{1}{12}, \frac{2}{12}, \ldots, \frac{119}{12}$,

$$(_tV + P^n/12)(1.06)^{\frac{1}{12}} = 100\,000\,(1.06)^{\frac{1}{24}}\,_{\frac{1}{12}}q_{55+t} + _{t+\frac{1}{12}}V\,_{\frac{1}{12}}p_{55+t},$$

and for $t = \frac{120}{12}, \frac{121}{12}, \ldots, \frac{238}{12}$ we have

$$_tV(1.06)^{\frac{1}{12}} = 100\,000\,(1.06)^{\frac{1}{24}}\,_{\frac{1}{12}}q_{55+t} + _{t+\frac{1}{12}}V\,_{\frac{1}{12}}p_{55+t}.$$

As in the previous question, the approach to calculating the premium is to set up a spreadsheet calculation with an arbitrary, but realistic, guess at the gross premium to calculate the net present value of the policy, and hence the profit margin, under this monthly premium. Once the spreadsheet is complete, we can use Solver to adjust the premium until it gives the required 15% profit margin.

We show the profit test details for the first three months and the last two months, based on the premium which generates a 15% profit margin.

Profit test using the correct premium.

t (1)	$_{t-1/12}V$ (2)	P_t (3)	E_t (4)	I_t (5)	EB_t (6)	EV_t (7)	Pr_t (8)
0			300				−300.00
1/12	0	394.27	0	2.38	15.89	356.94	23.82
2/12	357	394.27	9.86	4.48	16.03	715.53	14.33
3/12	716	394.27	9.86	6.65	16.17	1 075.79	14.75
⋮	⋮	⋮	⋮	⋮	⋮	⋮	⋮
239/12	99 035	0	0	598.66	144.50	99 372.59	116.52
240/12	99 516	0	0	601.57	100 000.44	0	117.08

As usual, the first row accounts for the initial expenses and each row from $t = 1/12$ to $t = 20$ considers the cash flows for that month, accumulated to the month end, assuming the policy is in force at the start of the month.

Column (1) is the time to which the month's cash flows are accumulated.

Column (2) shows the reserve brought forward, $_{t-1/12}V$, calculated from the above net premium recursion.

Column (3) shows the monthly premium, P_t, which equals $P/12$, for $t = 1/12, 2/12, \ldots, 10$, and 0 thereafter.

Column (4) shows the expenses, E_t.

Column (5) shows the interest earned during the month on the start of month cash flows,

$$I_t = (_{t-1/12}V + P_t - E_t) \times \left(1.075^{1/12} - 1\right).$$

Column (6) shows the expected cost of benefits at month end, given that the policy is in force at the start of the month. We assume that, on average, death benefits are paid half-way through the month of death. If the policyholder survives to the start of the final month, the full benefit is payable at the month end on survival, so

$$EB_t = 100\,000 \, _{\frac{1}{12}}q_{55+t-\frac{1}{12}}(1.075^{1/24}) \text{ for } t = \tfrac{1}{12}, \ldots, 19\tfrac{11}{12}$$

and

$$EB_{20} = 100\,000 \, _{\frac{1}{12}}q_{74\frac{11}{12}}(1.075^{1/24}) + 100\,000 \, _{\frac{1}{12}}p_{74\frac{11}{12}}.$$

Column (7) shows the expected cost of the reserve for continuing policies,

$$EV_t = \, _{\frac{1}{12}}p_{55+t-\frac{1}{12}} \, _tV.$$

Column (8) shows the profit vector

$$\text{Pr}_t = \, _{t-1/12}V + P_t - E_t + I_t - EB_t - EV_t.$$

The net present value of the policy using a risk discount rate of 12% per year is

$$\text{Pr}_0 + \sum_{k=1}^{240} 1.12^{-k/12} \, _{\frac{k-1}{12}}p_{55} \, \text{Pr}_{\frac{k}{12}}.$$

To obtain the profit margin, we divide this by the EPV of the premiums, i.e.

$$P \sum_{k=0}^{119} 1.12^{-k/12} {}_{k/12}p_{55}.$$

The value of P which gives a profit margin of 15% is \$4731.22, or \$394.27 per month.

E12.9 (a) Let P denote the single premium. We set P equal to the EPV of the expenses and death benefit at an effective interest rate of 4% per year.

At each policy anniversary, the expenses incurred are $0.03P$ if at least one life is alive. The probability that at least one of the lives is alive at time t is 1 minus the probability that both are dead at time t, i.e.

$$1 - (1 - {}_{t}p_{50})(1 - {}_{t}p_{50}) = 2\,{}_{t}p_{50} - {}_{t}p_{50:50}.$$

So the EPV of the premium related expenses is

$$0.03P \sum_{t=0}^{9} v^{t} \, (2\,{}_{t}p_{50} - {}_{t}p_{50:50}) = 0.25304\,P.$$

For the EPV of the death benefit, consider three possible situations for each policy year t to $t + 1$:

- 100 000 is payable at time $t + 1$ if both lives are alive at time t and exactly one of them dies during the year;

- 300 000 is payable at time $t + 1$ if both lives are alive at time t and both die during the year; and

- 200 000 is payable at time $t + 1$ if exactly one life is alive at time t and that life dies during the year (and note that this situation can only apply from the second year, as both lives are alive at time $t = 0$).

Then the EPV of the death benefit is

$$100\,000 \sum_{t=0}^{9} v^{t+1} {}_t p_{50:50} \, (2\, p_{50+t}\, q_{50+t})$$

$$+ 300\,000 \sum_{t=0}^{9} v^{t+1} {}_t p_{50:50} \, (q_{50+t})^2$$

$$+ 200\,000 \sum_{t=1}^{9} v^{t+1} \, 2 \, {}_t p_{50} \, (1 - {}_t p_{50}) \, q_{50+t}$$

$$= 3122.55 \, .$$

The single premium is then $P = \$4180.35$.

(b) The reserves can be calculated recursively. Let ${}_t V^{(1)}$ denote the reserve if only one life is alive at time t, and let ${}_t V^{(0)}$ denote the reserve if both lives are alive at time t.

The situation when only one life is alive at time t is simpler; we have

$$\left({}_t V^{(1)} - 0.03P \right) 1.04 = 200\,000 \, q_{50+t} + {}_{t+1} V^{(1)} \, p_{50+t} \, .$$

This can be calculated recursively, using ${}_{10} V^{(1)} = 0$, or by using standard functions as

$$ {}_t V^{(1)} = 200\,000 A^{\,1}_{50+t:\overline{10-t}|} + 0.03 P \ddot{a}_{50+t:\overline{10-t}|} \, .$$

If both lives are alive at time t we have

$$\left({}_t V^{(0)} - 0.03P \right) 1.04 = \left(100\,000 + {}_{t+1} V^{(1)} \right) (2\, p_{50+t}\, q_{50+t})$$
$$+ 300\,000 \, q^2_{50+t} + {}_{t+1} V^{(0)} \, p^2_{50+t}$$

since if exactly one of the lives dies aged $50 + t$, a death benefit and a reserve $({}_{t+1} V^{(1)})$ are required at the year end, if both lives die, a death benefit of $300\,000$ is required, and if both lives survive, a reserve $({}_{t+1} V^{(0)})$ is required. The recursion can be used in conjunction with values of ${}_t V^{(1)}$, backwards, using the fact that ${}_{10} V^{(0)} = 0$. This should generate ${}_0 V = P$, which is the reserve immediately after receipt of the single premium.

(c) We calculate the profit signature by evaluating first two separate profit vectors; one assuming that only one life is alive at the start of the policy year, denoted $\mathrm{Pr}^{(1)}$, and the other assuming that both lives are alive at the start of the policy year, denoted $\Pr^{(0)}$. We then multiply these by the appropriate probabilities to obtain the overall profit signature.

We show here an excerpt from the profit test table for calculating the emerging profit at time t in the case that both lives are alive at time $t - 1$.

t (1)	$_{t-1}V^{(0)}$ (2)	E_t (3)	I_t (4)	EB_t (5)	$EV_t^{(0)}$ (6)	$EV_t^{(1)}$ (7)	$\Pr_t^{(0)}$ (8)
0		62.71					−62.71
1	4180.35	0.00	334.43	241.85	3965.77	9.52	297.64
2	3975.37	65.21	312.81	266.39	3727.71	9.86	219.01
3	3737.66	67.82	293.59	293.96	3452.69	10.09	206.69
⋮	⋮	⋮	⋮	⋮	⋮	⋮	⋮

We account separately for the initial expenses as a time 0 outgo.

Column (2) shows the reserve brought forward in the tth year, $_{t-1}V^{(0)}$, calculated from the above net premium recursion, given that both lives are alive at time $t - 1$. Note that we include the single premium in the first year's cash flows in column (2), as $_0V^{(0)}$, for convenience.

Column (3) shows the expenses in the tth year, $E_t = 0.015P(1.04^{t-1})$.

Column (4) shows the interest earned during the year on the start-year cash flows, $I_t = 0.08\left(_{t-1}V^{(0)} - E_t\right)$.

Column (5) shows the expected cost of benefits at year end, given that both lives are alive at the start of the year, EB_t. If one of the lives dies, and the other survives, the benefit is $100\,000$. If both lives die, the benefit is $300\,000$, so

$$EB_t = (2\,p_{50+t-1}\,q_{50+t-1})\,100\,000 + (q_{50+t-1})^2\,300\,000.$$

Column (6) shows the expected cost of the reserve for continuing policies, for the case when both lives survive to the year end

$$EV_t^{(0)} = (p_{50+t-1})^2\,_tV^{(0)}.$$

Column (7) shows the expected cost of the reserve for continuing policies, for the case when exactly one life survives to the year end

$$EV_t^{(1)} = (p_{50+t-1})(q_{50+t-1})\,_tV^{(1)}.$$

Column (8) shows the profit vector for the case when both lives are alive at the start of the year

$$\Pr_t^{(0)} = {}_{t-1}V^{(0)} - E_t + I_t - EB_t - EV_t^{(0)} - EV_t^{(1)}.$$

Next, we show an excerpt from the profit test to determine the profit emerging at time t when exactly one life survives to time $t - 1$. This is only possible for $t = 2, 3, \ldots, 10$, as we know that both lives are alive at the start of the policy.

t	${}_{t-1}V^{(1)}$	E_t	I_t	EB_t	$EV_t^{(1)}$	$\Pr_t^{(1)}$
(1)	(2)	(3)	(4)	(5)	(6)	(7)
2	3943.26	65.21	310.24	266.21	3704.36	217.73
3	3709.30	67.82	291.32	293.75	3433.50	205.55
$\vdots$	$\vdots$	$\vdots$	$\vdots$	$\vdots$	$\vdots$	$\vdots$

The entries in this table are similar to the $\Pr^{(0)}$ case above. The reserve brought forward in Column (2) is now the reserve for the one-survivor case. EB_t is the expected benefit cost in the tth year, given that only one life survived to the start of the year. Hence

$$EB_t = 200\,000\, q_{50+t-1}$$

and $EV^{(1)}$ is the expected cost of establishing the year-end reserve in the case that the life survives, that is

$$EV_t^{(1)} = p_{50+t-1}\, {}_t V^{(1)}.$$

For the profit signature, we multiply the profit vector elements by the appropriate survival probabilities up to time $t-1$, to give the unconditional expected emerging profits at time t. For $t = 0, 1$, we know that both lives are alive at time $t = 0$, so

$$\Pi_0 = \Pr_0^{(0)} \quad \text{and} \quad \Pi_1 = \Pr_1^{(0)}.$$

For $t = 2, 3, \ldots, 10$, we multiply $\Pr_t^{(0)}$ by the probability that both lives are alive at time $t - 1$, and we multiply $\Pr_t^{(1)}$ by the probability that exactly one life is alive at time $t - 1$, giving

$$\Pi_t = {}_{t-1}p_{50:50}\, \Pr_t^{(0)} + 2\,{}_{t-1}p_{50}\, {}_{t-1}q_{50}\, \Pr_t^{(1)}.$$

Some selected values from the profit signature are

$$\Pi_2 = 219.01, \quad \Pi_4 = 192.75, \quad \Pi_6 = 159.29, \quad \Pi_8 = 116.68, \quad \Pi_{10} = 62.52.$$

12.10 The reserve required at time 4 to zeroize the negative emerging surplus at time 5 is

$$_4V^Z = 217/1.05 = 206.67.$$

This reserve cannot be established from the emerging surplus of -55 at time 4, so the reserve required at time 3 is

$$_3V^Z = 55/1.05 + 206.67\, p_{x+3}/1.05 = 246.06$$

since a loss of 55 emerges for each policy in force at time 3 and a reserve of $_4V^Z$ is required only for policies still in force at time 4. This reserve cannot be established from the emerging surplus of 94 at time 3, but this surplus does contribute to the reserve. Hence, the reserve required at time 2 is

$$_2V^Z = -94/1.05 + 246.06\, p_{x+2}/1.05 = 141.30.$$

This amount is required in respect of policies in force at time 2, and so the emerging surplus at time 2 is

$$229 - 141.30\, p_{x+1} = 89.68.$$

Hence, the revised profit vector is

$$(-310,\ 436,\ 89.68,\ 0,\ 0,\ 0)'.$$

^{E}12.11 (a) Let P be the annual premium. The EPV of premium payments is

$$P\ddot{a}_{60:60:\overline{5}|} = 4.5628P$$

and the EPV of the annuity and expenses is

$$300 + 10\,200 \sum_{t=1}^{20} v^t\, (1 - {}_tp_{60})\, {}_tp_{60} = 8362.63$$

giving $P = \$1832.79$.

(b) First, we calculate the reserves. Let $_tV^{(1)}$ denote the reserve at time t if only the husband is alive and let $_tV^{(0)}$ denote the reserve if both the husband and wife are alive.

If the wife has died by time t, then the reserve must be sufficient to pay the annuity plus annuity expenses from time $t + 1$ to time 20, inclusive, so

$$_tV^{(1)} = 10\,200\, a_{60+t:\overline{20-t}|}\,.$$

The values can be determined from tables or recursively, backwards, given $_{20}V^{(1)} = 0$ and

$$_tV^{(1)}\, 1.04 = p_{60+t}\left(10\,200 + {_{t+1}}V^{(1)}\right).$$

Given the values for $_tV^{(1)}$, we can also calculate $_tV^{(0)}$ recursively: for $t = 0$

$$(P - 300)\, 1.04 = p_{60:60}\, {_1V^{(0)}} + p_{60}\, q_{60}\left(10200 + {_1V^{(1)}}\right),$$

for $t = 1, 2, 3, 4$,

$$\left(_tV^{(0)} + P\right) 1.04 = p_{60+t:60+t}\, {_{t+1}V^{(0)}} + p_{60+t}\, q_{60+t}\left(10\,200 + {_{t+1}V^{(1)}}\right),$$

and, as premiums cease after five years, for $t = 5, 6, \ldots, 19$,

$$_tV^{(0)}\, 1.04 = p_{60+t:60+t}\, {_{t+1}V^{(0)}} + p_{60+t}\, q_{60+t}\left(10\,200 + {_{t+1}V^{(1)}}\right).$$

The recursion can work backwards, as $_{20}V^{(0)} = 0$, or forwards, using $_0V^{(0)} = 0$, because the premium and reserve are calculated on the same basis.

We calculate two profit vectors each year (after the first). $\Pr_t^{(0)}$ is the expected profit emerging at time t, conditional on both partners surviving to time $t - 1$. $\Pr_t^{(1)}$ is the expected emerging profit at time t conditional on the husband surviving and the wife having died at time $t - 1$. The profit signature is calculated by multiplying each of these by the appropriate probability, and summing, to give the expected emerging profit at time t, conditional only on both partners being alive at the start of the policy.

We show here an excerpt from the profit test table for $\Pr^{(0)}$.

t (1)	$_{t-1}V^{(0)}$ (2)	P_t (3)	I_t (4)	EB_t (5)	$EV_t^{(0)}$ (6)	$EV_t^{(1)}$ (7)	$\Pr_t^{(0)}$ (8)
0							−300.00
1	0	1832.79	109.97	34.54	1136.59	422.96	348.66
2	1144.36	1832.79	178.63	38.53	2603.75	453.95	59.54
3	2623.61	1832.79	267.38	43.00	4105.50	486.15	89.13
⋮	⋮	⋮	⋮	⋮	⋮	⋮	⋮

We account separately for the initial expenses as a time 0 outgo; this is captured as $\text{Pr}_0^{(0)}$ in the table. The benefit expenses are accounted for with the benefit costs.

Column (2) shows the reserve brought forward in the tth year, $_{t-1}V^{(0)}$, calculated from the above net premium recursion, given that both lives are alive at time $t - 1$.

Column (3) shows the premiums, which are $P_t = 1832.79$ for the first five years, with $P_t = 0$ thereafter.

Column (4) shows the interest earned during the year on the start-year cash flows, $I_t = 0.06\,(_{t-1}V^{(0)} + P_t)$.

Column (5) shows the expected cost of benefits at year end, given that both partners are alive at the start of the year, EB_t. If the wife dies and the husband survives, the year-end benefit, including expenses, is \$10 200, so

$$EB_t = 10\,200\, p_{60+t-1}\, q_{50+t-1} \, .$$

Column (6) shows the expected cost of the reserve for continuing policies, for the case when both lives survive to the year end:

$$EV_t^{(0)} = (p_{60+t-1})^2 \,_t V^{(0)} \, .$$

Column (7) shows the expected cost of the reserve for continuing policies, for the case when only the husband survives to the year end:

$$EV_t^{(1)} = (p_{60+t-1})(q_{60+t-1}) \,_t V^{(1)} .$$

Column (8) shows the profit vector for the case when both partners are alive at the start of the year:

$$\text{Pr}_t^{(0)} = {}_{t-1}V^{(0)} + P_t + I_t - EB_t - EV_t^{(0)} - EV_t^{(1)} \, .$$

For the case when the husband is alive at the start of a policy year and the wife is not, the calculations are similar, but for an alive–dead model. We show an excerpt from the profit test table below.

t	$_{t-1}V^{(1)}$	I_t	EB_t	$EV_t^{(1)}$	$\mathrm{Pr}_t^{(1)}$
(1)	(2)	(3)	(4)	(5)	(6)
2	124 890	7493	10 161	119 725	2497.80
3	120 180	7211	10 157	114 831	2403.60
4	115 319	6919	10 152	109 780	2306.38
⋮	⋮	⋮	⋮	⋮	⋮

Combining the profit vectors with the appropriate probabilities, we obtain the profit signature. We have

$$\Pi_0 = -300, \qquad \Pi_1 = \mathrm{Pr}_1^{(0)}$$

and for $t = 2, 3, \ldots, 20$,

$$\Pi_t = {}_{t-1}p_{60:60}\,\mathrm{Pr}_t^{(0)} + {}_{t-1}q_{60}\,{}_{t-1}p_{60}\,\mathrm{Pr}_t^{(1)}.$$

The net present value is

$$\sum_{t=0}^{20} 1.15^{-t}\,\Pi_t = \$779.26.$$

E12.12 (a) Let P denote the single premium. Then, noting that the return of premium applies on death before age 66,

$$P = 20\,020\,(1.06^{-5})\,{}_5p_{60}\,a_{65}{}^{5\%} + \sum_{t=0}^{5} 1.06^{-(t+1)}(1.05^{t+1}\,P)\,{}_t|q_{60} + 275,$$

giving $P = \$192\,805.84$.

(b) We calculate reserves recursively. We have

$$(_0V + P - 275)(1.06) = q_{60}\,P(1.05) + p_{60}\,{}_1V,$$

$$_tV\,(1.06) = q_{60+t}\,P(1.05)^{t+1} + p_{60+t}\,{}_{t+1}V$$

for $t = 1, 2, 3, 4,$

$$_5V\,(1.05) = q_{65}\,P(1.05)^6 + p_{65}\,(20\,020 + {}_6V),$$

and

$$_tV\,(1.05) = p_{60+t}\,(20\,020 + {}_{t+1}V)$$

for $t = 6, 7, \ldots$ The recursions can be applied forwards (premiums and reserves are calculated using the same assumptions, so $_0V = 0$), or backwards, using an appropriately high assumption for the maximum lifetime, or set $_6V = 20\,020\,a_{66}$ at 5% effective interest, and use recursions for the values for earlier years.

(c) (i) Note that the mortality basis for the profit test is different from the premium and reserve basis.

We show an excerpt from the profit test table, and explain each column in more detail below.

t (1)	$_{t-1}V + P_t - E_t$ (2)	I_t (3)	EB_t (4)	EV_t (5)	Pr_t (6)	Π_t (7)
0	−275				−275	−275
1	192 806	15 424	688	203 394	4 148	4 148
2	204 088	16 327	806	215 526	4 083	4 069
3	216 346	17 308	945	228 379	4 330	4 298
⋮	⋮	⋮	⋮	⋮	⋮	⋮
12	219 787	13 187	19 786	210 719	2 469	2 303
13	213 207	12 792	19 758	203 815	2 427	2 237
14	206 516	12 391	19 726	196 796	2 385	2 170
⋮	⋮	⋮	⋮	⋮	⋮	⋮

Column (2): the first row accounts for the initial expenses. The second row accounts for the single premium. The other entries in this column are the reserve values from the calculations in part (b).

Column (3): the interest earned at 8% (before vesting) or 6% (after vesting) on the Column (2) cash flow, for $t = 1, 2, 3, \ldots$

Column (4): EB_t is the expected cost of the year-end benefits, given that the contract is in force at the start of the year. For $t = 1, 2, 3, 4, 5$ this is the expected cost of the return of premium with interest. For $t = 6$, we allow for the return of premium, if the policyholder dies during the year, and for the annuity payment and expenses, if the policyholder survives. For $t = 7, 8, 9, \ldots$ the expected benefit is the expected cost of the annuity. That is

$$EB_t = \begin{cases} P(1.05)^t\, q_{60+t-1} & \text{for } t = 1, 2, 3, 4, 5. \\ P(1.05)^t\, q_{60+t-1} + 20\,020\, p_{60+t-1} & \text{for } t = 6, \\ 20\,020\, p_{60+t-1} & \text{for } t = 7, 8, \ldots \end{cases}$$

Column (5): EV_t is the expected cost of the year-end reserve for continuing contracts, so for $t = 1, 2, 3, \ldots$

$$EV_t = {}_tV \, p_{60+t-1}.$$

Column (6): Pr_t is the profit emerging at time t, conditional on the contract being in force at time $t - 1$ (for $t = 1, 2, \ldots$), so

$$\text{Pr}_t = \begin{cases} -275 & \text{for } t = 0, \\ P + I_t - EB_t - EV_t & \text{for } t = 1, \\ {}_{t-1}V + I_t - EB_t - EV_t & \text{for } t = 2, 3, 4, \ldots \end{cases}$$

Column (7): the profit signature, Π_t, is the profit emerging at time t, per policy issued, so

$$\Pi_0 = \text{Pr}_0 \text{ and } \Pi_t = {}_{t-1}p_{60} \, \text{Pr}_t \text{ for } t = 1, 2, 3, \ldots$$

(ii) Using a risk discount rate of 10% per year, the net present value of the contract is

$$\sum_{t=0}^{\omega-60} 1.1^{-t} \, \Pi_t = 28\,551.36$$

(where ω is a suitable limiting age, e.g. 145), and dividing this by the single premium gives the profit margin as 14.8%.

E12.13 We have a survival model, as shown in Figure 12.2 of AMLCR, with two parameterizations, one for profit testing and one for the calculation of the gross premium and the reserves. The difference between the parameterizations is that the former allows for withdrawals, whereas the latter does not.

Let ${}_tp_x^{ij*}$ denote the probability that a life in state i at age x will be in state j at age $x + t$ given the parameterizations allowing for withdrawals and let ${}_tp_x^{ij}$ denote the corresponding probability when withdrawals are not included. The following probabilities are useful in our calculations.

For $0 \leq t \leq 10$,

$$_t p_{55}^{00*} = \exp\left\{-\int_0^t (\mu_{55+s}^{01} + \mu_{55+s}^{02} + \mu_{55+s}^{03})\, ds\right\} = \exp\{-0.035t\},$$

$$_t p_x^{00} = \exp\left\{-\int_0^t (\mu_{x+s}^{01} + \mu_{x+s}^{02})\, ds\right\} = \exp\{-0.025t\},$$

$$_t p_x^{11*} = \exp\{-0.03t\} = {}_t p_x^{11},$$

$$_t p_{55}^{01*} = \int_0^t {}_s p_{55}^{00*}\, \mu_{55+s}^{01}\, {}_{t-s} p_{55+s}^{11*}\, ds$$

$$= \int_0^t \exp\{-0.035s\}\, 0.01\, \exp\{-0.03(t-s)\}\, ds$$

$$= 2(\exp\{-0.03t\} - \exp\{-0.035t\}),$$

$$_t p_{55}^{01} = \int_0^t {}_s p_{55}^{00}\, \mu_{55+s}^{01}\, {}_{t-s} p_{55+s}^{11}\, ds$$

$$= \int_0^t \exp\{-0.025s\}\, 0.01\, \exp\{-0.03(t-s)\}\, ds$$

$$= 2(\exp\{-0.025t\} - \exp\{-0.03t\}),$$

$$_t p_x^{12*} = 1 - \exp\{-0.03t\} = {}_t p_x^{12}.$$

Further, for $55 \leq x \leq 64\frac{11}{12}$,

$$_{\frac{1}{12}} p_x^{12*} = 1 - \exp\{-0.03/12\} = {}_{\frac{1}{12}} p_x^{12},$$

$$_{\frac{1}{12}} p_x^{02*} = \frac{5}{7}(1 - \exp\{-0.035/12\}) - 2(\exp\{-0.03/12\} - \exp\{-0.035/12\}),$$

$$_{\frac{1}{12}} p_x^{02} = 1 - 3\exp\{-0.025/12\} + 2\exp\{-0.03/12\},$$

$$_{\frac{1}{12}} p_x^{03*} = \frac{2}{7}(1 - \exp\{-0.035/12\}),$$

$$_{\frac{1}{12}} p_x^{01*} = 2(\exp\{-0.03/12\} - \exp\{-0.035/12\}),$$

$$_{\frac{1}{12}} p_x^{01} = 2(\exp\{-0.025/12\} - \exp\{-0.03/12\}).$$

(a) Let P' denote the monthly premium calculated on the net premium policy value basis, so that withdrawals are ignored. Then

$$P' \sum_{t=0}^{119} {}_{\frac{t}{12}} p_{55}^{00}\, v^{\frac{t}{12}} = 50\,000\ {}_{10} p_{55}^{00}\, v^{10} + 50\,000 \sum_{t=0}^{119} \left({}_{\frac{t}{12}} p_{55}^{00}\, {}_{\frac{1}{12}} p_{55+\frac{t}{12}}^{01} + {}_{\frac{t}{12}} p_{55}^{01}\, {}_{\frac{1}{12}} p_{55+\frac{t}{12}}^{12}\right) v^{\frac{t+1}{12}}$$

$$+ 100\,000 \sum_{t=0}^{119} {}_{\frac{t}{12}} p_{55}^{00}\, {}_{\frac{1}{12}} p_{55+\frac{t}{12}}^{02}\, v^{\frac{t+1}{12}}.$$

Using the formulae we have developed, we can calculate that

$$\sum_{t=0}^{119} \tfrac{1}{12} p_{55}^{00} \, v^{\frac{t}{12}} = 85.13$$

and

$$\sum_{t=0}^{119} \tfrac{1}{12} p_{55}^{01} \, v^{\frac{t}{12}} = 3.65$$

giving $P' = \$452.00$.

(b) Let $_t V^{(0)}$ and $_t V^{(1)}$ denote the net premium policy values at policy duration t years given that the policyholder is healthy and disabled, respectively. If t is an exact number of months, then the policy value is calculated before payment of a premium and after payment of any benefits due at that time.

Then

$$_{10} V^{(0)} = {}_{10} V^{(1)} = 0$$

and we can calculate the policy values recursively for $t = 9\frac{11}{12}, 9\frac{10}{12}, \dots, \frac{1}{12}, 0$ from these starting values using the formulae

$$({}_t V^{(0)} + P') \, 1.05^{\frac{1}{12}} = \tfrac{1}{12} p_{55+t}^{00} \,\, _{t+\frac{1}{12}} V^{(0)} + \tfrac{1}{12} p_{55+t}^{01} \, (50\,000 + {}_{t+\frac{1}{12}} V^{(1)}) + 100\,000 \, \tfrac{1}{12} p_{55+t}^{02}$$

and

$$_t V^{(1)} \, 1.05^{\frac{1}{12}} = \tfrac{1}{12} p_{55+t}^{11} \,\, _{t+\frac{1}{12}} V^{(1)} + 50\,000 \, \tfrac{1}{12} p_{55+t}^{12}.$$

Policy values for a selection of durations are shown in Table 12.1.

Table 12.1 *Net premium policy values.*

t years	$_t V^{(0)}$	$_t V^{(1)}$	t years	$_t V^{(0)}$	$_t V^{(1)}$
0	0.00	–	$7\frac{11}{12}$	36 252.19	2 876.14
$\frac{1}{12}$	279.32	10 301.49	8	36 761.39	2 769.93
$\frac{2}{12}$	560.40	10 244.19	$8\frac{1}{12}$	37 273.82	2 663.02
$\vdots$	$\vdots$	$\vdots$	$\vdots$	$\vdots$	$\vdots$
$3\frac{11}{12}$	15 237.52	7 234.67	$9\frac{10}{12}$	48 818.44	247.86
4	15 613.44	7 157.17	$9\frac{11}{12}$	49 407.35	124.34
$4\frac{1}{12}$	15 991.75	7 079.16	10	0.00	0.00

(c) Let P denote the monthly gross premium. Then, using the equivalence principle,

$$0.95\,P\sum_{t=0}^{119} {}_{\frac{t}{12}}p_{55}^{00}\,v^{\frac{t}{12}} = 50\,000\,{}_{10}p_{55}^{00}\,v^{10}$$

$$+50\,000\sum_{t=0}^{119}\left({}_{\frac{t}{12}}p_{55}^{00}\,{}_{\frac{1}{12}}p_{55+\frac{t}{12}}^{01} + {}_{\frac{t}{12}}p_{55}^{01}\,{}_{\frac{1}{12}}p_{55+\frac{t}{12}}^{12}\right)v^{\frac{t+1}{12}}$$

$$+100\,000\sum_{t=0}^{119} {}_{\frac{t}{12}}p_{55}^{00}\,{}_{\frac{1}{12}}p_{55+\frac{t}{12}}^{02}\,v^{\frac{t+1}{12}} + 1000$$

where the rate of interest is now 5.25% per year. Hence, we now have

$$\sum_{t=0}^{119} {}_{\frac{t}{12}}p_{55}^{00}\,v^{\frac{t}{12}} = 84.26$$

and

$$\sum_{t=0}^{119} {}_{\frac{t}{12}}p_{55}^{01}\,v^{\frac{t}{12}} = 3.59,$$

giving $P = \$484.27$.

(d) The emerging surplus at the end of each month is calculating in two parts: first we assume the life is healthy at the start of the month and then we assume the life is disabled at the start of the month. Parts of the calculation are shown in Tables 12.2 and 12.3.

Table 12.2 *Emerging surplus assuming the life is healthy at the start of the month.*

t years (1)	${}_{t-\frac{1}{12}}V^{(0)}$ (2)	P (3)	E_t (4)	I_t (5)	Dis. ben. (6)	Dis. res. (7)	Death ben. (8)	With'l ben. (9)	Healthy res. (10)	$\Pr_t^{(0)}$ (11)
0			1024.21							−1024.21
$\frac{1}{12}$	0.00	484.27	0.00	2.74	41.55	8.56	124.92	0.32	278.50	33.15
$\frac{2}{12}$	279.32	484.27	24.21	4.18	41.55	8.51	124.92	0.51	558.77	9.29
⋮	⋮	⋮	⋮	⋮	⋮	⋮	⋮	⋮	⋮	⋮
$9\frac{10}{12}$	48 233.24	484.27	24.21	275.32	41.55	0.21	124.92	32.43	48 676.26	93.24
$9\frac{11}{12}$	48 818.44	484.27	24.21	278.63	41.55	0.10	124.92	32.82	49 263.46	94.27
10	49 407.35	484.27	24.21	281.96	41.55	0.00	124.92	33.21	49 854.38	95.30

The key to the columns in Table 12.2 is as follows.

(1) denotes the time interval from $t - \frac{1}{12}$ to t, measured in years, except that $t = 0$ denotes time 0.

(2) denotes the reserve held at the start of the time interval for a life who is healthy at that time, $_{t-\frac{1}{12}}V^{(0)}$. No reserve is required for $t = 0$ or $t = \frac{1}{12}$ since $_0V^{(0)} = 0$.

(3) denotes the gross premium, \$484.27, payable at the start of the month.

(4) denotes the expenses payable in the time interval. The entry for $t = 0$ includes all the initial expenses, so that

$$1024.21 = 1000 + 0.05 \times P = 1000 + 0.05 \times 484.27.$$

The entry for $t = \frac{1}{12}$ is zero since all the initial expenses have been assigned to the row for $t = 0$. For other rows the expense is $0.05P$, which is assumed to be incurred at the start of the month.

(5) denotes the interest earned during the month at the assumed rate of 7% per year effective, so that

$$I_t = (1.07^{\frac{1}{12}} - 1)(_{t-\frac{1}{12}}V^{(0)} + P - E_t).$$

(6) is the expected disability benefit payable at the end of the month, $50\,000\,\frac{1}{12}p^{01*}_{55+t}$, in respect of a life who was healthy at the start of the month but disabled at the end of the month.

(7) is the expected cost of setting up the required reserve at the end of the month for a life who was healthy at the start of the month but disabled at the end of the month. This expected cost is $\frac{1}{12}p^{01*}_{55+t}\,{}_tV^{(1)}$.

(8) is the expected death benefit payable at the end of the month for a life who was healthy at the start of the month. This expected cost is $100\,000\,\frac{1}{12}p^{02*}_{55+t}$.

(9) is the expected cost of the withdrawal benefit. This is

$$\frac{1}{12}p^{03*}_{55+t}\left(_{t-\frac{1}{12}}V^{(0)} + P\right) \times 0.8.$$

(10) denotes the expected cost of setting up the reserve required at the start of the following month for a life who remains healthy throughout the month. This expected cost is $\frac{1}{12}p^{00*}_{55+t}\,{}_tV^{(0)}$.

(11) denotes the expected surplus emerging at the end of the month in respect of a policyholder who was healthy at the start of the month, so that

$$\Pr_t^{(0)} = (2) + (3) - (4) + (5) - (6) - (7) - (8) - (9) - (10).$$

The key to the columns in Table 12.3 is as follows.

Table 12.3 *Emerging surplus assuming the life is disabled at the start of the month.*

t years (1)	$_{t-\frac{1}{12}}V^{(1)}$ (2)	I_t (3)	Death ben. (4)	Disabled res. (5)	$\Pr_t^{(1)}$ (6)
$\frac{1}{12}$	0.00	0.00	0.00	0.00	0.00
$\frac{2}{12}$	10 031.49	58.25	124.84	10 218.61	16.28
$\frac{3}{12}$	10 244.19	57.92	124.84	10 161.08	16.19
$\vdots$	$\vdots$	$\vdots$	$\vdots$	$\vdots$	$\vdots$
$9\frac{10}{12}$	370.58	2.10	124.84	247.24	0.59
$9\frac{11}{12}$	247.86	1.40	124.84	124.03	0.39
10	124.34	0.70	124.84	0.00	0.20

(1) denotes the time interval from $t - \frac{1}{12}$ to t, measured in years.

(2) denotes the reserve held at the start of the time interval for a life who is disabled at that time, $_{t-\frac{1}{12}}V^{(1)}$. No cash flows are included for the first month, corresponding to $t = \frac{1}{12}$, since the life is healthy when the policy is issued.

(3) denotes the interest earned during the month, at the rate of 7% per year effective, on the reserve held at the beginning of the month.

(4) is the expected death benefit payable at the end of the month for a life who was disabled at the start of the month. This expected cost is $50\,000 \, _{\frac{1}{12}}p_{55+t}^{12*}$.

(5) denotes the expected cost of setting up the reserve required at the start of the following month for a life who remains disabled throughout the month. This expected cost is $_{\frac{1}{12}}p_{55+t}^{11*} \, _tV^{(1)}$.

(6) denotes the expected surplus emerging at the end of the month in respect of a policyholder who was disabled at the start of the month, so that

$$\Pr_t^{(1)} = (2) + (3) - (4) - (5).$$

(e) The profit signature vector, $\Pi = (\Pi_0, \Pi_{\frac{1}{12}}, \dots, \Pi_{9\frac{11}{12}}, \Pi_{10})'$, is calculated as

$$\Pi_0 = \Pr_0^{(0)}$$

and for $t = \frac{1}{12}, \frac{2}{12}, \dots, 10$,

$$\Pi_t = \Pr_t^{(0)} \, _{t-\frac{1}{12}}p_{55}^{00*} + \Pr_t^{(1)} \, _{t-\frac{1}{12}}p_{55}^{01*}.$$

Values of $\Pr_t^{(0)}$, $_{t-\frac{1}{12}}p_{55}^{00*}$, $\Pr_t^{(1)}$, $_{t-\frac{1}{12}}p_{55}^{01*}$ and Π_t for selected values of t are shown in Table 12.4.

Table 12.4 *Calculation of the profit signature.*

t years	$\Pr_t^{(0)}$	$_{t-\frac{1}{12}}p_{55}^{00*}$	$\Pr_t^{(1)}$	$_{t-\frac{1}{12}}p_{55}^{01*}$	Π_t
0	-1024.21	1.00	–	0.00	-1024.21
$\frac{1}{12}$	33.15	1.00	0.00	0.00	33.15
$\frac{2}{12}$	9.29	0.9971	16.28	0.0008	9.27
$\vdots$	$\vdots$	$\vdots$	$\vdots$	$\vdots$	$\vdots$
$3\frac{11}{12}$	34.82	0.8744	11.55	0.0338	30.84
4	35.48	0.8719	11.43	0.0345	31.33
$4\frac{1}{12}$	36.13	0.8694	11.31	0.0351	31.81
$\vdots$	$\vdots$	$\vdots$	$\vdots$	$\vdots$	$\vdots$
$7\frac{11}{12}$	71.38	0.7602	4.71	0.0607	54.55
8	72.27	0.7580	4.54	0.0612	55.06
$8\frac{1}{12}$	73.16	0.7558	4.38	0.0617	55.56
$\vdots$	$\vdots$	$\vdots$	$\vdots$	$\vdots$	$\vdots$
$9\frac{10}{12}$	93.24	0.7109	0.59	0.0710	66.33
$9\frac{16}{12}$	94.27	0.7088	0.39	0.0714	66.85
10	95.30	0.7067	0.20	0.0719	67.37

The internal rate of return is the rate of interest, r, per year such that

$$\sum_{k=0}^{120} \Pi_{\frac{k}{12}} (1+r)^{-\frac{k}{12}} = 0.$$

This gives an internal rate of return of 32.7% per year.

(f) The net present value, NPV, is given by

$$\text{NPV} = \sum_{k=0}^{120} \Pi_{\frac{k}{12}} (1+0.15)^{-\frac{k}{12}} = \$992.29.$$

The profit margin, i.e. the NPV as a percentage of the EPV of gross premiums, is

$$\text{NPV} \bigg/ \left(P \sum_{k=0}^{119} {}_{\frac{k}{12}}p_{55}^{00*} (1+0.15)^{-\frac{k}{12}} \right) = 3.84\%,$$

and the NPV as a percentage of the acquisition costs is

$$\text{NPV} / (0.05\,P + 1\,000) = 97.0\%.$$

The discounted payback period is $m/12$ years, where m is the smallest integer such that

$$\sum_{k=0}^{m} \Pi_{\frac{k}{12}} (1 + r)^{-\frac{k}{12}} \geq 0.$$

This gives a discounted payback period of 5 years and 5 months.

Solutions for Chapter 13

13.1 Let AV_t and AS_t denote the account value and asset share, respectively, at the end of year t. Recall that the asset share at time t is the accumulated income minus outgo, expressed per policy in force at time t.

We have $AV_4 = 30$ and $AS_4 = 20$, so

$$AV_5 = 1.06\ (AV_4 + 20 - 2 - 7) = 43.46$$

and

$$AS_5 = \frac{1.08\ (AS_4 + 20 - 2) - 0.001 \times 1000 - 0.05\ (AV_5 - 20)}{1 - 0.001 - 0.05} = 40.96.$$

13.2 Let CV_t and AV_t denote the cash (surrender) value and the account value, respectively, at the end of the tth month; CoI_t is the cost of insurance in the tth month.

The effective monthly rate of credited interest is $0.054/12 = 0.0045$. This is also the CoI interest rate. We have

$$AV_{11} = CV_{11} + 500 = 1700.00,$$
$$AV_{13} = CV_{13} + 125 = 1927.94,$$

$$CoI_{12} = 0.002 \times 50\,000/1.0045 = 99.55,$$
$$CoI_{13} = 0.003 \times 50\,000/1.0045 = 149.33,$$

$$AV_{12} = 1.0045\ (AV_{11} + 300(1 - W) - 99.55 - 10)$$
$$= 1898.96 - 301.35W,$$

$$AV_{13} = 1.045\,(AV_{12} + 300 \times 0.85 - 149.33 - 10)$$
$$= 2003.60 - 302.71W$$
$$= 1927.94,$$

giving $W = 0.25$.

13.3 First, we calculate the CoI and account values for the first two years as

$$\text{CoI}_1 = 0.0054 \times 200\,000/1.06 = 1018.87,$$
$$\text{CoI}_2 = 0.0060 \times 200\,000/1.06 = 1132.08,$$

$$AV_1 = 1.06\,(5000 - 1018.87 - 100) = 4114.00,$$
$$AV_2 = 1.06\,(4114.00 + 5000 - 1132.08 - 100) = 8354.84.$$

So the cash value at the end of the second year is expected to be

$$CV_2 = 0.93 \times 8354.84 = 7770.00.$$

Next, calculate the probability of surrender in the second-year, say $_{1|1}q_{60}^{(w)}$,

$$_{1|1}q_{60}^{(w)} = (1 - 0.0034)\,(1 - 0.06)\,(1 - 0.0038)\,0.06 = 0.055995.$$

Then the EPV of the second-year surrender benefit is

$$0.055995 \times 7770.00\,v_{7\%}^2 = 380.01.$$

13.4 (a) First, calculate the reserves and cash values for the year, denoting the start of the year as time $t - 1$. Then

$$_{t-1}V = 100\,000\,A_{40\ (4\%)} = 17\,758.80,$$
$$_tV = 100\,000\,A_{41\ (4\%)} = 18\,426.14,$$
$$CV_t = 100\,000\,A_{41\ (5\%)} = 12\,665.17.$$

Next, project the expected surplus emerging at the year end (time t), per policy in force at the start of the year (time $t - 1$):

$$\Pr_t = 1.06\,(_{t-1}V - 20) - 0.0004 \times 100\,000$$
$$- 0.9996 \times 0.08\,CV_t - 0.9996 \times 0.92\,_tV = 805.05.$$

The policyholder's share is 80%, or $644.04 per policy in force at time $t - 1$.

The dividend is only paid to policyholders who are still in force at time t, so the projected dividend per policy in force is

$$\frac{644.07}{0.9996 \times 0.92} = 700.32.$$

(b) The projected surplus at time t, per policy in force at time $t - 1$, ignoring surrenders, is

$$\text{Pr}_t = 1.06 \,(_{t-1}V - 20) - 0.0004 \times 100\,000 - 0.9996 \times {}_tV = 344.35.$$

The dividend is 80% of this surplus, shared between the projected in-force policyholders. It is not proposed that surrender rates are changed, nor that surrendering policyholders share in the profit distribution. This means that the denominator in the dividend calculation is the same as in part (a), so the revised projected dividend is

$$\frac{0.8 \times 344.35}{0.9996 \times 0.92} = 299.56.$$

Comments:

(i) If profit sharing has been marketed specifically as sharing in investment profits, it is reasonable not to include surrender profits in the dividend calculations.

(ii) On the other hand, if profit sharing is presented as an 80/20 split of profits between policyholders and shareholders, it would seem unreasonable to omit surrender profits.

(iii) In either case, it would be more equitable to include surrendering policyholders in the profit distribution, as they have contributed to the investment profits for the policy year.

13.5 (a) In the first year there is no bonus, according to the information from Example 13.2

At the end of the second year, the cash dividend value is $Div_2 = \$228.36$, (as for Example 13.2), per policy in force at time 1.

The dividend is paid out as reversionary bonus, $\widetilde{B}_2$, which impacts the policyholders as follows.

(i) If the policyholder dies in the second year, the bonus is paid in full at the year end.

(ii) If the policyholder survives and the policy remains in force, the reserve carried forward must be increased by the cost of the bonus, $\widetilde{B}_2 A_{62}$, under the reserve basis. That is

$$_{2+}V = {}_{2-}V + \widetilde{B}_2 A_{62}.$$

(iii) If the policyholder surrenders at time t, the cash value is $h_t \times {}_tV$. The cost of the bonus for each surrendering policyholder is

$$h_t({}_{t+}V - {}_{t-}V) = h_t \widetilde{B}_t A_{60+t}.$$

So, equating the value of the bonus at time 2 with the cash dividend emerging for each policy in force at time 1 we have

$$Div_2 = p_{61}^{0d} \widetilde{B}_2 + p_{61}^{0w} h_2 \widetilde{B}_2 A_{62} + p_{61}^{00} \widetilde{B}_2 A_{62}$$

$$\Rightarrow 228.36 = \widetilde{B}_2 \left(p_{61}^{0d} + p_{61}^{0w} h_2 A_{62} + p_{61}^{00} A_{62} \right)$$

$$\Rightarrow \widetilde{B}_2 = \$756.50 \text{ and } \widetilde{RB}_2 = \$756.50,$$

as $p_{61}^{0d} = 0.00379$, $p_{61}^{0w} = 0.04981$, $p_{61}^{00} = 0.94640$, $h_2 = 0$, and $A_{62} = 0.31495$.

For the third year, we have to calculate the emerging profit, per policy in force at time 2, before distribution of profits (i.e. assume, first, no bonus payment at time 3).

The reserve carried forward comes from the pre-dividend reserve at time 2, plus the value of the bonus at time 2 for in-force policyholders. That is

$$_{2+}V = (S + \widetilde{RB}_1)A_{62} - P^*\ddot{a}_{62} + \widetilde{B}_2 A_{62} = (S + \widetilde{RB}_2)A_{62} - P^*\ddot{a}_{62}$$

$$= 2033.60.$$

The year-end reserve before bonus declaration, for in-force policies, is

$$_{3-}V = (S + \widetilde{RB}_2)A_{63} - P^*\ddot{a}_{63} = 3892.90.$$

So

$$Pr_{3-} = 1.06\,({}_{2+}V + P - E) - p_{62}^{0d}(S + \widetilde{RB}_2) - p_{62}^{0w} h_3\,{}_{3-}V - p_{62}^{00}\,{}_{3-}V$$

$$= 378.46,$$

and $Div_3 = 0.9\,Pr_{3-} = 340.61$.

Following the previous argument,

$$340.61 = \widetilde{B}_3 \left(p_{62}^{0d} + p_{62}^{0w} h_3 A_{63} + p_{62}^{00} A_{63} \right),$$

giving $\widetilde{B}_3 = \$1083.47$ and $\widetilde{RB}_3 = \$1839.97$.

Similarly, $Div_4 = 462.70$ and $\widetilde{B}_4 = \$1413.82$.

(b) In this approach, the share of profit is expressed as an addition to the sum insured before distribution to the exiting policyholders. The policyholders in force at the start of each year are in one of three groups at the end of the year, the deaths, the withdrawals and the continuing.

Under the cash dividend distribution, the distribution to each group is the same – in the second year, for example, each policyholder receives \$228.36.

Under the distribution described in Example 13.2, a cash dividend is paid to the deaths and withdrawals, but an addition to the sum insured is paid to continuing policyholders. The cash dividend is the same as would be paid on a pure cash dividend basis, so the deaths and withdrawals groups receive the same benefit as under the cash dividend system. The continuing policyholders benefit from an addition to the sum insured.

Under the distribution described in the question, the dividend is converted to sum insured before distribution. This impacts the deaths and withdrawals payouts substantially. Withdrawing policyholders only receive partial recovery of the dividend, because the surrender value is a proportion (h_t) of the policy value. In fact, in the early years, the withdrawing policyholders receive no benefit from the profit share, as $h_t = 0$ for $t = 1, 2, 3, 4$. On the other hand, converting the dividend into additional sum insured increases the benefits for policies with death claims – we see in the first year that the death claim policies receive \$756.50 under this distribution plan, compared with \$228.36 under the previous two schemes. There is also a small impact on the value of bonus for continuing policyholders.

13.6 As this is a Type B policy, the additional death benefit is constant, at \$50 000.

The account value at time $t = 11$ months, $= AV_{11}$, say, is $860 + 500 = 1360$. So

$$AV_{12} = 1.0045 \left(AV_{11} + 300 - 0.2 \times 300 - 20 - 0.002 \, v_{4\%}^{\frac{1}{12}} \, 50\,000 \right)$$

$$= 1486.99.$$

Similarly,

$$AV_{13} = 1.0045 \left(AV_{12} + 300 - 0.15 \times 300 - 10 - 0.003 \, v_{4\%}^{\frac{1}{12}} \, 50\,000 \right)$$

$$= 1589.60.$$

Deducting the second-year surrender penalty of 125 gives the cash value as $1464.60.

E13.7 (a) (i) Let P denote the annual premium, and let $S = 75\,000$ denote the sum insured before bonuses. Then we have the following EPVs, where all calculations are at 4% per year interest, using the Standard Select Survival Model. The EPV of premium income is

$$P \, \ddot{a}_{[55]} = 18.0611 \, P,$$

the EPV of the death benefit is

$$S A_{[55]} = 22\,900.74,$$

and the EPV of expenses is

$$160 + 65 \, \ddot{a}_{[55]} + 0.725P + 0.025P \, \ddot{a}_{[55]} + 200 A_{[55]}$$
$$= 1395.04 + 1.1765 \, P,$$

giving $P = \$1438.94$.

(ii) The only change from part (i) is that the EPV of the death benefit is now

$$S A_{[55]} + 0.02S \, (IA)_{[55]} = 35\,715.06$$

as $(IA)_{[55]} = 8.54288$. This gives the revised premium as $2197.87.

(b) There is no bonus distributed in the first policy year. So we start the analysis for the policy year from time 1 to time 2.

Let $_{t-}V^g$ denote the gross premium policy value at time t, before consideration of bonus declared at time t, for $t = 1, 2, \ldots$, and let $_{t+}V^g$ denote the gross premium policy value immediately after the bonus declaration at time t. We have $P = 2197.87$ from part (a)(ii); let $E = 65 + 0.025P = 119.95$ denote the expenses incurred at the start of each year after the first.

Let $_{t-}V$ and $_{t+}V$ denote the reserve at time t, before consideration of bonus declared and immediately after the bonus declaration at time t, respectively. Let B_t denote the reversionary bonus declared at the end of the tth year, and let RB_t denote the total reversionary bonus declared up to, and including, time t. Then, for $t = 1, 2, \ldots$

$$_{t-}V^g = (S + RB_{t-1} + 200) A_{[55]+t} - (0.975P - 65) \ddot{a}_{[55]+t},$$

$$_{t+}V^g = {}_{t-}V^g + B_t A_{[55]+t},$$

$$_tV = \max({}_tV^g, 0).$$

So, in the second policy year, we have $RB_1 = 0$ and

$$_{1+}V^g = 75\,200 A_{[55]+1} - 2077.92\, \ddot{a}_{[55]+1} = -13\,140$$

giving $_{1+}V = 0$, and

$$_{2-}V^g = 75\,200 A_{57} - 2077.92\, \ddot{a}_{57} = -11\,687$$

giving $_{2-}V = 0$. The surplus at time 2, per policy in force at time 1, is

$$Pr_2 = 1.04\, (_{1+}V + P - E) - q_{[55]+1}(S + 200) - p_{[55]+1}\, _{2-}V$$
$$= 2003.12.$$

Recall that the profit, Pr_2, is distributed amongst all the policyholders alive at time 1 as an additional sum insured of B_2. The equation of value for B_2 is

$$Pr_2 = q_{[55]+1} B_2 + p_{[55]+1} B_2 A_{57}$$

giving

$$B_2 = \frac{2003.12}{q_{[55]+1} + p_{[55]+1} A_{57}} = \$6087.7.$$

In the third policy year we have $RB_2 = 6087.7$ and

$$_{2+}V^g = (75\,200 + 6087.7) A_{57} - 2077.92\, \ddot{a}_{57} = -9693$$

giving $_{2+}V = 0$, and

$$_{3-}V^g = (75\,200 + 6087.7) A_{58} - 2077.92\, \ddot{a}_{58} = -8139$$

giving $_{3-}V = 0$. Then

$$Pr_3 = 1.04\, (_{2+}V + P - E) - q_{57}\, (S + RB_2 + 200) - p_{57}\, _{3-}V$$
$$= 1\,961.14$$

and hence

$$B_3 = \frac{1961.14}{q_{57} + p_{57} A_{57}} = \$5755.55.$$

Table 13.1 *Bonus calculations for Exercise 13.7 (b), using gross premium policy values.*

t	$_{(t-1)+}V$	$P - E$	I	EDB_{t-}	$E_{t-}V$	Pr_{t-}	B_t	RB_t	Bonus Rate
2	0	2 077.9	83.1	158.1	0	2 003	6 087	6 087	8.1%
3	0	2 077.9	83.1	199.9	0	1 961	5 756	11 843	7.7%
4	0	2 077.9	83.1	238.2	0	1 923	5 452	17 295	7.3%
5	0	2 077.9	83.1	281.9	0	1 879	5 149	22 444	6.9%
6	1 030	2 077.9	124.3	331.8	2 900	0	0	22 444	0.0%
7	2 910	2 077.9	199.5	370.2	4 817	0	0	22 444	0.0%
8	4 836	2 077.9	276.5	413.4	6 777	0	0	22 444	0.0%
9	6 806	2 077.9	355.3	461.9	8 777	0	0	22 444	0.0%
10	8 819	2 077.9	435.9	516.3	10 816	0	0	22 444	0.0%

The reason for the negative $_tV^g$ values is that the premiums are calculated to support the 2% simple bonus rate, but the $_tV^g$ values are calculated assuming a level sum insured.

In Table 13.1 we show the emerging surplus calculations for the first 10 years of the contract, using gross premium policy values. The bonus rates, expressed as simple reversionary bonus, are given in the final column.

(c) The calculations are very similar to part (b), except in place of gross premium policy values, we use net premium policy values, $_tV$, say, where the net premium is $P^n = 75\,000\,A_{[55]}/\ddot{a}_{[55]} = 1267.96$, and

$$_{t-}V = (S + RB_{t-1})A_{[55]+t} - P^n\,\ddot{a}_{[55]+t}\,,$$

$$_{t+}V = (S + RB_t)A_{[55]+t} - P^n\,\ddot{a}_{[55]+t}$$

$$= {}_{t-}V + B_t\,A_{[55]+t}.$$

The results are given in Table 13.2.

(d) In this example, the premium is loaded with a view to creating surplus for distribution as bonus. In part (b), we see how the gross premium policy value approach allows all of the surplus from the extra premiums to emerge in the first few years. This creates large bonuses at early durations, but soon the bonuses decline to zero, as all the future extra premiums are effectively taken into account early in the contract. This has two important disadvantages.

1. The purpose of the reversionary bonus system is to create flexibility, so

Table 13.2 *Bonus calculations for Exercise 13.7 (c), using net premium policy values.*

t	$_{(t-1)+}V$	$P-E$	I	EDB_{t-}	$E_{t-}V$	Pr_{t-}	B_t	RB_t	Bonus Rate
2	1 193	2 077.9	130.8	158.1	2 402	841.9	2 559	2 559	3.4%
3	3 245	2 077.9	212.9	191.2	4 503	841.9	2 471	5 029	3.3%
4	5 352	2 077.9	297.2	219.5	6 666	841.9	2 387	7 416	3.2%
5	7 521	2 077.9	384.0	251.8	8 890	841.8	2 307	9 723	3.1%
6	9 754	2 077.9	473.3	288.6	11 175	841.7	2 230	11 952	3.0%
7	12 050	2 077.9	565.1	330.4	13 521	841.6	2 156	14 108	2.9%
8	14 409	2 077.9	659.5	378.1	15 927	841.5	2 085	16 193	2.8%
9	16 831	2 077.9	756.4	432.3	18 392	841.4	2 017	18 210	2.7%
10	19 315	2 077.9	855.7	494.0	20 913	841.3	1 952	20 163	2.6%

the insurer can have more freedom in its investment strategy for the benefits which are not guaranteed. Once the bonus is declared, it is guaranteed, so under the gross premium policy value method, the flexibility is quickly lost.

2. The bonus system may also be used to retain policyholders, with an expectation of future profit sharing. Using the gross premium policy value method, there is little incentive to stay in the contract after the first few years, provided the cash values reflect the bonuses declared. If the cash values do not reflect the bonus distribution, there will be problems with fair treatment of surrendering policyholders.

In contrast, in part (c) we see that the net premium policy value approach generates a fairly stable bonus rate. The bonuses are far lower in the early years than under the gross premium policy value method, which allows the insurer to take advantage of the investment flexibility for a longer period. Also, the emerging bonus rates are stable, which may be more attractive to policyholders, as well as more equitable where surrendering policyholders get to benefit from the declared bonuses.

The steady emergence of distributable surplus was used for many years as a justification for the net premium policy value approach. A similar result can be obtained using the gross premium policy value approach, allowing for some specified smoothing process for bonus distributions.

13.8 From the question, using the notation of AMLCR, we have the following information:

$$FA = 100\,000, \quad \gamma_t = 1.95, \quad q^*_{x+t-1} = 0.005, \quad v_q = v_{4\%},$$
$$EC_t = 0.004\,AV_{t-1} + 25, \quad AV_{t-1} = 49\,500, \quad i^c_t = 5\%.$$

So

$$AV_t = 1.05\,(AV_{t-1} - 0.004\,AV_{t-1} - 25 - CoI_t)$$
$$= 51\,740.85 - 1.05\,CoI_t.$$

First, assume the ADB (Additional Death Benefit) is $FA - AV_t$. Then

$$CoI^f_t = q^*_{x+t-1} v_q\,(100\,000 - AV_t)$$
$$= 0.005\,v_{4\%}\left(100\,000 - \left(51740.85 - 1.05\,CoI^f_t\right)\right)$$
$$= 232.02 + 0.005048\,CoI^f_t$$

which gives $CoI^f_t = 233.19$, $AV^f_t = 51\,496.00$, and $ADB^f_t = 48\,504.00$.

Secondly, assume the ADB is based on the corridor factor, which means that

$$ADB_t = \gamma_t AV_t - AV_t = (\gamma_t - 1)AV_t.$$

Then

$$CoI^c_t = q^*_{x+t-1} v_q(cf_t - 1)AV_t$$
$$= 0.005\,v_q\,0.95\,(51\,740.85 - (1.05)CoI^c_t)$$
$$= 236.32 - 0.004796\,CoI^c_t$$

which gives $CoI^c_t = 235.19$, $AV^c_t = 51\,493.90$ and $ADB^c_t = 48\,919.20$.

The CoI is the greater of the two values calculated, so we have $CoI_t = 235.19$ and hence $ADB_t = 48\,919.20$.

13.9 The account value immediately after premiums and deductions at time 5 is

$$AV_{5+} = 2029 + 200 - 400 - 60 = 1769.$$

The EPV of the guaranteed term insurance is

$$100\,000\,A^{\,1}_{45:\overline{20}|} = 100\,000 \times 0.02391 = 2391.29.$$

So the no-lapse guarantee reserve is $2391.29 - 1769.00 = \$622.29$.

^{E}13.10 (a) First, project the account values and the death benefit, assuming the policy remains in force for four years. In general,

$$AV_t = (AV_{t-1} + P - EC - CoI)(1 + i_t^c)$$

and

$$DB_t = \max(12\,000, 1.5\,AV_t).$$

The calculations are set out in the following table.

t	AV_{t-1}	P	EC	CoI	i^c	AV_t	DB_t
1	0.00	3 000	120.00	25	4.0%	2 969.20	12 000.00
2	2 969.20	3 000	111.88	25	4.5%	6 094.78	12 000.00
3	6 094.78	3 000	124.38	25	5.5%	9 437.40	14 156.09
4	9 437.40	3 000	137.75	25	5.5%	12 949.75	19 424.63

Next, use AV_t and DB_t from this projection to profit test the insurer's cash flows. At time $t = 0$, we have the pre-premium expenses of \$200, giving $Pr_0 = -200$. For $t = 1, 2, 3, 4$, the emerging profit at the year end for a policy in force at the start of the year is

$$Pr_t = (AV_{t-1} + P - E)(1 + i_t) - q_{65+t-1}\,DB_t - p_{65+t-1}\,AV_t.$$

The full profit vector calculation is tabulated below.

t	AV_{t-1}	P	E	I	EDB_t	EAV_t	Pr_t
0			200.00				-200.00
1	0.00	3 000	50.00	132.75	70.98	2 951.64	60.14
2	2 969.20	3 000	51.00	325.50	79.42	6 054.44	109.84
3	6 094.78	3 000	52.02	587.78	104.88	9 367.47	158.18
4	9 437.40	3 000	53.06	804.98	161.16	12 842.31	185.84

The profit signature, Π, is the vector of emerging profits per policy issued, where $\Pi_t = {}_{t-1}p_{65}\,Pr_t$ for $t = 1, 2, 3, 4$, and $\Pi_0 = Pr_0$. So

$$\Pi = (-200.00, 60.14, 109.19, 156.20, 182.16)'$$

and

$$NPV = \Pi_0 + \sum_{t=1}^{4} \Pi_t\, v_{8\%}^t = 207.19.$$

(b) Given that the policyholder dies in the first year, the profit signature is

$$\Pi = (-200, \ -8\,917.25, \ 0, \ 0, \ 0)'.$$

Note that the profit signature and profit vector are the same when there is no uncertainty about the year of death.

We see that there is no impact on $\Pr_0$, as the value was not dependent on survival in any case. The second term is from the year 1 cashflows, given that the death benefit is paid in the first year:

$$\Pi_1 = 1.045\,(3000 - 50) - 12\,000 = -8917.25.$$

The NPV is $-\$8456.71$.

(c) The calculations are similar to those in part (a), but assuming the policyholder survives the term. For example

$$\Pi_1 = 1.045\,(3000 - 50) - AV_1 = 113.55,$$
$$\Pi_2 = 1.055\,(AV_1 + 3000 - 51) - AV_2 = 148.92.$$

The profit signature, given survival to the end of the term, is

$$\Pi = (-200, \ 113.55, \ 148.92, \ 193.14, \ 239.57)',$$

and the NPV is $\$362.23$.

(d) (i) The calculations are similar to those in part (c), but assuming the policy-holder survives to time 2, and then receives the full account value, AV_2, and there are no further cash flows. Using part (c), we have

$$\Pi = (-200, \ 113.55, \ 148.92, \ 0, \ 0)',$$

and the NPV is $\$32.82$.

(ii) Assuming the policyholder survives to time 2, and then receives 90% of the account value, we have

$$\Pi_2 = 1.055\,(AV_1 + 3\,000 - 51) - 0.9\,AV_2 = 758.40,$$

giving

$$\Pi = (-200, \ 113.55, \ 758.40, \ 0, \ 0)',$$

and the NPV is $\$555.35$.

(e) The profit margin, denoted *pm*, for policyholders who remain in force throughout the contract is

$$pm = \frac{\text{NPV}}{\text{PV Premiums}} \quad \text{given survival to the contract end}$$

$$= \frac{\text{NPV}}{3000\,\ddot{a}_{\overline{4}|\,8\%}} = \frac{362.23}{10\,731.29} = 3.38\%.$$

The profit margin for a policyholder who surrenders at time 2 is

$$pm = \frac{\text{NPV}}{\text{PV Premiums}} \quad \text{given surrender at time 2}$$

$$= \frac{\text{NPV}}{3000\,(1 + v_{8\%})} = \frac{\text{NPV}}{5777.78}.$$

Setting this profit margin equal to 3.38% gives

$$\text{NPV} = 0.0338 \times 5777.78 = 195.02,$$

and so, since we also have $\text{NPV} = \sum_{k=0}^{2} \Pi_k\, v_{8\%}^{k}$,

$$195.02 = -200 + 113.55\, v_{8\%} + \Pi_2\, v_{8\%}^{2},$$

giving $\Pi_2 = 338.12$. Then, if α represents the surrender penalty,

$$338.12 = 1.055\,(2969.20 + 3000 - 51) - (1 - \alpha)\,AV_2$$

giving $\alpha = 3.1\%$. So a cash value of 96.9% of the account value would generate the 3.38% profit margin required from policyholders surrendering during the second policy year.

(f) We see from part (a) that, ignoring surrenders, there will be a profit for the insurer, at the 8% risk discount rate, of $207.19 per policy. (The profit margin is 1.95%.) However, part (b) shows that early death is quite costly, as we would expect from a policy with a term insurance component. On the other hand, survivals generate a small profit in NPV terms, of $362.23 each. The mix of more severe losses from death benefit claims, which are assumed to be relatively rare, and smaller gains from survivals, which are more common, gives the average result found in part (a).

If the policyholder surrenders at time 2, we see from part (d) that the cash value determination is significant. If there is no surrender penalty, so policyholders take the full account value on early exit, the NPV is very small, at

$32.82; the profit margin (which is a useful measure as it adjusts for fewer premiums) is 0.6% in this case, compared with 1.95% overall.

If the cash value is reduced to 90% of the account value, the NPV is much stronger, at $555.35, representing a profit margin of 9.61%. At this level of penalty, the insurer gains an NPV greater than that earned from the full term survivors in part (c). It is not ideal to have surrenders generating significantly higher returns than those who stay – it creates perverse incentives for insurers to stimulate higher withdrawal rates, and indicates a lack of equitable treatment for leavers compared with stayers.

From part (e) we see that a cash value of 96.9% of the account value for the time 2 surrenders would generate the same profit margin for leaving policyholders as for those who stay throughout the term. This would appear to be more equitable. The NPV generated by the surrendering policyholders is less than for those staying for the full term, but is slightly more than the overall expected NPV, which allows for mortality but not for surrenders.

^{E}13.11 (a) Let S denote the initial sum insured, that is, $S = 100\,000$, and let P denote the annual premium. The EPV of premiums is

$$P\,\ddot{a}_{70} = 12.0083\,P,$$

the EPV of the death benefit is

$$S\left(v\,q_{70} + 1.025\,v^2\,_{1|}q_{70} + 1.025^2\,v^3\,_{2|}q_{70} + \cdots\right) = 62\,902.50,$$

and the EPV of expenses is

$$200 + 50\,\ddot{a}_{70} + 0.58\,P + 0.02P\,\ddot{a}_{70} = 800.42 + 0.82017\,P.$$

Hence $P = \$5693.79$.

(b) The net premium, used to determine net premium policy values, is

$$P^n = \frac{100\,000\,A_{70}}{\ddot{a}_{70}} = 3565.67,$$

using the Standard Ultimate Survival Model and interest at 5% per year.

The calculations for the first three values of the profit vector and profit signature are shown in detail here.

We have initial expenses, before the premium income, of $200, and the net premium policy value (i.e. the reserve) is $_0V = 0$, so

$$\text{Pr}_0 = -200.$$

For the first policy year, from time 0 to time 1, we have

$$_0V = 0,$$
$$E_1 = 50 + 0.60P = 3466.27,$$
$$I_1 = 0.05\,(_0V + P - E_1) = 468.52,$$
$$EDB_1 = q_{70}\,100\,000 = 1041.33,$$
$$E\,_1V = p_{70}\,_1V = p_{70}\,(102\,500\,A_{71} - P^n\,\ddot{a}_{71})$$
$$= p_{70}\,(3840.54) = 3800.55,$$

giving

$$\text{Pr}_1 = {}_0V + P - E_1 + I_1 - EDB_1 - E_1V = -2502.99$$

and $\Pi_1 = \text{Pr}_1 = -2502.99$.

Similarly, for the second policy year we have

$$_1V = 3840.54,$$
$$E_2 = 50 + 0.02P = 163.88,$$
$$I_2 = 0.05\,(_1V + P - E_2) = 468.52,$$
$$EDB_2 = q_{71}\,102\,500 = 1196.18,$$
$$E\,_2V = p_{71}\,_2V = p_{71}\,(105\,062.5\,A_{72} - P^n\,\ddot{a}_{72})$$
$$= p_{71}(7835.96) = 7744.51,$$

giving

$$\text{Pr}_2 = 898.29 \text{ and } \Pi_2 = p_{71}\,\text{Pr}_2 = 888.93.$$

Notice the death benefit increasing by 2.5% in the EDB and $E\,_tV$ calculations.

We continue for policy years up to $t = 40$ (after which time the survival probabilities are sufficiently small that there is no impact on the calculations). Excerpts from the profit test table are shown in Table 13.3. The final column is the partial NPV vector, where

$$\text{NPV}_t = \sum_{k=0}^{t} \Pi_k\,v_{10\%}^k$$

Table 13.3 *Profit vector, profit signature and partial NPV values for Exercise 13.11, part (b).*

t	Pr_t	Π_t	NPV_t
0	−200.00	−200.00	−200.00
1	−2 502.99	−2 502.99	−2 475.44
2	898.29	888.93	−1 740.79
3	829.08	810.87	−1 131.57
⋮	⋮	⋮	⋮
11	174.59	145.02	789.86
12	82.12	65.99	810.88
13	−11.93	−9.24	808.21
14	−107.19	−79.58	787.25
⋮	⋮	⋮	⋮
⋮	⋮	⋮	⋮
39	−419.85	−0.40	238.05
40	−231.13	−0.09	238.05

The NPV, as shown at the end of the partial NPV column, is $238.05. The EPV of premiums is $48 794, so the profit margin is 0.49%.

(c) This case differs from part (b) above, in that the bonuses are determined according to the emerging surplus, after the first policy year. Expenses and premiums are the same as in (b). Reserves and death benefits are different, as the bonuses are different. We use the subscript t_- to denote the values for the expected reserve cost and profit vector *before* bonus is determined, and subscript t to denote the values after bonus distribution.

For $t = 0$, $Pr_0 = \Pi_0 = -200$, as before.

For $t = 1$ we have no bonus, and

$$_0V = 0,$$
$$E_1, I_1, EDB_1 \text{ are as above}$$
$$E_{1-}V = p_{70}\, _1V = p_{70}\,(100\,000 A_{71} - P^n \ddot{a}_{71})$$
$$= p_{70}\, 2731.06 = 2702.62,$$

giving

$$Pr_1 = _0V + P - E_1 + I_1 - EDB_1 - E_1V = -1405.06$$

and hence $\Pi_1 = -1405.06$.

For $t = 2$ we have P and E_2 as in part (b). Also

$$_1V = 2731.06$$
$$EDB_1 = 100\,000\,q_{71} = 1167.00$$
$$E\,_{2-}V = p_{71}\,(100\,000A_{72} - P^n\,\ddot{a}_{72}) = 5444.56,$$
$$\text{Pr}_{2-} = 2062.46.$$

So, the distributable surplus emerging at time 2 is \$2062.46, for each policy in force at time 1. The policies terminating through death in the year do not receive any of the surplus. The policies in force at the year end receive a bonus of B_2, giving the bonus equation of value as:

$$2062.46 = p_{71}\,B_2\,A_{72} \Rightarrow B_2 = \frac{2062.46}{p_{71}\,A_{72}} = 4539.74.$$

The revised expected cost of the year-end reserve is

$$E\,_2V = p_{71}\,(104\,539.74\,A_{72} - P^n\,\ddot{a}_{72}) = 7507.02,$$

and the revised profit vector element is

$$\text{Pr}_2 = {}_1V + P - E_2 + I_2 - EDB_2 - E_2V = 0.$$

Note that $Pr_2 = \text{Pr}_{2-} - (E\,_{2-}V - E\,_2V)$, and

$$E\,_{2-}V - E\,_2V = p_{71}\,B_2\,A_{72} = \text{Pr}_{2-}\,.$$

So the zero value for Pr_2 is by design – all the profit is distributed in the form of bonus, so the emerging profit after bonus is 0.

The compound bonus rate in the second year is $B_2/S = 4.54\%$, considerably higher than the 2.5% loading in the premium. However, later bonuses fall below the premium assumption. In Table 13.4 we show excerpts from the profit test, including the profit signature, partial NPV and the emerging compound bonus rates.

The NPV for the contract is −\$1477, and the profit margin is −3.0%.

(d) In these examples, we have a policy which is priced to provide a 2.5% compound bonus, assuming interest at 5% and the expenses specified in the premium basis. The profit tests assume the same interest rate and expenses as the premium basis, and the reserve also uses the same interest rates, but different expense assumptions implicit in the net premium approach.

Table 13.4 *Profit vector, profit signature, partial NPV values, and compound bonus rates for Exercise 13.11, part (c).*

t	Pr_{t-}	B_t	$E_t V$	Pr_t	NPV_t	Bonus rate
0	−200.00			−200.00		
1	−1 405.06	0.00	2 702.62	−1 405.06	−1 477.32	0.00%
2	2 062.46	4 539.74	7 507.02	0.00	−1 477.32	4.54%
3	2 062.46	4 392.14	12 414.40	0.00	−1 477.32	4.20%
4	2 062.46	4 253.11	17 416.94	0.00	−1 477.32	3.90%
⋮	⋮	⋮	⋮	⋮	⋮	⋮
39	2 062.46	5 308.55	89 212.17	0.00	−1 477.32	2.31%
40	2 062.46	5 888.98	82 599.42	0.00	−1 477.32	2.50%

We see in part (b) that the mismatch between reserves and premium/profit test assumptions creates a small profit. However, there is a problem in the policy design. It is unsatisfactory to have negative emerging surplus projected during the term of the contract. Negative values for Pr_t imply a need for further injections of capital while the contract is in force. Prudent capital management requires that all projected capital requirements are allowed for at the start of the policy. One way to do this would be to set more conservative reserves – for example, using a reserve interest rate of 3.5% in place of 5% would eliminate the negative surplus, at the cost of extra capital during the early years of the policy. This reduces the profit margin to −1.6%.

In part (c) we show the effect of distributing profit as it emerges. The emerging profit before distribution is stable at $2062.46. We can identify where this number comes from, as follows. For $t = 2, 3, \ldots$, the premium is $P = 5693.79$, expenses are $E = 163.88$ and the net premium is $P^n = 3565.67$. Let RB_t denote the total bonus declared up to and including the end of the tth year, and let $i = 5\%$. Both $_{t-1}V$ and $_{t-}V$ are determined using a total sum insured of $S + RB_{t-1}$. For easier interpretation, we denote this as DB_{t-1}. So

$$
\begin{aligned}
\text{Pr}_{t-} &= (_{t-1}V + P - E)(1 + i) - q_{x+t-1} DB_{t-1} - p_{x+t-1}\,{}_{t-}V \\
&= (DB_{t-1} A_{x+t-1} - P^n \ddot{a}_{x+t-1} + P - E)(1 + i) \\
&\quad - q_{x+t-1} DB_{t-1} - p_{x+t-1}(DB_{t-1} A_{x+t} - P^n \ddot{a}_{x+t}) \\
&= DB_{t-1} A_{x+t-1}(1 + i) - P^n \ddot{a}_{x+t-1}(1 + i) + (P - E)(1 + i) \\
&\quad - q_{x+t-1} DB_{t-1} - p_{x+t-1} DB_{t-1} A_{x+t} + p_{x+t-1} P^n \ddot{a}_{x+t}\,.
\end{aligned}
$$

Recall that

$$A_{x+t-1} = q_{x+t-1}\, v + p_{x+t-1}\, v A_{x+t}\,,$$

$$\ddot{a}_{x+t-1} = 1 + p_{x+t-1}\, v\, \ddot{a}_{x+t}\,.$$

So

$$\Pr\nolimits_{t-} = DB_{t-1}\,(q_{x+t-1} + p_{x+t-1} A_{x+t})$$

$$- P^n((1+i) + p_{x+t-1}\,\ddot{a}_{x+t}) + (P-E)(1+i)$$

$$- q_{x+t-1} DB_{t-1} - p_{x+t-1} DB_{t-1} A_{x+t} + p_{x+t-1} P^n \ddot{a}_{x+t}$$

$$= (P - P^n - E)(1+i) = 2062.46.$$

The profit is constant because P, P^n, E and i are all constant for $t \geq 2$. Further, we see that $P - P^n$ is the loading in the gross premium for expenses and bonus, and E is the part that is used for renewal expenses. So $P - P^n - E$ is the gross premium that is not required for reserves or renewal expenses, at the start of the year. Multiplying by $(1 + i)$ gives the year-end value. Under the assumptions in part (c), this is all distributed as bonus. The problem is that some of this loading is actually designed to recover the outstanding acquisition expenses. The distribution strategy in part (c) does not allow for this, resulting in a negative NPV and profit margin. This could be turned around if bonuses were postponed to the third policy year, for example.

We also see in part (c) that the strategy of distributing surplus as it emerges leads to high rates of compound reversionary bonus in the early contract years, with rates declining as the duration increases, before rising again for the very old-age survivors. The result is higher benefits in the variable bonus case – but that is not surprising, given that the insurer is over-distributing the profits, because of the unrecovered acquisition expenses. Comparing the resulting death benefits with the level bonus case, we have, for example, the values below.

Year	Death benefit level bonus rate	Death benefit variable bonus rate
5	110 381	113 185
10	124 886	132 644
15	141 297	149 758
20	159 865	165 360

Solutions for Chapter 14

^{E}14.1 (a) The fund value at the end of the year is $F_1 = 97R$, where $R \sim LN(0.09, 0.18^2)$. Hence

$$\begin{aligned}
\Pr[F_1 < 100] &= \Pr[97R < 100] \\
&= \Pr[\log 97 + \log R < \log 100] \\
&= \Pr\left[\frac{\log R - 0.09}{0.18} < \frac{\log 100 - \log 97 - 0.09}{0.18}\right] \\
&= \Pr[Z < -0.3308] \quad \text{where} \quad Z \sim N(0, 1) \\
&= 0.37040.
\end{aligned}$$

(b) The mean of F_1 is

$$E[F_1] = 97\,E[R] = 97\exp\{0.09 + 0.5 \times 0.18^2\} = \$107.87.$$

(c) For a standard normal random variable, Z, the lower 5% point is -1.64485. Hence

$$\Pr\left[\frac{\log R - 0.09}{0.18} < -1.64485\right] = 0.05$$
$$\implies \Pr[R < \exp\{-0.18 \times 1.64485 + 0.09\}] = 0.05$$
$$\implies \Pr[R < 0.81377] = 0.05.$$

(d) From part (c) we know that

$$\Pr[R > 0.81377] = 0.95.$$

Hence

$$\Pr[97R > 97 \times 0.81377] = 0.95$$

$$\implies \Pr[100 - 97R < 100 - 97 \times 0.81377] = 0.95$$

$$\implies \Pr[\max(100 - 97R, 0) < 100 - 97 \times 0.81377] = 0.95$$

$$\text{since } 100 - 97 \times 0.81377 > 0$$

$$\implies \Pr[L_0 < (100 - 97 \times 0.81377)e^{-0.05} - 0.5] = 0.95$$

$$\implies Q_{0.95}(L_0) = (100 - 97 \times 0.81377)e^{-0.05} - 0.5$$

$$\implies Q_{0.95}(L_0) = \$19.54.$$

(e) (i) Let f denote the probability density function of R. The random variable L_0 has the following distribution:

$$L_0 = \begin{cases} -0.5 & \text{if } R > 100/97, \\ (100 - 97R)e^{-0.05} - 0.5 & \text{if } R \le 100/97. \end{cases}$$

Hence

$$E[L_0] = -0.5 + \int_0^{100/97} (100 - 97x)\, e^{-0.05}\, f(x)\, dx$$

$$= -0.5 + 100\, e^{-0.05}\, \Pr[R < 100/97] - 97\, e^{-0.05} \int_0^{100/97} x\, f(x)\, dx$$

$$= \$3.46.$$

(ii) $\text{CTE}_{0.95}(L_0)$ is $E[L_0 \mid L_0 > Q_{0.95}(L_0)]$ (as $Q_{0.95}(L_0)$ lies in the continuous part of the distribution of L_0). Note first that

$$\Pr[L_0 > Q_{0.95}(L_0)] \equiv \Pr[R < 0.81377] = 0.05.$$

Then

$$\text{CTE}_{0.95}(L_0) = E[L_0 + 0.5 \mid L_0 > Q_{0.95}(L_0)] - 0.5$$

$$= e^{-0.05} E[(L_0 + 0.5)e^{0.05} \mid L_0 > Q_{0.95}(L_0)] - 0.5$$

$$= e^{-0.05} E[(L_0 + 0.5)e^{0.05} \mid R < 0.81377] - 0.5$$

$$= e^{-0.05} E[\max(100 - 97R, 0) \mid R < 0.81377] - 0.5$$

$$= e^{-0.05} E[100 - 97R \mid R < 0.81377] - 0.5$$

$$\text{since } 100 - 97R > 0 \text{ for } R < 0.81377$$

$$= 100e^{-0.05} - 0.5 - \frac{97e^{-0.05}}{\Pr[R < 0.81377]} \int_0^{0.81377} x\, f(x)\, dx$$

$$= \$24.83.$$

(f) The values are simulated using random $N(0, 1)$ numbers to generate 100 different values for R, say $R_1, R_2, \ldots, R_{100}$. Use these to generate 100 values for F_1 and 100 values for L_0.

   (a) If n is the number of simulated values of F_1 less than 100, then the estimate of $\Pr[F_1 < 100]$ is $n/100$.

   (b) The estimate of $E[F_1]$ is the average of the 100 simulated values of F_1.

(c), (d) The 5th percentile of the distribution of R and the 95th percentile of the distribution of L_0 can be found using spreadsheet functions. Note that the Excel PERCENTILE function uses a smoothed approach, so that the estimated 5th percentile is interpolated between the 5th and 6th values.

   (e)(i) The estimate of $E[L_0]$ is the average of the 100 simulated values of L_0.

   (e)(ii) The estimate of $\text{CTE}_{0.95}(L_0)$ is the average of the five largest simulated values of L_0.

E14.2 Let P denote the annual premium. We use the following notation:

I_t is the return on investments in the tth year.

E_t is the total expense incurred at time $t - 1$ per policy in force at the start of the tth year. All the expenses at time 0 are included in E_0 rather than E_1, so that

$$E_0 = 0.1P + 100; \quad E_1 = 0; \quad E_t = 0.06P \text{ for } t = 2, 3, 4, 5.$$

Pr_t is the profit emerging at the end of the tth year per policy in force at the start of the year.

Π_t is $_{t-1}p_{50}\, \text{Pr}_t$.

$_tV$ is the reserve required at time t for a policy still in force at that time.

The profit, Pr_t, is calculated as follows:

$$\text{Pr}_0 = -E_0 ,$$
$$\text{Pr}_t = (_{t-1}V + P - E_t)(1 + I_t) - 10\,000\, q_{50+t-1} - {_tV}\, p_{50+t-1} \quad \text{for } t = 2, 3, 4,$$
$$\text{Pr}_5 = (_4V + P - E_5)(1 + I_5) - 10\,000\, q_{54} - 20\,000\, p_{54} .$$

(a) In this part, we have $I_t = 0.08$ for $t = 1, 2, \ldots, 5$. The EPV of future profit, or NPV, as a function of P, is given by

$$NPV = \Pr_0 + \sum_{t=1}^{5} v^t {}_{t-1}p_{50} \Pr_t$$

where $v = 1/1.1$. Requiring $NPV = P/3$ gives $P = \$3739.59$.

(b) For this part, we first generate 500 simulated values of $\{1 + I_t\}_{t=1}^{5}$, each with a $LN(0.07, 0.13^2)$ distribution. For each set of simulated values of the investment returns, we calculate $\{\Pr_t\}_{t=0}^{5}$ using $P = \$3740$.

(i) We are interested in the probability of a loss in the final year, given that the contract is in force at the start of that year, which is the probability that $\Pr_5$ is negative. Let N denote the number of simulations (out of 500) for which $\Pr_5$ is negative. Then $N \sim B(500, p)$ where $p = \Pr[\Pr_5 < 0]$, so that an estimate of p is $\hat{p} = N/500$, and the standard error of this estimate is $\sqrt{p(1-p)/500}$, which can be estimated as $\sqrt{\hat{p}(1-\hat{p})/500}$. In our projections, we find that 263 simulated values of $\Pr_5$ have a negative value, out of 500 simulations, so the estimate of p is $263/500 = 0.526$, and an approximate 95% confidence interval for p is

$$\hat{p} \pm 1.96 \sqrt{\hat{p}(1-\hat{p})/500}$$

which is $(0.482, 0.570)$.

(ii) The formula for $\Pr_5$ is

$$\Pr_5 = (1 + I_5)(15\,000 + 0.94 \times 3740)$$
$$-10\,000 \times 0.001797 - 20\,000 \times 0.998203.$$

Hence, the probability that $\Pr_5$ is negative can be calculated as

$$\Pr[1 + I_5 < 1.0792] = \Phi\left(\frac{\log 1.0792 - 0.07}{0.13}\right) = 0.519.$$

The 95% confidence interval calculated in part (i) contains the true value of p, as we might expect given the high level of confidence.

(iii) For each of the 500 simulations, we can calculate the NPV using a risk discount rate of 10%. In our calculations, 254 simulations have a NPV greater than $3740/3$ and so meet the profit objective. Then the estimated probability that the profit objective will be met is

$254/500 = 0.508$, and an estimated 95% confidence interval for this probability is

$$0.508 \pm 1.96 \sqrt{0.508(1 - 0.508)/500}$$

which is $(0.464, 0.552)$.

E14.3 (a) We assume the policy stays in force until at least the start of the final year. Let F_{t-} denote the fund value at time t, $t = 0, 1, \ldots, 4$, just before payment of the premium and deduction of the management charge. Then the management charge at time t, MC_t, is $0.03(F_{t-} + 100)$. F_{t-} can be calculated recursively as follows: $F_{0-} = 0$, and for $t = 1, 2, 3, 4$,

$$F_{t-} = 1.08 \times (1 - 0.03)(F_{t-1-} + 100).$$

The table of projected fund values and management charges is as follows. We also show the implied additional death benefit (ADB_t) for the insurer, which is the difference between the death benefit ($500) and the end-year fund, if positive.

t	$F_{t-1} + P$ before charges	MC_t	F_t	ADB_t
1	100.00	3.00	104.76	395.24
2	204.76	6.14	214.51	285.49
3	314.51	9.44	329.48	170.52
4	429.48	12.88	449.92	50.08
5	549.92	16.50	576.10	0.00

(b) The profit test table is shown below.

t	MC_t	E_t	I_t	EB_t	Pr_t	Π_t
1	3.00	2.00	0.06	0.79	0.27	0.27
2	6.14	4.10	0.12	0.80	1.37	1.37
3	9.44	6.29	0.19	0.55	2.79	2.77
4	12.88	8.59	0.26	0.19	4.37	4.33
5	16.50	11.00	0.33	0.00	5.83	5.76

Note that we are told that the insurer does not establish reserves for this contract.

MC_t is from the policyholder fund projection in part (a), and is an item of income for the insurer.

E_t denotes the insurer's expenses incurred at the start of the tth year.

I_t is the interest earned on the insurer's funds,

$$I_t = (MC_t - E_t)0.06.$$

EB_t is the expected cost of benefits. Note that the insurer only pays for the excess over the policyholder's funds, which is ADB_t from part (a). There is no projected liability for the maturity benefit, as in the projection in part (a), $F_5 > 500$, so the guaranteed minimum payment has no projected cost.

$\Pr_t$ is the emerging profit at time t for a policy in force at time $t - 1$, so

$$\Pr_t = MC_t - E_t + I_t - EB_t .$$

The profit signature is

$$\Pi_t = {}_{t-1}p_x \Pr_t .$$

(c) The calculations in parts (a) and (b) do not show any negative cash flows for the insurer and so it may appear that it is unnecessary to set up reserves for this contract. However, these calculations are based on assumptions, most notably concerning fund growth, which may or may not be realized. It would be prudent for the insurer to carry out a stochastic analysis, possibly using simulation, to determine the extent of any liabilities arising from different scenarios and then to decide if reserves are required to cover these liabilities.

(d) Suppose, for simplicity, that interest rate risk is the only source of future uncertainty when the policy is issued. In practice all assumptions – expenses, mortality, growth of the insurer's fund – are uncertain, but uncertainty about future interest rates is likely to have the greatest impact. We would choose an appropriate stochastic model for future interest rates, possibly the independent lognormal model. We would then generate a large number of future interest rate scenarios and, for each scenario, calculate the EPV of the future loss, after paying any initial expenses. Let L_i denote the EPV of the future loss calculated from the ith scenario. The 99% quantile reserve required at time 0 is then the 99th percentile of the distribution of L as given by the simulated values $\{L_i\}$, provided this is positive, and zero otherwise. The 99% CTE reserve required at time 0 is $E[L \mid L > Q_{0.99}(L)]$, which would be estimated by taking the average of the simulated values $\{L_i\}$ which are greater than the (estimated) value of the 99% quantile reserve.

(e) (i) There will be a payment under the guarantee if the fund at the end of the year is less than $500. Let the accumulation factor for the fifth year be denoted $1 + i_5$, so that

$$1 + i_5 \sim LN(0.09, 0.18^2).$$

The fund just before the start of the year is $485, so the fund at the end of the year will be $\$(1 + i_5)\,0.97\,(485 + 100)$. Hence, the required probability is

$$\Pr[1 + i_5 < 500/(0.97 \times 585)] = 0.114.$$

(ii) The insurer's liability at the end of year 5 is the same, $\max(500 - F_{5-}, 0)$, whether the policyholder survives or dies in the year. The management charge at the start of the year is given by

$$MC_4 = 0.03(485 + 100) = \$17.55,$$

the insurer's expenses at the start of the year are

$$0.02(485 + 100) = \$11.70,$$

and F_{5-} is given by

$$F_{5-} = 0.97(485 + 100)(1 + i_5).$$

Hence, the present value of the future loss at time 4, L_4, is given by

$$L_4 = \max(500 - F_{5-}, 0)/1.06 + 11.70 - 17.55.$$

We know from part (i) that there is a probability of $0.114\ (> 0.01)$ that $500 - F_{5-}$ will be positive. Hence, the 99% point of the distribution of L_4, $Q_{0.99}(L_4)$, will be the 99% point of the random variable

$$(500 - 0.97(485 + 100)(1 + i_5))/1.06 - 5.85.$$

This is equal to

$$500 - 0.97(485 + 100)\exp\{0.09 + 0.18z_{0.01}\}/1.06 - 5.85$$

where $z_{0.01}\ (= -2.3263)$ is the 1% point of the $N(0, 1)$ distribution, so that $\exp\{0.09 + 0.18z_{0.01}\}$ is the 1% point of the distribution of $1 + i_5$. This gives

$$Q_{0.99}(L_4)$$
$$= (500 - 0.97(485 + 100)\exp\{0.09 - 0.18 \times 2.3263\})/1.06 - 5.85$$
$$= \$80.50.$$

14.4 Note that the values in Table 14.10 have, conveniently, been ordered by size.

(a) There are 54 values in Table 14.10 which are larger than 10. Hence, the estimate of $\Pr[L_0 > 10]$ is $54/1000 = 0.054$.

(b) The variance of the estimate in part (a) is

$$p(1 - p)/1000,$$

where $p = \Pr[L_0 > 10]$. This can be estimated by

$$0.054(1 - 0.054)/1000 = 5.108 \times 10^{-5}.$$

The 99.5% point of the $N(0, 1)$ distribution is 2.5758. Hence, an approximate 99% confidence interval for p is

$$0.054 \pm 2.5758 \sqrt{5.108 \times 10^{-5}}$$

which is $(0.036, 0.072)$.

(c) Since there are 1000 simulated values of L_0, the estimate of the 99% point of the distribution is between the 10th and 11th largest values. We may estimate $Q_{0.99}(L_0)$ by taking take the mid-point between these values, giving an estimate of

$$(17.357 + 17.248)/2 = \$17.30.$$

Note that there are other ways to determine an appropriate estimate between the 10th and 11th largest values. The smoothed empirical estimation of the p-quantile from an ordered sample of n values uses interpolation to find the p(n + 1)th value, which in this case would be the 990.99th value, which is 17.36.

(d) The estimate of $CTE_{0.99}(L_0)$ is the average of the ten largest simulated values of L_0. Hence

$$CTE_{0.99}(L_0) = (26.140 + 24.709 + \cdots + 17.774 + 17.357)/10 = \$21.46.$$

^{E}14.5 (a) First project the policyholder's fund assuming the policy remains in force throughout. Let A_t denote the tth allocated premium (paid at time $t - 1$), let F_{t-} denote the fund at time t before the deduction of the management charge, let F_t denote the fund at time t after the deduction of the management charge, and let MC_t denote the management charge deducted at time t for a policy in force at time $t - 1$.

Then

$$A_1 = 0.25 \times 0.95 \times 750 = 178.13,$$

and for $t = 2, \ldots, 5$,

$$A_t = 1.025 \times 0.95 \times 750 = 730.31.$$

For $t = 1, 2, \ldots, 5$

$$F_{t-} = (A_t + F_{t-1})\,1.065, \quad MC_t = 0.01\,F_{t-}, \quad \text{and} \quad F_t = 0.99\,F_{t-}.$$

This gives the table of projected fund values shown below.

t	F_{t-1}	A_t	MC_t	F_t
1	0.00	178.13	1.90	187.81
2	187.81	730.31	9.78	968.02
3	968.02	730.31	18.09	1 790.64
4	1 790.64	730.31	26.85	2 657.96
5	2 657.96	730.31	36.09	3 572.43

The profit emerging at time 0, Pr_0, arises only from the insurer's initial expenses, so that $Pr_0 = -(150 + 0.1P) = -\$225$.

In each of the five years, assuming the contract is in force at the start of the tth year, the insurer is assumed to receive income from the unallocated premium, say $UP_t = 750 - A_t$ at the start of the year, and from the management charge at the end of the year, as well as from interest earned during the year at 5.5%. Outgo comprises the incurred expenses, the expected cost of death benefits and the expected cost of the maturity benefit. So, the profit table is as follows:

t (1)	UP_t (2)	E_t (3)	I_t (4)	MC_t (5)	EB_t (6)	Pr_t (7)	Π_t (8)
0	0	225.00				−225.00	−225.00
1	571.88	0	31.45	1.90	3.40	601.83	601.83
2	19.69	83.75	−3.52	9.78	2.70	−60.51	−54.40
3	19.69	83.75	−3.52	18.09	1.78	−51.27	−41.43
4	19.69	83.75	−3.52	26.85	0.56	−41.29	−29.98
5	19.69	83.75	−3.52	36.09	356.60	−388.10	−281.34

The expenses at time 0 have been included in the calculation of Pr_0 and so are not included in the calculation of Pr_1.

The cost to the insurer of the death benefit is the cost of the extra amount, if any, above the bid value of the units; there is a cost to the insurer in the final year from maturities of 10% of the bid value of the units. These costs are all included in the EB_t column.

For $t \geq 1$, Pr_t is the expected profit emerging at time t given that the contract is in force at time $t - 1$. The profit signature element for time t, Π_t, is the expected profit emerging at time t per policy issued. We must allow for the probability that the policyholder has not died or surrendered before time $t - 1$ to find Π_t from Pr_t, so

$$\Pi_0 = Pr_0 ,$$

$$\Pi_t = {}_{t-1}p_{50} (0.9)^{t-1} Pr_t \text{ for } t = 1, 2, 3, 4,$$

and

$$\Pi_5 = {}_4p_{50} (0.9)^3 Pr_5 .$$

The EPV of the profit is

$$\sum_{t=0}^{5} v^t \Pi_t = \$42.30$$

and the EPV of the premiums is

$$P \sum_{t=1}^{5} v^t 0.9^{\min(t-1,3)} {}_{t-1}p_{50} = \$2704.75,$$

where v is calculated at the risk discount rate, so that $v = 1/1.085$. Hence, the profit margin is $42.30/2704.75 = 0.0156$ or 1.56%.

(b) (i) The deterministic profit test in part (a) shows negative cash flows for the insurer at the end of years 2, 3, 4 and 5. Reserves should be established to meet these future liabilities.

(ii) The effect of introducing reserves is shown in the revised profit test table below.

t (1)	UP_t (2)	$_{t-1}V$ (3)	E_t (4)	I_t (5)	MC_t (6)	EB_t (7)	EV_t (8)	Pr_t
0			225.00					−225.00
1	571.88	0.00	0.00	31.45	1.90	3.40	359.56	242.26
2	19.69	400	83.75	18.48	9.78	2.70	359.52	1.97
3	19.69	400	83.75	18.48	18.09	1.78	359.47	11.25
4	19.69	400	83.75	18.48	26.85	0.56	374.39	6.32
5	19.69	375	83.75	17.10	36.09	356.60	0.00	7.52

To understand these calculations, consider, for example, the effect of the reserve of $400 required at the start of the fourth year. This has to be set up at the end of the third year, for policies which are continuing at that time. The expected cost, given that the policy is in force at the start of the third year, is EV_3 in the table above, where

$$EV_3 = {}_3V \times p_{52} \times 0.9$$

allowing for survival and for the probability that the policyholder does not surrender the contract.

The effect on Pr_3 is to reduce it by EV_3. The effect of this reserve on Pr_4 is to increase it by 1.055×400, since it is assumed the reserve will earn interest at 5.5% throughout the fourth year.

The overall effect of introducing reserves is to reduce the profit margin to 0.0051 or 0.51%. The negative cash flows in years 2 to 5 have been eliminated by setting aside, as a reserve, some of the profit that emerged at time 1. Note that Pr_1 reduces from $601.83 in part (a) to $242.26 in this table. The reserve is assumed to earn interest at 5.5% per year rather than the (higher) risk discount rate of 8.5% per year. This reduces the insurer's NPV and hence the profit margin.

(c) Let $\{z_t\}_{t=1}^5$ denote the random standard normal deviates given in the question. The simulated rates of return in successive years, $\{1 + i_t\}_{t=1}^5$, are calculated as

$$1 + i_t = \exp\{0.07 + 0.2z_t\}$$

for $t = 1, 2, \ldots, 5$. These rates of return are then used in place of the fixed rate 1.055 for projecting the growth of the policyholder's fund and hence the calculation of the management charge, the death benefit and the cost to the insurer of the maturity benefit.

With these changes, the calculations follow as in part (b)(ii).

The revised profit margin is -0.0143 or -1.43%.

Solutions for Chapter 15

15.1 Formulae (15.8) and (15.9) in AMLCR give the expressions we require to answer this question, namely

$$c(t) = S_t \, \Phi(d_1(t)) - K \, e^{-r(T-t)} \, \Phi(d_2(t)),$$

$$d_1(t) = \frac{\log(S_t/K) + (r + \sigma^2/2)(T-t)}{\sigma \sqrt{T-t}},$$

$$d_2(t) = d_1(t) - \sigma \sqrt{T-t}.$$

Then

$$\frac{d}{dS_t} c(t) = S_t \, \frac{d}{dS_t} \Phi(d_1(t)) + \Phi(d_1(t)) - Ke^{-r(T-t)} \frac{d}{dS_t} \Phi(d_2(t))$$

$$= S_t \, \phi(d_1(t)) \, \frac{d}{dS_t} d_1(t) + \Phi(d_1(t)) - Ke^{-r(T-t)} \, \phi(d_2(t)) \, \frac{d}{dS_t} d_2(t)$$

where $\phi(x) = \exp\{-x^2/2\}/\sqrt{2\pi}$ is the standard normal density function.

Now

$$\frac{d}{dS_t} d_1(t) = \frac{d}{dS_t} d_2(t) = \frac{1}{S_t \, \sigma \sqrt{T-t}}$$

so that

$$S_t \, \phi(d_1(t)) \, \frac{d}{dS_t} d_1(t) = \frac{\phi(d_1(t))}{\sigma \sqrt{T-t}}.$$

Next,

$$\phi\,(d_2(t)) = \frac{\exp\{-d_2(t)^2/2\}}{\sqrt{2\pi}}$$

$$= \frac{\exp\{-\left(d_1(t) - \sigma\,\sqrt{T-t}\right)^2/2\}}{\sqrt{2\pi}}$$

$$= \phi\,(d_1(t))\exp\left\{d_1(t)\sigma\,\sqrt{T-t} - \frac{\sigma^2}{2}\,(T-t)\right\},$$

and as

$$d_1(t)\sigma\,\sqrt{T-t} - \frac{\sigma^2}{2}\,(T-t) = \log(S_t/K) + (r + \sigma^2/2)(T-t) - \frac{\sigma^2}{2}\,(T-t)$$

$$= \log(S_t/K) + r(T-t),$$

we have

$$\phi\,(d_2(t)) = \phi\,(d_1(t))\,\frac{S_t}{K}\,\exp\{r(T-t)\}.$$

Thus

$$Ke^{-r(T-t)}\,\phi\,(d_2(t))\,\frac{d}{dS_t}d_2(t) = \frac{\phi\,(d_1(t))}{\sigma\,\sqrt{T-t}}$$

and hence

$$\frac{d}{dS_t}c(t) = \Phi(d_1(t)).$$

15.2 (a) Under the Q-measure,

$$S_n = S_0\,u^r\,d^{n-r}$$

for $r = 0, 1, 2, \ldots, n$ (i.e. r upward stock price movements and $n - r$ downward ones) with probability

$$\binom{n}{r}(1 - q)^r\,q^{n-r},$$

where

$$q = \frac{u - e^r}{u - d}.$$

Thus

$$E^Q[S_n] = \sum_{r=0}^{n} S_0 \, u^r \, d^{n-r} \binom{n}{r}(1-q)^r \, q^{n-r}$$

$$= S_0 \sum_{r=0}^{n} \binom{n}{r}(u(1-q))^r \, (d\,q)^{n-r}$$

$$= S_0 \, (u(1-q) + d\,q)^n$$

$$= S_0 \left(u\frac{e^r - d}{u - d} + d\frac{u - e^r}{u - d}\right)^n$$

$$= S_0 \, e^{rn}.$$

(Note that the second line is simply the binomial expansion of the third.)

(b) Under the Q-measure in the Black–Scholes–Merton model, S_n/S_0 has a lognormal distribution with parameters $(r - \sigma^2/2)n$ and $\sigma^2 n$. From Appendix A in AMLCR we know that if $X \sim LN(\mu, \sigma^2)$ then $E[X] = \exp\{\mu + \sigma^2/2\}$. From this it follows that

$$E[S_n/S_0] = \exp\{(r - \sigma^2/2)n + \sigma^2 n/2\} = \exp\{rn\},$$

i.e. $E[S_n] = S_0 \, e^{rn}$.

15.3 (a) Consider an investment of $\$a$ in zero-coupon bonds and $\$100b$ (i.e. b units) in the security. To construct the replicating portfolio at time $t = 0$ we require

$$a \, e^{0.06} + 110b = 20$$

(i.e. the payoff is replicated if the security price goes up) and

$$a \, e^{0.06} + 90b = 0$$

(i.e. the payoff is replicated if the security price goes down). Differencing these identities gives $b = 1$, and hence

$$a = -90 \, e^{-0.06} = -84.76.$$

Thus, the replicating portfolio comprises one unit of the security and $-\$84.76$ in zero-coupon bonds, and hence the option price is $100 - 84.76 = \$15.24$.

(b) Consider the situation at time $t = 1$ if the security price has increased to 110. If $\$a_u$ is invested in zero-coupon bonds and b_u units of the security are purchased, then we require

$$a_u e^{0.06} + 121b_u = 20,$$
$$a_u e^{0.06} + 110 \times 0.9b_u = 0,$$

since a security price of $S_2 = 110 \times 0.9 = 99 < S_0$, giving a payoff of $0 under the option. Differencing these identities gives

$$(121 - 99)b_u = 20,$$

so that $b_u = \frac{10}{11}$ and hence

$$a_u = -99b_u e^{-0.06} = -84.76.$$

Hence the replicating portfolio at time $t = 1$ has value $110b_u + a_u = \$15.24$ if the security price goes up in the first time period.

Now consider the situation at time $t = 1$ if the security price has decreased to 90. At time $t = 2$ the security price will either be 99 or 81. Thus, the security price will be below $S_0 = 100$, and hence the option will be worth 0 at time $t = 2$. The replicating portfolio at time $t = 1$ therefore consists of $0 in zero-coupon bonds and 0 units of the security. (You can also see this by setting up equations.)

To find the replicating portfolio at time $t = 0$ we consider an investment of $\$a$ in zero-coupon bonds and $\$100b$ in the security. Then we require

$$a e^{0.06} + 110b = 15.24,$$
$$a e^{0.06} + 90b = 0,$$

so that $b = 15.24/20 = 0.7621$ and hence

$$a = -90b e^{-0.06} = -64.59.$$

The option price is thus

$$100 \times 0.7621 - 64.59 = \$11.61.$$

15.4 (a) Under the P-measure the payoff under Option A is

3	with probability	$0.5^2 = 0.25$,
2	with probability	$2 \times 0.5^2 = 0.5$,
1	with probability	$0.5^2 = 0.25$.

Hence the EPV of the payoff is

$$e^{-2\times0.04879} \left(3 \times 0.25 + 2 \times 0.5 + 1 \times 0.25\right) = 2e^{-0.09758} = 1.81.$$

Under the P-measure the payoff under Option B is

$$
\begin{array}{lll}
1 & \text{with probability} & 0.5^2 = 0.25, \\
2 & \text{with probability} & 2 \times 0.5^2 = 0.5, \\
3 & \text{with probability} & 0.5^2 = 0.25.
\end{array}
$$

Hence the EPV of the payoff is

$$e^{-2\times0.04879} \left(1 \times 0.25 + 2 \times 0.5 + 3 \times 0.25\right) = 2e^{-0.09758} = 1.81.$$

(b) We can price the options using the same approach as calculating the expected present values in (a), except that we replace the true probability of up and down moves with the artificial Q-measure values. From equation (15.2) we see that the Q-measure 'probability' of an up movement in each time period is

$$\frac{e^r - d}{u - d} = 0.4$$

where u is the proportionate increase in the security price on an up move, which is 1.2 in this case, and d is the proportionate decrease on a down move, 0.95 in this case. The option prices are then

Option A: $e^{-2r} \left(3 \times 0.4^2 + 2 \times (2 \times 0.4 \times 0.6) + 1 \times 0.6^2\right) = 1.633$,

Option B: $e^{-2r} \left(1 \times 0.4^2 + 2 \times (2 \times 0.4 \times 0.6) + 3 \times 0.6^2\right) = 1.995$.

(c) We price options using the principle of replication. As the payoffs differ under the two options, the values of the replicating portfolios must differ, firstly at time $t = 1$, then at time $t = 0$.

Intuitively, Option A is less expensive because its payoff moves in the same direction as the stock, and the up-side move of the stock is bigger, relatively, than the down-side move; when we hedge, we benefit from the extra return on the up-side. The starting replicating portfolios for the two options are as follows, where a is the value of the risk free asset, and b is the value of the security, at time $t = 0$:

Option A: $a = -2.18$ and $b = 3.81$,

Option B: $a = 5.81$ and $b = -3.81$.

E15.5 (a) The put-call parity formula (see equation (15.11)) is

$$c(t) + K e^{-r(T-t)} = p(t) + S_t.$$

We have $t = 0$, $T = \frac{1}{2}$, $r = 0.07$, $S_0 = 400$, $K = 420$ and $c(0) = 41$. The price of the put option is thus

$$p(0) = c(0) + K e^{-r/2} - S_0$$
$$= 41 + 420 e^{-0.035} - 400$$
$$= \$46.55.$$

(b) The implied volatility is the value of σ implied by the price of the European call option. Inserting the parameter values from part (a) into formula (15.8) in AMLCR we have

$$c(0) = 41 = 400 \, \Phi(d_1(0)) - 420 \, e^{-0.035} \, \Phi(d_2(0))$$

where

$$d_1(0) = \frac{\log(4/4.2) + \frac{1}{2}(0.07 + \sigma^2/2)}{\sigma \sqrt{1/2}}$$

and $d_2(0) = d_1(0) - \sigma \sqrt{1/2}$.

This can only be solved numerically for σ. Using Solver in Excel we find that $\sigma = 38.6\%$.

(c) The delta of the option at time t is $dc(t)/dS_t$, which, from Exercise 15.1, is $\Phi(d_1(t))$. Thus, with $t = 0$ and σ as in part (b), we have

$$d_1(0) = \frac{\log(4/4.2) + \frac{1}{2}(0.07 + 0.386^2/2)}{0.386 \sqrt{1/2}} = 0.08595$$

and $\Phi(0.08595) = 0.5342$, so the delta of the option is 53.42%.

(d) Formula (15.8) in AMLCR tells us that

$$41 = 400 \, \Phi(d_1(0)) - 420 \, e^{-0.035} \, \Phi(d_2(0))$$

and the right-hand side gives the self-financing replicating portfolio at time 0 as

$$400 \, \Phi(d_1(0)) = \$213.6981 \text{ in stock,}$$
$$-420 \, e^{-0.035} \, \Phi(d_2(0)) = -\$172.6982 \text{ in bonds.}$$

The total holding for 10 000 units of the call option is then $2 136 981 in stock, i.e. 5342.45 units of stock, and $-\$1\,726\,982$ in bonds, i.e. a short holding of 17 270 bonds with face value $100.

15.6 (a) Under the risk neutral measure the probability of an upward movement is

$$\frac{1.1 - 0.8}{1.25 - 0.8} = \frac{2}{3}$$

and the probability of a downward movement is $1/3$.

(b) Consider the situation at time $t = 1$ if the security price has increased to 125. If $\$a_u$ is invested in zero-coupon bonds and b_u units of the security are purchased, then we require

$$1.1a_u + 156.25b_u = 1,$$
$$1.1a_u + 100b_u = 2,$$

giving $b_u = -1/56.25 = -0.01778$ and

$$a_u = (2 - 100b_u)/1.1 = 3.4343.$$

Thus, the replicating portfolio has value $P_u = a_u + 125b_u = 1.2121$.

Next, if at time $t = 1$ the security price has decreased to 80, and if $\$a_d$ is invested in zero-coupon bonds and b_d units of the security are purchased, then we require

$$1.1a_d + 100b_d = 2,$$
$$1.1a_d + 64b_d = 0,$$

giving $b_d = 2/36 = 0.05556$ and

$$a_d = -64b_d/1.1 = -3.2323.$$

Thus, the replicating portfolio has value $P_d = a_d + 80b_d = 1.2121$, which is the same as P_u.

Thus, the amount required at time 1 is 1.2121 regardless of the movement in the security price in the first time period. We can replicate this by investing $\$1.2121/1.1$ in cash, so $D_0 = \$1.1019$.

(c) The hedging strategy at time $t = 0$ is to hold $\$1.1019$ of the risk free asset only, i.e. do not hold any of the security. The hedging strategy at time $t = 1$ is to have $\$3.4343$ in the risk free asset and a short holding of 0.01778 units of the security if $S_1 = 125$, and to be short $\$3.2323$ in the risk free asset and hold 0.05556 units of the security if $S_1 = 80$.

(d) The hedging strategy at time $t = 0$ is unusual in that it involves holding the risk free asset only. Although different replicating portfolios are required at time $t = 1$ depending on the value of S_1, these replicating portfolios have the same *value* at time $t = 1$, so the time $t = 1$ liability is certain. We always hedge a certain liability with the risk free investment.

15.7 (a) Under the risk neutral measure the probability of an upward movement is

$$\frac{1.04 - 0.8}{1.25 - 0.8} = 0.5333$$

and the probability of a downward movement is 0.4667.

(b) The option price is the expected present value under the risk neutral probability measure. The option pays \$10 if the stock price rises twice or falls twice, and the risk neutral expected present value is therefore

$$10\left(1.04^{-2}\right)\left(0.5333^2 + 0.4667^2\right) = 4.6433.$$

Solutions for Chapter 16

16.1 (a) The single premium is $P = \$100$ and the value of the GMMB is

$$\pi(0) = 0.95^9 \,_{10}p_{60}\, \mathrm{E}_0^Q \left[e^{-10r} \left(0.85P - P(1-m)^{11} S_{10} \right)^+ \right],$$

where the term 0.95^9 allows for withdrawals at the end of years 1 to 9, and $m = 0.02$ so that the term $(1-m)^{11}$ allows for both the front-end expense loading and the annual management charge. We can rewrite this as

$$\pi(0) = 0.95^9 \,_{10}p_{60}\, P(1-m)^{11} \mathrm{E}_0^Q \left[e^{-10r} \left(\frac{0.85}{(1-m)^{11}} - S_{10} \right)^+ \right].$$

Using formula (15.10) in AMLCR (with $t = 0$, $T = 10$ and $K = 0.85/(1-m)^{11}$) we have

$$\mathrm{E}_0^Q \left[e^{-10r} \left(\frac{0.85}{(1-m)^{11}} - S_{10} \right)^+ \right] = \frac{0.85\, e^{-10r}}{(1-m)^{11}} \, \Phi\left(-d_2(0)\right) - S_0\, \Phi(-d_1(0))$$

where $S_0 = 1$,

$$d_1(0) = \frac{\log\left((1-m)^{11}/0.85\right) + \left(0.04 + 0.2^2/2\right) 10}{0.2\sqrt{10}} = 0.85427$$

and

$$d_2(0) = d_1(0) - 0.2\sqrt{10} = 0.22182.$$

Hence

$$\mathrm{E}_0^Q \left[e^{-10r} \left(\frac{0.85}{(1-m)^{11}} - S_{10} \right)^+ \right] = 0.09685$$

and $\pi(0) = \$4.61$.

(b) The value of annual risk premiums of c is $c\,\ddot{a}_{60:\overline{10}|}$ at rate $i^* = m/(1-m) = 0.0204$, which is $6.7562c$. Equating this to $\pi(0)$ gives $c = 0.68$ or 0.68% of the fund.

(c) At time 2 years we have $S_2 = 0.95$. The value of the GMMB is

$$0.95^7 \,{}_8p_{62}\, P(1-m)^{11} \, \mathrm{E}_0^Q\!\left[e^{-8r}\left(\frac{0.85}{(1-m)^{11}} - S_{10}\right)^+\right]$$

and

$$\mathrm{E}_2^Q\!\left[e^{-8r}\left(\frac{0.85}{(1-m)^{11}} - S_{10}\right)^+\right] = \frac{0.85\,e^{-8r}}{(1-m)^{11}}\,\Phi\left(-d_2(2)\right) - S_2\,\Phi(-d_1(2))$$

where

$$d_1(2) = \frac{\log\left((1-m)^{11}\,S_2/0.85\right) + \left(0.04 + 0.2^2/2\right)8}{0.2\sqrt{8}} = 0.65230$$

and

$$d_2(2) = d_1(0) - 0.2\sqrt{8} = 0.08661.$$

Hence

$$\mathrm{E}_0^Q\!\left[e^{-8r}\left(\frac{0.85}{(1-m)^{11}} - S_{10}\right)^+\right] = 0.11456$$

and the value of the GMMB is $6.08.

E16.2 (a) The death benefit payable at time t, conditional on death in the previous month, is $\max(P, 1.05\,F_t)$, where $P = \$10\,000$ is the single premium, and $F_t = P\,e^{-0.03t}\,S_t$ (with $S_0 = 1$) since there is a management charge of 3% per year, deducted daily. We can write this death benefit as

$$1.05\,F_t + \max(P - 1.05\,F_t, 0) = 1.05\,F_t + 1.05\,P\,e^{-0.03t}\left(\frac{e^{0.03t}}{1.05} - S_t\right)^+.$$

As the fund will provide F_t at time t, we need to price the additional benefit payable on death, of

$$0.05\,F_t + 1.05\,P\,e^{-0.03t}\left(\frac{e^{0.03t}}{1.05} - S_t\right)^+$$

at time t. To value this benefit, use equation (16.3), where in this example

$$v(0,t) = \mathrm{E}_0^Q\!\left[e^{-rt}\left(0.05\,F_t + 1.05\,P\,e^{-0.03t}\left(\frac{e^{0.03t}}{1.05} - S_t\right)^+\right)\right].$$

Consider the first part:

$$E_0^Q \left[0.05\, F_t\, e^{-rt} \right] = E_0^Q \left[0.05\, e^{-0.03t}\, P\, S_t\, e^{-rt} \right] = 0.05\, e^{-0.03t}\, P\, E_0^Q \left[S_t\, e^{-rt} \right]$$

and we know that $E_0^Q[S_t] = S_0\, e^{rt}$, from the risk neutral quality of the Q-measure, so that

$$E_0^Q \left[e^{-rt}\, 0.05\, F_t \right] = 0.05\, P\, e^{-0.03t}.$$

The price at time 0 of this component of the death benefit is

$$P \sum_{t=1}^{120} 0.05\, e^{-0.03t} \,\, {}_{\frac{t-1}{12}}\big|_{\frac{1}{12}} q_{60} = 24.1436.$$

The price of the second component of the death benefit, conditional on the benefit being paid at time t, is

$$E_0^Q \left[e^{-rt}\, 1.05\, P\, e^{-0.03t} \left(\frac{e^{0.03t}}{1.05} - S_t \right)^+ \right]$$

which can be found as

$$1.05\, P\, e^{-0.03t} \left(\frac{e^{0.03t}}{1.05}\, e^{-rt}\, \Phi(-d_2(0,t)) - S_0\, \Phi(-d_1(0,t)) \right)$$

where

$$d_1(0,t) = \frac{\log(1.05\, e^{-0.03t}) + (r + \sigma^2/2)t}{\sigma\, \sqrt{t}}$$

where $r = 0.04$ and $\sigma = 0.25$, and

$$d_2(0,t) = d_1(0,t) - \sigma\, \sqrt{t}.$$

The price of this second component of the death benefit is then

$$P \sum_{t=1}^{120} \left(e^{-rt}\, \Phi(-d_2(0,t)) - 1.05\, e^{-0.03t}\, S_0\, \Phi(-d_1(0,t)) \right) {}_{\frac{t-1}{12}}\big|_{\frac{1}{12}} q_{60}$$

$$= 83.6097.$$

Hence the price of the death benefit at issue is

$$24.1436 + 83.6097 = \$107.75.$$

(b) The value of the risk premium deductible continuously from the fund (as part of the $m = 3\%$ per year management charge), at a rate c per year, is

$$P\, c\, \bar{a}_{60:\overline{10}|\, \delta=m} = 8.4465\, c\, P.$$

Equating this to the benefit cost $\$107.75$ gives $c = 0.128\%$ of the fund.

^{E}16.3 (a) Under the P-measure, $S_{10}/S_0 \sim LN(10\mu, 10\sigma^2)$ where $\mu = 0.08$ and $\sigma^2 = 0.25^2$. Setting $S_0 = 1$ we have

$$F_{10} = 0.97^{10} \times 100\,000 \times S_{10}$$

as there is a 3% management charge at the start of each year. The GMMB matures in the money if $F_{10} < 100\,000$. The required probability is thus

$$\Pr\left[0.97^{10}\, S_{10} < 1\right] = \Pr\left[\log S_{10} < -10\log 0.97\right]$$
$$= \Pr\left[Z < \frac{-10\log 0.97 - 10\mu}{\sigma\sqrt{10}}\right] \quad \text{where } Z \sim N(0, 1)$$
$$= \Phi(-0.6266) = 0.26545.$$

(b) Under the Q-measure, $S_{10}/S_0 \sim LN(10(r - \sigma^2/2), 10\sigma^2)$ where $r = 0.04$. Proceeding exactly as in part (a), the required probability is

$$\Pr\left[Z < \frac{-10\log 0.97 - 10\left(r - \sigma^2/2\right)}{\sigma\sqrt{10}}\right] = \Phi(0.2746) = 0.60819.$$

(c) The EPV of the option payoff is

$$E^P\left[e^{-10r}\left(100\,000 - 0.97^{10} \times 100\,000\, S_{10}\right)^+\right]$$

which can be written as

$$100\,000 \times 0.97^{10} \times e^{-10r}\, E^P\left[\left(0.97^{-10} - S_{10}\right)^+\right].$$

Let f denote the probability density function of S_{10} under the P-measure (we still have $S_0=1$). Then

$$E^P\left[\left(0.97^{-10} - S_{10}\right)^+\right] = \int_0^{0.97^{-10}} \left(0.97^{-10} - x\right) f(x)\, dx$$
$$= 0.97^{-10}\, \Pr[S_{10} \le 0.97^{-10}] - \int_0^{0.97^{-10}} x\, f(x)\, dx.$$

From Appendix A of AMLCR we can write

$$\int_0^{0.97^{-10}} x\, f(x)\, dx = \exp\left\{10\mu + \frac{10\sigma^2}{2}\right\} \Phi\left(\frac{\log 0.97^{-10} - 10\mu - 10\sigma^2}{\sigma\sqrt{10}}\right)$$
$$= \exp\{1.1125\}\, \Phi(-1.4172) = 0.23791,$$

and from part (a) we know that $\Pr[S_{10} \le 0.97^{-10}] = 0.26545$. Hence the EPV of the option payoff under the P-measure is \$6033.

(d) The price of the option is

$$E_0^Q \left[e^{-10r} \max \left(100\,000 - 0.97^{10} \times 100\,000\, S_{10}, 0 \right) \right]$$

which can be written as

$$0.97^{10} \times 100\,000\, E_0^Q \left[e^{-10r} \left(0.97^{-10} - S_{10} \right)^+ \right].$$

Now

$$E_0^Q \left[e^{-10r} \left(0.97^{-10} - S_{10} \right)^+ \right] = 0.97^{-10}\, e^{-10r}\, \Phi(-d_2(0)) - S_0\, \Phi(-d_1(0))$$

where

$$d_1(0) = \frac{\log\left(0.97^{10}\right) + \left(r + \sigma^2/2\right) 10}{\sigma \sqrt{10}} = 0.51597$$

and

$$d_2(0) = d_1(0) - \sigma \sqrt{10} = -0.27460.$$

Thus $E_0^Q \left[e^{-10r} \left(0.97^{-10} - S_{10} \right)^+ \right] = 0.24991$ and the price of the option is $\$18\,429$.

(e) Using the P-measure ignores the fact that the guarantee risk is non-diversifiable. For diversifiable risk, the P-measure expectation will be close to the true cost, provided enough contracts are sold for the diversification benefit from the central limit theorem. For non-diversifiable risk, the central limit theorem does not apply, and the P-measure expectation may be a long way from the true cost. The use of the Q-measure indicates that what we are valuing is not an expected value in the conventional sense, but the cost of replicating the option payoff. This is achieved by taking the EPV under the Q-measure.

(f) We start by simulating 1000 values from the standard normal distribution. In Excel, this can be done using the random number generation tool. Let z_i be the ith such random number. We then calculate our ith simulated value of S_{10} as

$$S_{10,i} = 100\,000 \exp\left\{ 10(r - \sigma^2/2) + z_i\, \sigma\, \sqrt{10} \right\}.$$

The simulated fund value at time 10 is then $F_{10,i} = 0.97^{10}\, S_{10,i}$ and the simulated payoff is

$$h_i(10) = \max(100\,000 - F_{10,i}, 0).$$

The estimate of the price of the option is then the average of the present values (at the risk free rate) of the simulated payoffs,

$$\frac{1}{1000} \sum_{i=1}^{1000} e^{-0.04 \times 10} h_i(10).$$

The result will depend on the random numbers used; our calculations give an estimate of $18\,385$, which is close to the true price calculated in part (d).

^{E}16.4 (a) The policyholder's fund value at time t years is

$$F_t = 100 \times 0.97 \times 0.99^t \, S_t$$

where $S_0 = 1$. As $F_5 = 110$ we have

$$S_5 = 1.1/(0.97 \times 0.99^5) = 1.19246.$$

The value at time 5 of the original guarantee is

$$E_5^Q \left[e^{-5r} \, (100 - F_{10})^+ \right]$$

$$= 100 \times 0.97 \times 0.99^{10} \, E_5^Q \left[e^{-5r} \left(\frac{1}{0.97 \times 0.99^{10}} - S_{10} \right)^+ \right]$$

and

$$E_5^Q \left[e^{-5r} \left(\frac{1}{0.97 \times 0.99^{10}} - S_{10} \right)^+ \right]$$

$$= \frac{e^{-5r}}{0.97 \times 0.99^{10}} \, \Phi(-d_2(5, 10)) - S_5 \, \Phi(-d_1(5, 10))$$

where

$$d_1(5, 10) = \frac{\log(S_5 \times 0.97 \times 0.99^{10}) + (r + \sigma^2/2)5}{\sigma \sqrt{5}} = 0.93432$$

since $r = 0.05$ and $\sigma = 0.18$, and

$$d_2(5, 10) = d_1(5, 10) - \sigma \sqrt{5} = 0.53183.$$

Thus the value of the original guarantee is

$$100 \left(e^{-5r} \, \Phi(-0.53183) - 0.99^5 \times 1.1 \, \Phi(-0.93432) \right) = \$4.85.$$

Under the reset guarantee, the guarantee changes to 110. The value at time 5 of this guarantee is

$$E_5^Q \left[e^{-10r} \left(110 - F_{15} \right)^+ \right]$$

$$= 100 \times 0.97 \times 0.99^{15} E_5^Q \left[e^{-5r} \left(\frac{1.1}{0.97 \times 0.99^{15}} - S_{15} \right)^+ \right]$$

and

$$E_5^Q \left[e^{-5r} \left(\frac{1.1}{0.97 \times 0.99^{15}} - S_{15} \right)^+ \right]$$

$$= \frac{1.1 \, e^{-10r}}{0.97 \times 0.99^{15}} \, \Phi(-d_2(5, 15)) - S_5 \, \Phi(-d_1(5, 15))$$

where

$$d_1(5, 15) = \frac{\log\left(S_5 \times 0.97 \times 0.99^{15} / 1.1 \right) + (r + \sigma^2/2)10}{\sigma \sqrt{10}} = 0.98645$$

and

$$d_2(5, 15) = d_1(5, 15) - \sigma \sqrt{10} = 0.41724.$$

Thus the value of the reset guarantee is

$$100 \left(1.1 \, e^{-10r} \, \Phi(-0.41724) - 0.99^{10} \times 1.1 \, \Phi(-0.98645) \right) = \$6.46.$$

(b) The threshold value has to be found by numerical methods. We calculate the values of the original and reset guarantees as in part (a), except we set the value of S_5 to be $(1 + x)/(0.97 \times 0.99^5)$. For a given value of x, we can calculate the value of the guarantees. Solving numerically, for example using Excel Solver, we determine that $x = 0.03433$, so that $F_5 = 103.43$ and each guarantee has value \$6.07.

^{E}16.5 (a) The single premium is $P = \$100\,000$ and the value of the GMMB is

$$\pi(0) = {}_5p_{60} \, E_0^Q \left[e^{-5r} (100\,000 - F_5)^+ \right]$$

where $F_5 = 100\,000(1 - 0.0025)^{60} S_5$, with $S_0 = 1$. Now

$$E_0^Q \left[e^{-5r} (100\,000 - F_5)^+ \right]$$

$$= 100\,000 \times 0.9975^{60} E_0^Q \left[e^{-5r} (0.9975^{-60} - S_5)^+ \right]$$

and

$$E_0^Q \left[e^{-5r} (0.9975^{-60} - S_5)^+ \right]$$

$$= 0.9975^{-60} \, e^{-5r} \, \Phi(-d_2(0)) - S_0 \, \Phi(-d_1(0))$$

where

$$d_1(0) = \frac{\log(0.9975^{60}) + (r + \sigma^2/2)5}{\sigma \sqrt{5}} = 0.44679$$

since $r = 0.05$ and $\sigma = 0.2$, and

$$d_2(0) = d_1(0) - \sigma \sqrt{5} = -0.00042.$$

Thus

$$\pi(0) = {}_5p_{60} \, 100\,000 \left(e^{-5r} \, \Phi(0.00042) - 0.9975^{60} \, \Phi(-0.44679)\right)$$

$$= 0.97874 \times 10\,769.16$$

$$= 10\,540.21.$$

The value of risk premiums of c per month deducted from the fund is

$$cP \sum_{t=0}^{59} 0.9975^t \, {}_tp_{60} = 55.26545c\,P,$$

and setting this equal to $\pi(0)$ gives $c = 0.19\%$ of the fund.

(b) (i) We illustrate the calculation for time 2 months, i.e. $t = \frac{1}{6}$ years. At this time, the cost of the option is

$$_{4\frac{5}{6}}p_{60\frac{1}{6}} \, E^Q_{1/6}\left[e^{-4\frac{5}{6}r}(100\,000 - F_5)^+\right]$$

which can be written as

$$100\,000 \times 0.9975^{60} \, {}_{4\frac{5}{6}}p_{60\frac{1}{6}} \, E^Q_{1/6}\left[e^{-4\frac{5}{6}r}(0.9975^{-60} - S_5)^+\right].$$

Now

$$E^Q_{1/6}\left[e^{-4\frac{5}{6}r}(0.9975^{-60} - S_5)^+\right]$$

$$= 0.9975^{-60} \, e^{-4\frac{5}{6}r} \, \Phi(-d_2(\tfrac{1}{6}, 5)) - S_{1/6} \, \Phi(-d_1(\tfrac{1}{6}, 5))$$

where

$$d_1(\tfrac{1}{6}, 5) = \frac{\log(S_{1/6} \times 0.9975^{60} + (r + \sigma^2/2)4\frac{5}{6}}{\sigma \sqrt{4\frac{5}{6}}} = 0.35264$$

and

$$d_2(\tfrac{1}{6}, 5) = d_1(\tfrac{1}{6}, 5) - \sigma \sqrt{4\frac{5}{6}} = -0.08706.$$

Thus, the cost of the option is

$$100\,000 \, {}_{4\frac{5}{6}}p_{60\frac{1}{6}} \, (e^{-4\frac{5}{6}r} \, \Phi(0.08706) - 0.9975^{60}S_{1/6} \, \Phi(-0.35264)),$$

so that the stock part of the hedge is

$$100\,000 \,_{4\frac{5}{6}}p_{60\frac{1}{6}} \times 0.9975^{60}\, S_{1/6}\, \Phi(-0.35264) = -\$29\,528$$

and the bond part of the hedge is

$$100\,000 \,_{4\frac{5}{6}}p_{60\frac{1}{6}}\, e^{-4\frac{5}{6}r}\, \Phi(0.08706) = \$41\,120.$$

Thus, the cost of the option at time $t = \frac{1}{12}$ is

$$-29\,528 + 41\,120 = \$11\,592.$$

The hedge at time $t = \frac{1}{12}$ comprised $-29\,737$ of stock and $41\,668$ in bonds. At time $t = \frac{1}{6}$ this has value

$$-29\,737\,\frac{S_{1/6}}{S_{1/12}} + 41\,668\, e^{r/12} = \$11\,701.$$

The rebalancing cost at time $t = \frac{1}{6}$ is therefore

$$11\,592 - 11\,701 = -\$109.$$

If $H(t)$ denotes the hedge rebalancing cost at time t years (so that $H(\frac{1}{6}) = -109$), then the present value of the hedge rebalancing costs is

$$\sum_{t=1}^{60} 1.05^{-t/12}\, H(t/12) = -\$1092.35.$$

(ii) Again, we illustrate the calculation using time $t = 2$ months as an example. The fund at time 2 months is

$$F_2 = 100\,000\, S_2 \times 0.9975^2 = \$96\,261.88.$$

The management cost is

$$0.0025 \times F_2 = \$240.65,$$

the expenses are

$$0.00065 \times F_2 = \$62.57,$$

and, from part (i), the hedge rebalancing cost is $-\$109.16$. Thus, the emerging profit is

$$\text{Pr}_2 = 240.65 - 62.57 + 109.16 = \$287.24.$$

The profit margin is calculated as

$$\sum_{t=0}^{60} 1.1^{-t/12} {}_{t/12}p_{60} \, \mathrm{Pr}_t / 100\,000 = -1.23\%.$$

(iii) In part (a) we calculated that the initial hedge cost converts to a monthly outgo of 0.19% of the fund. The incurred renewal expenses are 0.065% of the fund, so the monthly cost of these two items is 0.255% of the fund. As the monthly management fees are 0.25% of the fund, we would not expect the contract to be profitable.